Exploring Metalworking

Fundamentals of Technology

by
John R. Walker
Charlottesville, Virginia

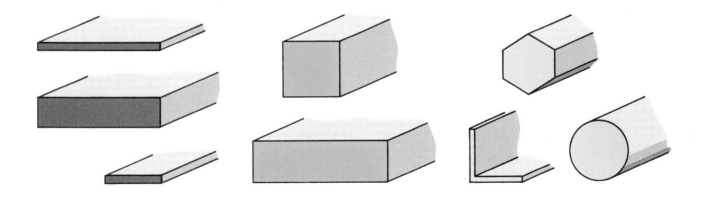

Publisher
The Goodheart-Willcox Company, Co.
Tinley Park, Illinois

Copyright 1995

by

THE GOODHEART-WILLCOX COMPANY, INC.

Previous Editions Copyright 1987, 1976

Library of Congress Catalog Card Number 94 31819
International Standard Book Number 1-56637-153-8

3 4 5 6 7 8 9 10   95

Library of Congress Cataloging in Publication Data

Walker, John R.
  Exploring metalworking: fundamentals of
technology / by John R. Walker.

    p.   cm.
  Includes index.
  ISBN 1-56637-153-8
  1. Metal-work. I. Title.
TT205.W33   1995
684'.09--dc20   94-31819
                                                CIP

IMPORTANT SAFETY NOTICE

Work procedures and shop practices described in this book are effective methods of performing given operations. Use special tools and equipment as recommended. Carefully follow all safety warnings and cautions. Note that these warnings are not exhaustive. Proceed with care and under proper supervision to minimize the risk of personal injury or injury to others.

This book contains the most complete and accurate information that could be obtained from various authoritative sources at the time of publication. The Goodheart-Willcox Company, Inc. cannot assume responsibility for any changes, errors, or omissions.

Introduction

EXPLORING METALWORKING is a first course in the fundamentals of working with metal, using both hand and power tools.

EXPLORING METALWORKING is written in easy-to-understand language. It contains an abundance of illustrations. Extra color is used to clarify details, and to illustrate major processes in steelmaking.

EXPLORING METALWORKING provides constructional details on carefully selected projects. It also includes alternate designs and design variations which will help you design your own projects. The text tells and shows how to organize and operate a small manufacturing business in your school lab. You learn how to mass produce items with proven student-appeal.

Using selected material, EXPLORING METALWORKING may be used to present a six, nine, eighteen, or thirty-six week metalworking program.

EXPLORING METALWORKING emphasizes the important place metals occupy in our everyday lives. It explores metalworking career opportunities.

John R. Walker

Contents

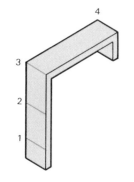

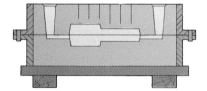

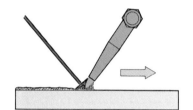

The field of metalworking technology offers many new opportunites. The concern for environmental protection and energy conservation, for example, has required the development of new metals and manufacturing techniques.
The experimental vehicle shown uses a gas turbine to drive a generator to charge the batteries. A gas turbine with continuous combustion and high operating temperatures has far lower polluting emissions than a piston engine. The high operating temperatures require metals able to withstand heat for long operating periods without failing.
The car has three modes of operation. The first mode is pure electric for pollution-free city driving with a range of 50 miles. In the second (hybrid) mode, the turbine is automatically activated to drive the generator when battery power declines to a certain level. In the third mode, the turbine alone is used when maximum power is required in emergency situations.
(Volvo Cars of North America, Inc.)

Unit 1 . . . .

Careers in Metalworking Technology

After studying this unit, you will be able to identify the many job opportunities in the metalworking industries. You will also discover the importance of leadership skills in both school and career. And you will learn how to write a resume for use in your job search.

TECHNOLOGY is defined as the "know-how" that links science and the industrial arts. Its purpose is to solve problems and enhance (improve in value and/or quality) the natural and human-made environment. In the process, creativity, human skills, tools, machines, and resources are used.

HIGH TECHNOLOGY and STATE-OF-THE-ART TECHNOLOGY means that the area of technology to which reference is made employs the very latest ideas, techniques, research, tools, and machines available, Fig. 1-1.

Fig. 1-1. Two-stage-to-orbit launch vehicle. In this artist's concept, the smaller stage of the launch vehicle is shown as it separates from the first stage supersonic airplane that began its boost towards space. The construction of these vehicles will require state-of-the-art metalworking technology.
(Boeing Defense & Space Group)

Fig. 1-2. Robotic work stations. The robots spot weld various body panels together. Productivity and quality is increased as the result of these robots.

Through METALWORKING TECHNOLOGY it is possible to change raw materials into finished products, Fig. 1-2. As an area of employment, it can provide interesting and challenging work.

Work has been found to be very important to life, well-being and security to the average person. Selecting an occupation is a serious and difficult task. It should not be done quickly. You must be ready to invest time and money to acquire the knowledge and skills needed to succeed in your chosen career.

There are many areas of specialization in metalworking technology. However, there are not many jobs for persons without the proper skills and training.

TYPES OF JOBS IN METALWORKING

Jobs in the metalworking industry fall into many categories. Yet all of them may be classified according to whether they are semiskilled, skilled, technical, or professional.

SEMISKILLED JOBS

Most semiskilled workers are employed in manufacturing where they:

1. Operate machines or equipment.
2. Assemble manufactured parts into complete units, Fig. 1-3.
3. Serve as helpers who assist skilled workers.
4. Work as inspectors or conduct tests to be sure manufactured parts are made to, and operate according to, specifications.

The majority of semiskilled workers work with their hands and require only a brief on-the-job training program. They are told what to do and how to do it. Frequently, semiskilled workers do the same job or operation over and over. Their work is closely supervised.

Some semiskilled workers are paid on the number of items they produce, and, therefore, make a good salary. However, most have annual earnings that are less than skilled workers.

8

Fig. 1-3. Many semiskilled workers assemble manufactured parts into complete units. They do not require a long training period. (Saturn)

Semiskilled workers are usually the first to lose their jobs when business slows down and are often the last to be rehired.

To qualify for better jobs, the semiskilled workers must enter an apprentice training program or attend classes at a community college, technical center, or night school.

SKILLED WORKERS

Skilled workers are considered the backbone of industry. They are the artisans who make the tools, machines, and equipment that transform raw materials, ideas, and designs into finished products.

Skilled workers may have acquired their skills through a formal apprentice training program, a lengthy on-the-job training program, or while in the Armed Forces, Fig. 1-4. Most such programs last 4 to 6 years. They are carefully planned to give the apprentice broad training in a specific area of

Fig. 1-4. The Armed Forces are one of the few places where it is possible to learn a trade. (U.S. Army)

interest: machinist, sheet metal specialist, welder, etc. The apprentice must also have a good background in math and be able to read and interpret drawings and prints.

Skilled workers are also able to work with their hands. They are expected to use independent judgment when using costly tools, machines, and raw materials.

Skilled workers continually update their skills as improvements and advances are made in technical processes. This is usually done through company sponsored educational programs.

There are many skilled trades in the metalworking industry. The MACHINIST operates and sets up machine tools such as lathes, drilling machines, milling machines, grinders, etc. Since they work to very close tolerances (the part must be precisely made), the machinist must be familiar with all types of precision measuring instruments.

The TOOL AND DIE MAKER is a highly skilled machinist who specializes in making tools and dies. These are needed to cut, shape, and form metal. They make jigs and fixtures used to guide cutting tools and position metal while it is being machined, formed, and assembled, Fig. 1-5.

Fig. 1-6. The instrument maker manufactures precise parts that make up the instruments and gauges used by industry, medicine, and science. (Master Lock Co.)

The INSTRUMENT MAKER, Fig. 1-6, makes precision parts for instruments used by industry, medicine, science, and government. They also repair, assemble, and test instruments.

A SET UP SPECIALIST, Fig. 1-7, sets up and adjusts machine tools so semiskilled workers can operate them.

Fig. 1-5. This tool and die maker is checking the dies used for molding a plastic pattern used to cast a jet engine component. Master tooling assures that other sections of the jet, made elsewhere in the United States, Israel, and Europe will fit together perfectly.
(Precision Castparts Corp.)

Fig. 1-7. The set up specialist prepares machine tools so that they can be operated by less skilled workers.
(Maho Machine Tool Corp.)

Fig. 1-8. Skilled steel erection workers had the dangerous job of building this bridge. Many of them travel all over the world to do this type of work. (Howard Bud Smith)

If you like working outside, you may want to be a skilled worker in the steel erection industry, Fig. 1-8. These experts have an adventurous (and dangerous) job.

The WELDER is highly skilled, Fig. 1-9. Types of work range from microwelding (welded pieces viewed through a microscope) to welding sections that weigh several hundred pounds.

Fig. 1-9. Welders are skilled craftworkers. They must be familiar with metal characteristics and be able to read and understand drawings. They work indoors and outdoors, in all types of weather. (Lincoln Electric Co.)

Fig. 1-10. Many highly skilled men and women are involved in the manufacture of this state-of-the-art firefighting amphibian aircraft. (Canadair Limited)

If you are interested in aircraft and rocketry, you may want to work in the aerospace industry, Fig. 1-10. Large numbers of highly skilled workers are employed in this segment of the economy.

Good SHEET METAL WORKERS are always in demand by the aircraft, building, heating, and air-conditioning industries.

These jobs are only a few of the many available in the metalworking industry that require the competence of the skilled worker. Regardless of what you choose to do, to be successful and advance in your job, you will need to complete high school. While there study mathematics, science, and vocational subjects.

TECHNICIANS

Advances in many areas of industry and science have brought about a demand for persons to do complex technical work. The men and women who do these jobs are called TECHNICIANS, Fig. 1-11. Technicians usually assist engineers in research, development, and design, Fig. 1-12. They construct and test experimental devices and machines, compile statistics, make cost estimates and prepare technical reports.

Fig. 1-11. This technician in training is learning the operation of CNC machine tools.
(William Schotta, Millersville University)

Fig. 1-12. This technician checks a device that speeds vehicle door alignment and installation on an auto assembly line. (Honda)

There are many excellent jobs in TEACHING. This is a challenging career for those who like to work with people.

ENGINEERING, Fig. 1-13, is one of the largest professional occupations. The minimum requirement for becoming an engineer is a bachelor's degree in some type of engineering. However, some men and women have entered the profession after experience as group leaders and engineering technicians.

There are many types of engineers. The INDUSTRIAL ENGINEER finds the safest and most efficient way to use machines, materials, and personnel, Fig. 1-14.

The design and development of new machines and ideas is the responsibility of the MECHANICAL ENGINEER.

A TOOL AND MANUFACTURING ENGINEER devises the methods for manufacturing and assembling a product, Fig. 1-15.

Where can you get training to become a technician? Start by taking all of the mathematics, science, computer, and vocational classes that you can fit into your high school schedule. English is also highly desirable. Most technicians must be able to understand and write technical reports.

Upon graduation from high school, you can get formal training from many sources. These include community colleges, vocational/technical centers, and technical institutes. In addition, many colleges offer two year technical programs. The programs stress mathematics, science, English, engineering, drafting, manufacturing processes, and computer science. Students also learn to handle tools, machines, and materials related to their area of interest.

THE PROFESSIONS

If you are planning to attend college, you may be interested in one of the professional occupations in metalworking.

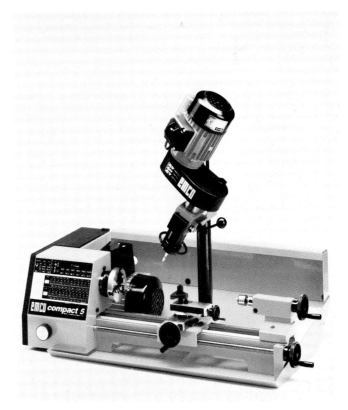

Fig. 1-13. Many engineering areas worked together to design, develop, and manufacture this combination lathe/milling machine used in many school metals technology labs. (Emco Maier Corp.)

13

Fig. 1-14. The industrial engineer planned the safest and most efficient way for this automated foundry to operate. It casts auto engine parts. (Saturn)

AERONAUTICAL ENGINEERS design and plan the manufacture of aerospace products. See Fig. 1-16.

METALLURGICAL ENGINEERS work with metals. They are concerned with the processing of metals, their conversion into commercial products, and the development of new metal alloys.

LEADERSHIP IN METALWORKING TECHNOLOGY

In your study of this unit, you have learned that metalworking technology requires a highly-skilled and educated work force. Strong and dynamic (energetic and aggressive) leadership is also needed.

LEADERSHIP is the ability to be a leader. A LEADER is a person who is in charge or command. The quality of leadership usually determines whether an organization will be a success or a failure.

WHAT MAKES A GOOD LEADER?

No one is quite sure what makes people work hard for one leader but not for another. This desire to work hard for a reason is MOTIVATION. It

Fig. 1-15. When a design is approved for production, tool and manufacturing engineers must devise the methods for manufacturing and assembling it. (Pontiac)

Fig. 1-16. The aeronautical engineer designs and plans the manufacture and testing of aircraft like this swept-forward-wing craft. (Grumman Aerospace Corp.)

is seldom based on standard rewards such as increased salaries and improved working conditions.

There are no tests to determine whether a person will be a strong leader. However, studies have shown that strong leaders have the following traits in common.

VISION. This is the talent for knowing what must be done. Short and long range goals with well defined plans are developed. A schedule is followed to achieve these goals. The status quo (existing conditions or situations) is always being updated and improved. Persons with vision enjoy the challenge of leadership and can inspire others.

COMMUNICATION. It is important to communicate in such a way that others will wish to assist and cooperate. A good leader has the ability to create situations where the energies and ideas of others can be used to reach desired goals or results.

PERSISTENCE. Persistence means the ability to stay on course, no matter what obstacles are met. However, a leader must still be flexible and willing to make changes when new ideas are presented. Persistent leaders will work long hours to achieve goals.

ORGANIZATIONAL ABILITIES. A good leader knows how to organize and direct the activities of a group. He or she learns from mistakes. The lesson learned is to improve efficiency and performance. It is important to be tactful (knowing the right thing to do or say). But it is also important to be autocratic (demand cooperation of others within the group) when necessary.

RESPONSIBILITY. Responsible persons accept responsibility for their actions. Also, they quickly give credit and recognition to others when deserved.

DELEGATES AUTHORITY. A good leader must not be afraid to assign tasks that may give others in the group opportunities for leadership. Helping others to develop leadership skills is an important quality.

GETTING LEADERSHIP EXPERIENCE

How can you get experience in leadership? The vocational education program and other clubs all need leaders. These activities offer good leadership training. See Fig. 1-17.

As a leader you will be expected to set a good example. Leadership also means that you get all

Fig. 1-17. Student groups like the Technology Student Association (TSA) and the Vocational Industrial Clubs of America (VICA) offer opportunities to build leadership skills. This student is competing in the annual VICA National Leadership Conference and United States Skill Olympics. (Howard Bud Smith)

members of the group involved in activities. This requires tact and encouragement.

A good leader does not have answers for every problem the group meets. Other members should give possible solutions. It will, however, be your job to decide which (if any) to use.

Leadership is not always easy. Decisions must be made that some of the group will not like. People, even friends, may have to be reproached or excused for poor behavior or attitude.

Do you have the traits (qualities) of a leader? Do you think you could develop them? Can you handle the unpleasant tasks that are part of leadership? Then, by all means, join a group where it will be possible for you to become a leader.

OCCUPATION AND LEADERSHIP INFORMATION

You can get more information on jobs in metalworking technology from many sources. The guidance office and your vocational education teacher are good starting points.

Most types of metalworking jobs are described in the OCCUPATIONAL OUTLOOK HANDBOOK. This is published by the United States Department of Labor. It can be found in libraries and guidance offices.

A local community college is also a good source. They will be glad to give information on the technical programs they offer.

Another outstanding source of information is your local State Employment Service. They can inform you of local job opportunities in metalworking.

The TECHNOLOGY STUDENT ASSOCIATION (TSA) will be happy to provide information on how to start a TSA chapter in your school. Included will be material on the leadership training program that is part of the club.

WHAT AN EMPLOYER EXPECTS OF YOU

Have you thought about what a company that employs you will look for in you? They often look for a return on the salary they pay you.

They will expect a fair day's work for a fair day's pay. They will count on you to do your assigned work to the best of your ability.

For your part, you should develop responsibility for the tools and equipment you use. These tools are very costly. Many employers have more than $100,000 invested in tools and equipment for each worker.

You must also remember that high school graduation is not the end of your training and/or education. If you want to keep and advance in a good job, you must keep up with technology advances. This may be done thorugh in-plant classes and/or advanced studies at community colleges or technical schools.

GETTING A JOB

Getting your first full-time job will be a very important task.

You must first decide what type of work you would like to do. Your guidance office and the local State Employment Service give tests that help find work areas where you may succeed. You can get more help by answering the following questions:

1. What have I accomplished with some degree of success?
2. What have I done that others have commended me for doing well?
3. What are the things I really like doing?
4. What are the things I DO NOT like to do?
5. What jobs have I held? Why did I leave them?

You might find that you have several areas of interest. List them. Start getting information on each of these areas. This can be done by reading, by talking with persons doing this kind of work, and/or by visiting industry.

The final step is to plan your school program. Prepare yourself for entry into the job or for advanced schooling, if it is required.

Now that you are ready to get a job, how would you go about it?

You must remember that some jobs are always available. Workers get promoted, retire, change jobs, quit, die, and are fired. Technological advances create new jobs. YOU MUST TRACK THEM DOWN.

Zero in on getting the job. MAKE YOUR JOB APPLICATION IN PERSON. Be specific about the type of job you are after. Do not just ask for a job or ask the employment office, "What job openings do you have?"

Prepare a JOB INFORMATION SHEET in advance, Fig. 1-18. This speeds up the task of filling out job applications. With this sheet, the responses you give will be the same on all applications. There will be little chance to supply confusing responses.

Finally, know where to look for a job. Review the "want ads" of local newspapers each day. Talk with friends and relatives. They may be aware of job openings before they become official or are advertised.

New office and factory buildings usually mean new job openings. You may also prepare a list of employers you would like to work for in your community. Visit their employment offices.

Remember, in most cases the job will not come to you. YOU must go to it.

JOB INFORMATION SHEET

This form has been designed to help you with the general information that will be required on most employment applications. Fill it out as completely as you can, making sure that the information is correct.

Name _____ Soc. Sec. #_____
last   first   middle

Address _____
Street   City   State   Zip

Telephone _____ How long living at present address? _____

Previous Address _____How long did you live there?_____

Age _____ Date of Birth _____

In case of emergency notify (usually nearest relative):

Name _____

Address_____ Phone _____

RECORD OF EDUCATION

	School	No. Yrs.	Name of School	Course	Graduate
Elementary					Yes ___ No ___
High School					Yes ___ No ___
College					Yes ___ No ___
Other Type					Yes ___ No ___

EMPLOYMENT RECORD

	Dates Mo. Yr.	Type of work performed
Present or last previous employer		
Address		Reason for Leaving
Rate of Pay		
Previous Employer		
Address		Reason for Leaving
Rate of Pay		

THREE PERSONAL REFERENCES (DO NOT GIVE RELATIVES)

Name	Address	Phone

Fig. 1-18. Prepare a job information sheet in advance to speed up the task of filling out job applications.

TEST YOUR KNOWLEDGE, Unit 1

Please do not write in the text. Place your answers on a separate sheet of paper.

1. Describe the meaning of technology.
2. Metalworking jobs fall into one of four classifications. Name them.
3. If you were a semiskilled worker in metalworking, what four jobs would you probably do?
4. There are disadvantages that semiskilled workers must face. Choose the disadvantages from the list below.
   a. Doing the same job over and over for long periods of time.
   b. Requires only a brief on-the-job training period.
   c. First to lose jobs when business slows down.
   d. All of the above.
   e. None of the above.
5. The formal apprentice program usually lasts _____ to _____ years.

MATCHING QUESTIONS: Match each of the following terms with their correct definitions.

a. Machinist.
b. Tool and die maker.
c. Instrument maker.
d. Set up specialist.
e. Technician.
f. Industrial engineer.
g. Mechanical engineer.
h. Aeronautical engineer.

6. __ Works between the shop and the engineering department
7. __ Finds the safest and most efficient way to use machines, materials, and personnel.
8. __ Designs and plans the manufacture of aerospace products.
9. __ Makes the tools and dies needed to cut, shape and form metal.
10. __ Designs and develops new machines and ideas.
11. __ Makes the parts for the instruments used by industry, medicine, science, and government.
12. __ Adjusts machines and tools so semiskilled workers can operate them.
13. __ Must be able to operate all kinds of machine tools.
14. The _____ engineer is concerned with the processing of metals and their conversion into commercial products.
15. What does the term leadership mean?
16. The person who is in charge or command is called a _____.
17. The quality of leadership often determines whether an organization will be a _____.

TECHNICAL TERMS TO LEARN

apprentice
careers
communications
creativity
design
enhance
industry
inspector
job application
leadership
manufacturing
metalworking
occupation

persistence
research
resources
semiskilled workers
skilled workers
skills
state-of-the-art
technician
technique
technology
vocational-technical center

ACTIVITIES

1. Metals play a very important part in our modern world. How many jobs can YOU name that make use of metal in some shape or form? Think of all those jobs that use metal directly (use metal to make things) or indirectly (only in machinery and tools).
2. Contact the TECHNOLOGY STUDENT ASSOCIATION (1914 Association Drive, Reston, VA 22091). Ask for information on how to start a TSA chapter in your school. Discuss the idea with your teacher before sending for the material.

Unit 2 . . . .

Metals We Use

In this unit you will learn about the many types of metals in use today. You will discover how metals are classified and which metals are used in school laboratories. You will be able to discuss the qualities of various metals we use and how these metals are shaped, measured, and purchased.

The metals we use have many properties. Some of them, like aluminum, magnesium, and titanium, are strong and light enough to be used to manufacture aircraft, Fig. 2-1.

Rocket and jet engines are subjected to great amounts of heat. The metals used on these engines must be able to withstand this heat. The fuel (uranium) that powers nuclear vessels, Fig. 2-2, is a metal. Only a few pounds are needed to power a ship around the world.

Fig. 2-1. The metals used to construct aircraft must be light and strong.   (Delta Air Lines)

Fig. 2-2. A metal fuel (uranium) powers this nuclear aircraft carrier. Only a few pounds are needed to propel it around the world. (U.S. Navy)

The racing car, Fig. 2-3, makes use of many kinds of metals. Each metal is selected for its special qualities: strength, lightness, and ability to dissipate heat.

Hundreds of metals and alloys are used by industry. The small internal combustion engine, Fig. 2-4, that powers a model plane, car, or boat costs only a few dollars. However, its construction makes use of more than a dozen different metals.

How many other products can you name that need metals with special qualities?

HOW METALS ARE CLASSIFIED

The metals you will use in your shop work are the same as those used by industry. They are available in a large number of shapes and sizes, Fig. 2-5.

For identification purposes, metals fall into several categories.

BASE METALS are pure metals like gold, copper, lead, and tin. They contain no other metals.

ALLOYS are combinations of several metals. They are fused (blended) together while in a molten state. For example, brass is an alloy of copper and zinc.

Fig. 2-3. Many different kinds of metal must be used in high performance racing cars. (Scott Gauthier)

Fig 2-4. Metals mined in all parts of the world (iron, aluminum, copper, brass, chrome, lead, tin, zinc, platinum, etc.) are needed to manufacture the various parts of this miniature engine.   (Cox Hobbies, Inc.)

Fig. 2-5. A few of the hundreds of different metal shapes available to industry.

Metals are further grouped into the following classes.

FERROUS METALS are alloys that contain iron as a major part of their composition. Steel is a ferrous metal.

NONFERROUS METALS contain no iron, except in very small amounts as impurities. Metals like aluminum, brass, and tin are nonferrous metals.

METALS USED IN SCHOOL LABORATORIES

The ferrous metals include carbon steels, tin plate, and galvanized sheet. Carbon steels are classified according to the amount of carbon they contain. The carbon is measured in PERCENTAGE or in POINTS (100 points equal 1 percent).

1. LOW CARBON STEELS do not contain enough carbon to be hardened (less than 0.30 percent or 30 points). They are relatively soft and are often called MILD STEEL. As they are easy to machine, weld, and form, they have

Fig. 2-6. This trivet is made from mild steel.

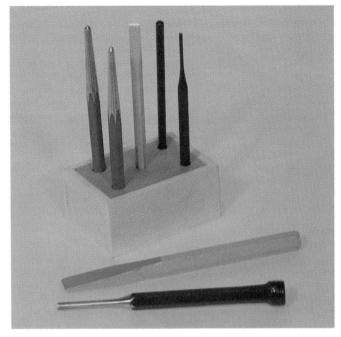

Fig. 2-8. Tools such as punches are made from tool steel.

many applications in bench metal work, Fig. 2-6. Mild steels are available as rods, bars, strips, and sheets.

2. MEDIUM CARBON STEELS contain 0.30 to 0.60 percent carbon (30 to 60 points). They are good for projects that need machining, Fig. 2-7.

3. HIGH CARBON STEELS are sometimes called TOOL STEELS. They contain 0.60 to 1.00 percent carbon. These steels are used to make tools because they can be heat-treated (this is the process of controlling the heating and cooling of metal to bring about certain desirable characteristics, such as hardness and toughness), Fig. 2-8.

Hot finished steel has a characteristic black coating (oxide). When cold finished, the steel has a surface that is smooth with no trace of the black scale, Fig. 2-9. TIN PLATE (tin cans are made from it) is a mild steel sheet to which a tin coating has been applied. GALVANIZED SHEET is a mild steel sheet on which a coating of zinc has been deposited.

Fig. 2-7. Medium carbon steel machines easily. It was used to make this small lathe.

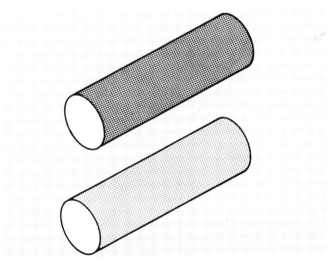

Fig. 2-9. Hot finished steel (top) has a characteristic black coating, while cold finished steel (bottom) has a smooth surface, with no trace of the black scale.

A recent addition is a mild steel sheet with a vinyl coating. It can be cut, shaped, formed, and joined like other steel sheets. Various colors and textured finishes arc available.

Many nonferrous metals are also used in the school laboratory.

ALUMINUM

Aluminum is a term used to identify an entire family of metals (there are over 100 different aluminum alloys). They range from almost pure aluminum which is very soft, to an aluminum alloy tough enough to be used as armor plate, Fig. 2-10.

Aluminum is similar to silver in color, but has a bluish tint. It is lighter weight than steel. Aluminum melts at about 1200°F (649°C), and can be worked using regular metalworking techniques.

Aluminum can be purchased as foil, sheet, rod, bar, plate, wire, or tubing.

BRASS

Brass is an alloy of copper and zinc. The color varies from a reddish bronze to a yellowish gold. Color depends upon the percentage of zinc the brass contains. Brass is easy to shape, cut, etch, solder, electroplate, and chemically color. Brass is used a great deal in art metal work, Fig. 2-11.

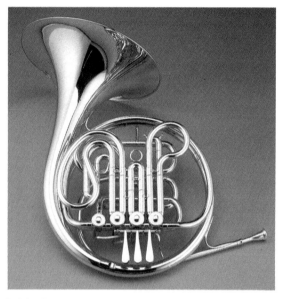

Fig. 2-11. Brass is widely used for making musical instruments. such as this French horn.   (G. Leblanc Corp.)

Brass is available in soft, half-hard, three-quarter, and hard tempers.

COPPER

Copper is an easily-worked metal. It is reddish brown in color and melts at 1981°F (1083°C). The metal takes a brilliant polish but, like brass, it must be sprayed with clear lacquer to keep the finish. Copper is worked like brass.

Fig. 2-10. Aluminum provides the strength and light weight needed to construct aircraft like this forest-fire-fighting water bomber.   (Canadair Limited)

Fig. 2-12. A great deal of copper is used in the windings of electric motors like these industrial models.   (Baldor)

Fig. 2-14. Modern pewter contains no lead. It can be used to serve food and drink.

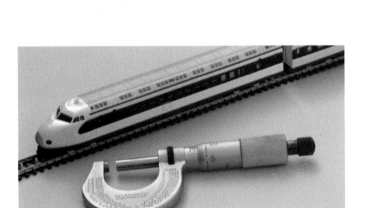

Fig. 2-13. Copper makes it possible to produce the small powerful motor that powers this miniature train.

and zinc. It works much like brass but is a bit more brittle.

STERLING SILVER

Silver combined with a small amount of copper (7 1/2 percent) is known as sterling silver. When polished, it is shiny, silvery-white in color. Sterling silver has outstanding working characteristics. It can be easily shaped and formed, and it hard solders well, Fig. 2-15.

Much copper is used in electric wiring and in electric motors. See Figs. 2-12 and 2-13.

PEWTER

Modern pewter, or Britannia metal, is an alloy of tin (91 percent), copper (1 1/2 percent) and antimony (7 1/2 percent). When polished, it has a fine silvery sheen. Modern pewter DOES NOT contain lead and can be used to serve food and drink, Fig. 2-14. However, old pewter may contain lead and should not be used to serve food or drink. Pewter is easy to work, but a good deal of skill is needed to join it properly.

NICKEL SILVER

Nickel silver, or German silver, is used as a substitute for silver in inexpensive jewelry. It is a copper base alloy with varying quantities of nickel

Fig. 2-15. Sterling silver has outstanding working characteristics. It was used to make this bowl and vase.

SHAPES OF METALS WE USE

Metals are produced in many shapes and sizes. A few of the standard metal shapes are illustrated in Fig. 2-16.

Fig. 2-17 presents several sheet metals commonly found in the school laboratory. The chart shows how they are measured and purchased.

Have you ever wondered how metal is shaped? Many shapes start as ingots which are heated and passed through rolling mills. There they are shaped into semifinished products called slags, blooms, or billets, Fig. 2-18. These pass on through other rolling mills, where rolls of different types and sizes turn them into plates, sheets, rods, and bars. The rolling process not only shapes the metal but also makes it tougher and stronger.

SHAPES		LENGTH	HOW MEASURED	*HOW PURCHASED	OTHER
	 Sheet less than 1/4 in. thick	to 144 in.	Thickness x width widths to 72 in.	Weight, foot, or piece	Available in coils of much longer lengths
	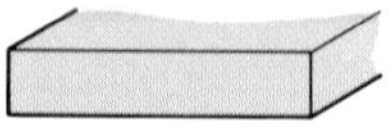 Plate more than 1/4 in. thick	to 20 ft.	Thickness x width	Weight, foot, or piece	
	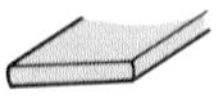 Band	to 20 ft.	Thickness x width	Weight or piece	Mild steel with oxide coating
	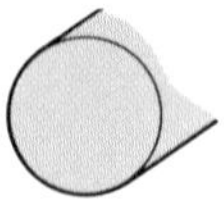 Rod	12 to 20 ft.	Diameter	Weight, foot, or piece	Hot-rolled steel to 20 ft. length; cold-finished steel to 12 ft. length; steel drill rod 36 in.
	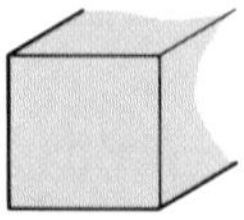 Square	12 to 20 ft.	Width	Weight, foot, or piece	
	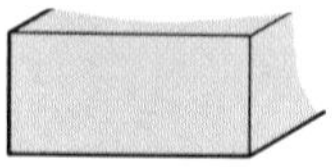 Flats	Hot rolled 20-22 ft. Cold finished	Thickness x width	Weight, foot, or piece	
	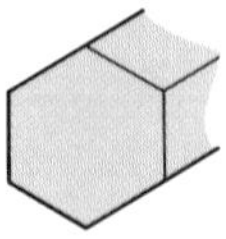 Hexagon	12 to 20 ft.	Distance across flats	Weight, foot, or piece	
	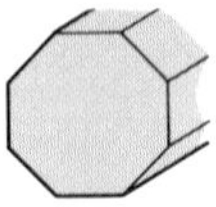 Octagon	12 to 20 ft.	Distance across flats	Weight, foot, or piece	
	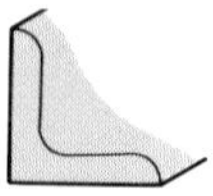 Angle	Lengths to 40 ft.	Leg length x leg length x thickness of legs	Weight, foot, or piece	
	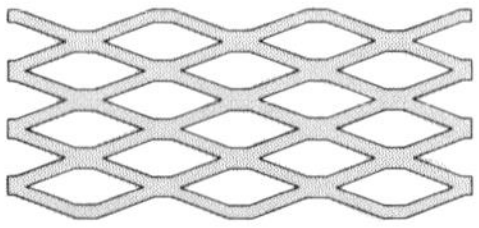 Expanded sheet	to 96 in.	Gauge number (U.S. Standard)	36 x 96 in. and size of openings	Metal is pierced and expanded (stretched) to diamond shape; also available rolled to thickness after it has been expanded
	 Perforated Sheet	to 96 in.	Gauge number (U.S. Standard)	30 x 36 in. 36 x 48 in. 36 x 96 in.	Design is cut in sheet; many designs available.

*Charge made for cutting to other than standard lengths.

Fig. 2-16. Metals we use . . . available shapes, how they are measured and purchased, and some of their characteristics.

MATERIAL (Sheet less than 1/4 in. thick)	HOW MEASURED	HOW PURCHASED	CHARACTERISTICS
Copper	Gauge number (Brown & Sharp & Amer. Std.)	24 x 96 in. sheet or 12 or 18 in. by lineal feet on roll	Pure metal
Brass	Gauge number (B & S and Amer. Std.)	24 x 76 in. sheet or 12 or 18 in. by lineal feet on roll	Alloy of copper and zinc
Aluminum	Decimal	24 x 72 in. sheet or 12 or 18 in. by lineal feet on roll	Available as commercially pure metal or alloyed for strength, hardness, and ductility
Galvanized Steel	Gauge number (U.S. Std.)	24 x 96 in. sheet	Mild steel sheet with zinc plating, also available with zinc coating that is part of sheet
Black Annealed Steel Sheet	Gauge number (U.S. Std.)	24 x 96 in. sheet	Mild steel with oxide coating- hot rolled
Cold Rolled Steel Sheet	Gauge number (U.S. Std.)	24 x 96 in. sheet	Oxide removed and cold rolled to final thickness
Tin Plate	Gauge number (U.S. Std.)	20 x 28 in. sheet 56 or 112 to pkg.	Mild steel with tin coating
Nickel Silver	Gauge number (Brown & Sharp)	6 or 12 in. wide by lineal sheet	Copper 50%, zinc 30%, nickel 20%

Fig. 2-17. Metals we use . . . how they are measured and purchased, and some of their characteristics.

Sheet stock is made by passing a metal slab between rolls, Fig. 2-19, until the desired thickness is obtained. As the slab becomes thinner, its length increases. The slab can be made wider by passing it crosswise through the rolls.

Bar, rod, and other forms are also shaped by rolling. However, the process differs from the rolling of sheet in that the rolls are grooved to produce the specific shape desired. The rolling process

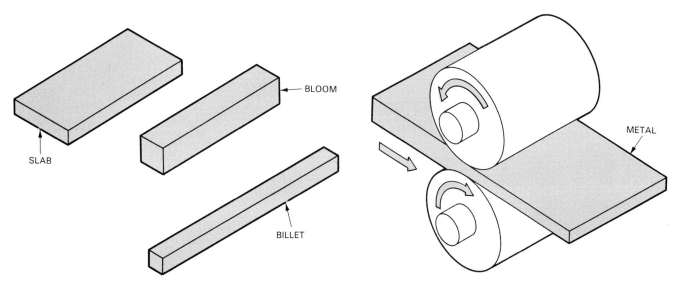

Fig. 2-18. Most metal shapes start as slabs, blooms or billets.　　Fig. 2-19. How sheet metal and plate are rolled to thickness.

starts with a billet which is gradually worked into the required shape. See Fig. 2-20.

Wire is made by a drawing process, Fig. 2-21. In wire drawing, the end of the rod is pointed and pulled through dies. These dies reduce the diameter of the rod until the required wire diameter is reached.

Seamless tubing is produced as shown in Fig. 2-22. A cylinder is cupped at one end and drawn through well-lubricated dies that reduce its diameter and increase its length.

Seamless tubing can also be made by the extrusion process, Fig. 2-23. Pressure is employed to force the metal through a die of the required shape and size. The extrusion process is also employed to produce other complex metal shapes, Fig. 2-24

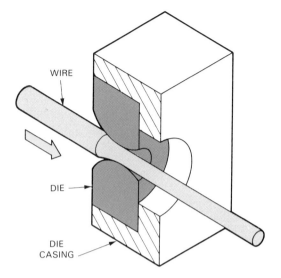

Fig. 2-21. Wire is made by pulling a rod through dies to reduce its diameter to the required size.

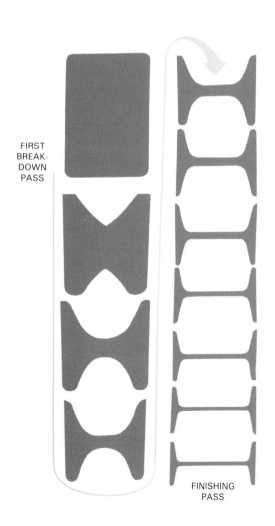

Fig. 2-20. When rolling structural shapes, the process starts with a billet that is gradually worked into the required shape.

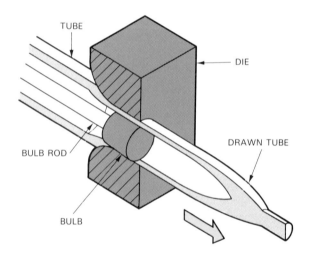

Fig. 2-22. One technique used to draw seamless tubing.

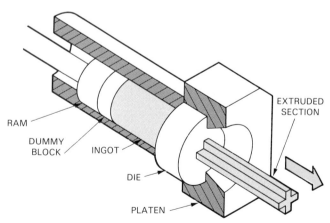

Fig. 2-23. In the extrusion process, metal is forced through a die of the required shape and size.

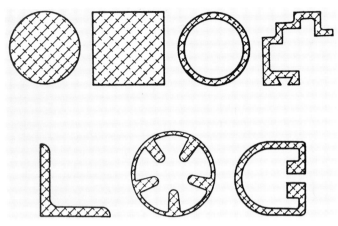

Fig. 2-24. A few of the extruded shapes available. Almost any shape can be produced by this process.

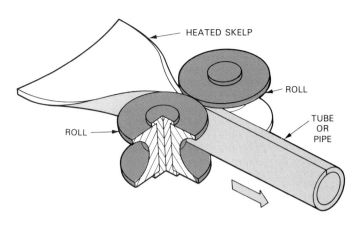

Fig. 2-25. How some pipe and tubing is made from flat metal sheet.

Butt welded pipe is made from a heated strip called skelp. Skelp is formed and welded together as shown in Fig. 2-25.

Metal is shaped by other techniques too. Many of the methods used will be described in this book.

MAJOR PROCESSES IN THE STEEL INDUSTRY

It is hard to imagine a person who does not use at least one of the many items made of steel during the course of a day. People depend on steel for such things as buildings, bridges, safety pins, and paper clips.

Although steel is familiar in our daily lives, it is also found at the frontiers of science. Few people understand the human effort required to produce it. The following flow charts, courtesy of American Iron and Steel Institute, show some of the things that must be done to produce steel.

The United States is the world's largest producer of raw steel. Markets in this country support many companies operating steelmaking or finishing facilities in 38 states. More than half of these companies make raw steel and finish it themselves. Others buy semifinished steel from which they make bars, wire, and wire products, hot and cold rolled sheets, plates, pipe and tubing. A wide variety of other products are also made. However, the public seldom sees these because they are processed further by the customers of the steel industry.

The modern steel industry is concerned with producing huge amounts of steel. It is also concerned with being a partner with individuals, communities, and governments working for ecological (relationship between living things and surrounding conditions) improvement. Each of the processes which follow has air and water quality control equipment designed into it.

FLOWLINE OF STEELMAKING

From iron ore, limestone, and coal in the earth's crust to space-age steels — this fundamental flowline shows only major steps in an intricate progression of processes with their many options.

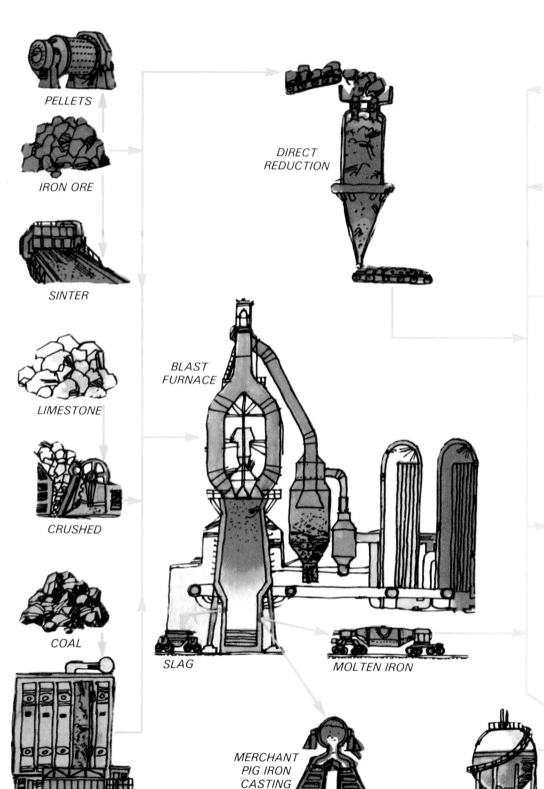

PELLETS

IRON ORE

SINTER

LIMESTONE

CRUSHED

COAL

COKE OVENS

DIRECT REDUCTION

BLAST FURNACE

SLAG

MOLTEN IRON

MERCHANT PIG IRON CASTING

SCRAP

LIME & FLUX

MOLTEN STEEL

ELECTRIC FURNACE

NOTE: Vacuum treatment of liquid steels is frequently used for making super-refined metals for advanced technology end-uses.

MOL STE

OPEN HEARTH FURNACE

NOTE: A modification of the basic oxygen furnace is the Q-BOP in which the oxygen and other gases are blown in from the bottom rather than the top as shown.

OXYGEN

MOL ST

BASIC OXYGEN FURNAC OR Q-BOP

Metals We Use

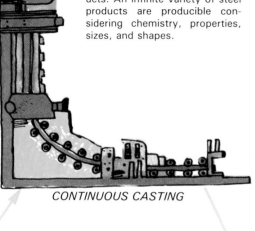

Molten steel must solidify before it can be made into finished products. An infinite variety of steel products are producible considering chemistry, properties, sizes, and shapes.

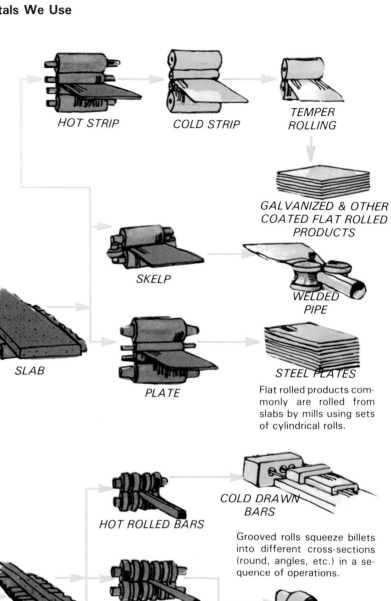

CONTINUOUS CASTING

HOT STRIP

COLD STRIP

TEMPER ROLLING

GALVANIZED & OTHER COATED FLAT ROLLED PRODUCTS

SKELP

WELDED PIPE

SLAB

PLATE

STEEL PLATES

Flat rolled products commonly are rolled from slabs by mills using sets of cylindrical rolls.

CONVENTIONAL INGOT TEEMING

INGOT BREAKDOWN MILL

HOT FORGING

NOTE: A small but significant percentage of heated ingot steel is squeezed in forging presses to make large shafts for power plants, nuclear plant components, and other products.

HOT ROLLED BARS

COLD DRAWN BARS

Grooved rolls squeeze billets into different cross-sections (round, angles, etc.) in a sequence of operations.

BILLET

RODS

WIRE & WIRE PRODUCTS

TUBE ROUNDS

SEAMLESS PIPE

Piercing is the process used to make seamless pipe and tubing from a semifinished product called tube rounds.

STRUCTURAL SHAPES

BLOOM

Sets of grooved rolls are used to roll blooms into heavy beams for construction or for rails.

RAILS

(American Iron and Steel Institute)

31

BLAST FURNACE IRONMAKING

A blast furnace is a cylindrical steel vessel, often as tall as a ten-story building, lined inside with a heat-resistant brick. Once it is fired up, the furnace runs continuously until this lining is worn out and must be replaced. Coke, iron ore, and limestone are charged into the top of the furnace. They proceed slowly down through the furnace being heated as they are exposed to a blast of super-hot air that blows upward from the bottom of the furnace. The blast of air burns the coke, releasing heat and gas which remove oxygen from the ore. The limestone acts as a cleansing agent.

Freed from its impurities, the molten iron collects in the bottom where it is drawn off every three-to-five hours as a white-hot stream of liquid iron. From there, the molten iron will be further refined in a steelmaking furnace.

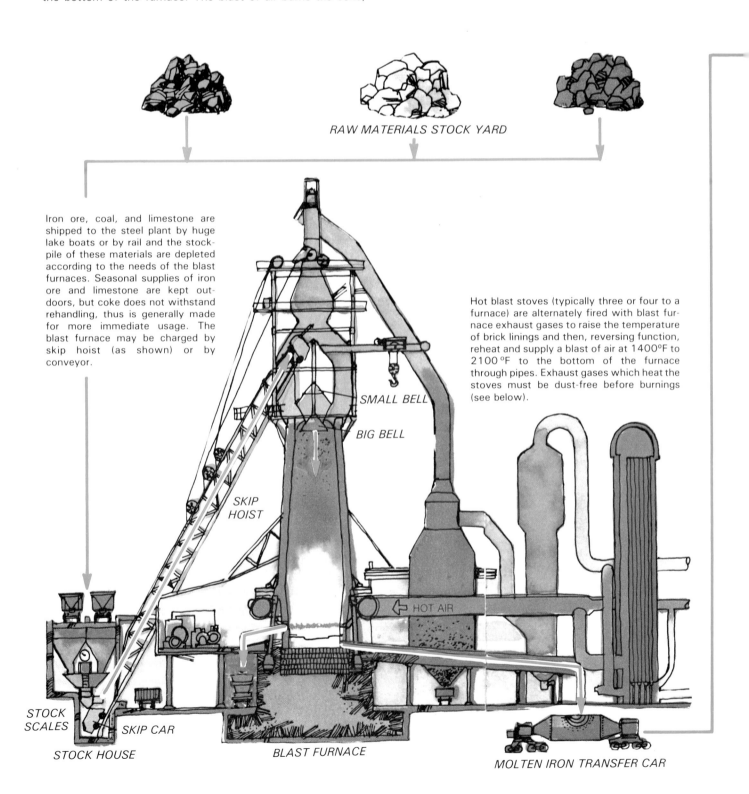

RAW MATERIALS STOCK YARD

Iron ore, coal, and limestone are shipped to the steel plant by huge lake boats or by rail and the stockpile of these materials are depleted according to the needs of the blast furnaces. Seasonal supplies of iron ore and limestone are kept outdoors, but coke does not withstand rehandling, thus is generally made for more immediate usage. The blast furnace may be charged by skip hoist (as shown) or by conveyor.

Hot blast stoves (typically three or four to a furnace) are alternately fired with blast furnace exhaust gases to raise the temperature of brick linings and then, reversing function, reheat and supply a blast of air at 1400°F to 2100°F to the bottom of the furnace through pipes. Exhaust gases which heat the stoves must be dust-free before burnings (see below).

SMALL BELL

BIG BELL

SKIP HOIST

← HOT AIR

STOCK SCALES

SKIP CAR

STOCK HOUSE

BLAST FURNACE

MOLTEN IRON TRANSFER CAR

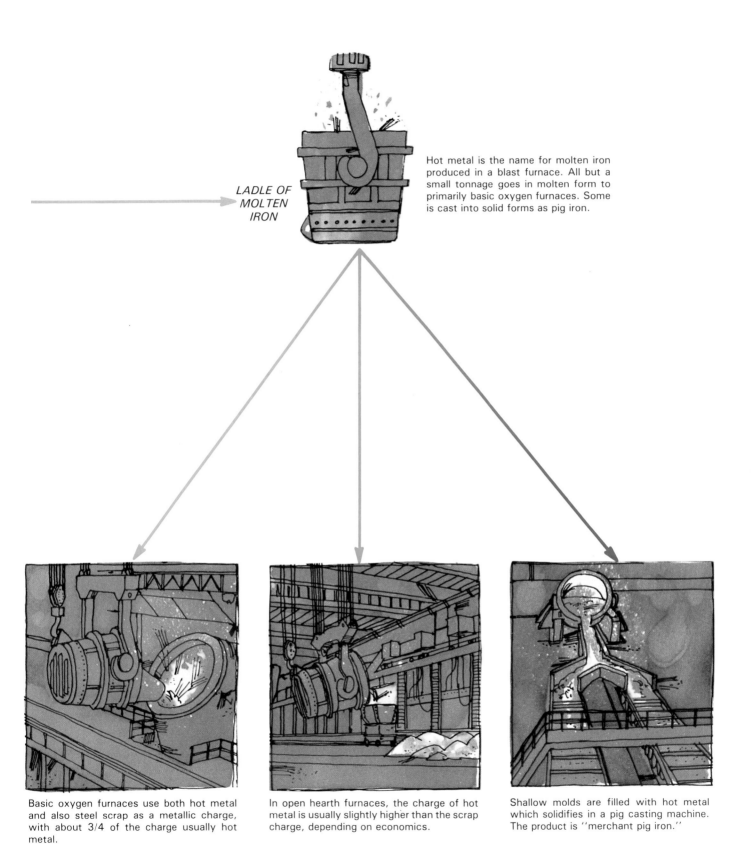

LADLE OF MOLTEN IRON

Hot metal is the name for molten iron produced in a blast furnace. All but a small tonnage goes in molten form to primarily basic oxygen furnaces. Some is cast into solid forms as pig iron.

Basic oxygen furnaces use both hot metal and also steel scrap as a metallic charge, with about 3/4 of the charge usually hot metal.

In open hearth furnaces, the charge of hot metal is usually slightly higher than the scrap charge, depending on economics.

Shallow molds are filled with hot metal which solidifies in a pig casting machine. The product is ''merchant pig iron.''

(American Iron and Steel Institute)

BASIC OXYGEN STEELMAKING

In the United States more steel is produced by basic oxygen furnaces (BOF's) than by any other means. They consume large amounts of oxygen to support the combustion of unwanted elements and so eliminate them. No other gases or fuels are used. BOF's make steel very quickly compared with the other major methods now in use — for example, 300 tons in 45 minutes as against several hours in open hearth and electric furnaces. Most grades of steel can be made in BOF's.

The actual furnaces are a small part of the facility, as this schematic drawing shows. Gas cleaning devices and materials handling equipment occupy most of the space.

GAS CLEANING EQUIPMENT

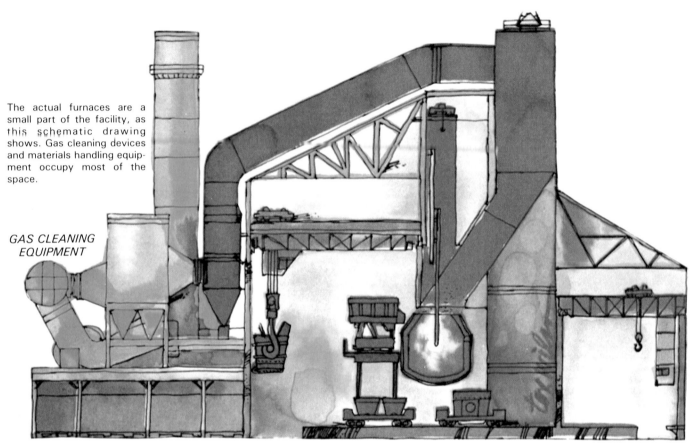

DIAGRAM OF BASIC OXYGEN FURNACE FACILITY

The first step for making a heat of steel in a BOF is to tilt the furnace and charge it with scrap. The furnaces are mounted on trunnions and can be rotated through a full circle.

Hot metal from the blast furnace accounts for up to 80 percent of the metallic charge and is poured from a ladle into the top of the tilted furnace.

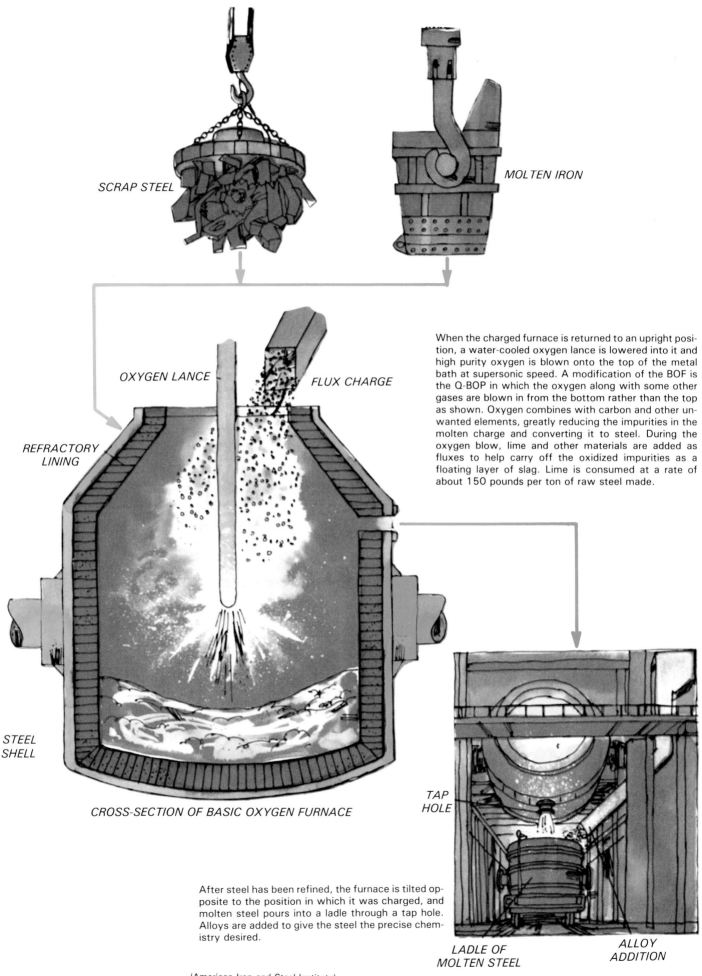

SCRAP STEEL

MOLTEN IRON

OXYGEN LANCE

FLUX CHARGE

REFRACTORY
LINING

STEEL
SHELL

CROSS-SECTION OF BASIC OXYGEN FURNACE

When the charged furnace is returned to an upright position, a water-cooled oxygen lance is lowered into it and high purity oxygen is blown onto the top of the metal bath at supersonic speed. A modification of the BOF is the Q-BOP in which the oxygen along with some other gases are blown in from the bottom rather than the top as shown. Oxygen combines with carbon and other unwanted elements, greatly reducing the impurities in the molten charge and converting it to steel. During the oxygen blow, lime and other materials are added as fluxes to help carry off the oxidized impurities as a floating layer of slag. Lime is consumed at a rate of about 150 pounds per ton of raw steel made.

TAP
HOLE

After steel has been refined, the furnace is tilted opposite to the position in which it was charged, and molten steel pours into a ladle through a tap hole. Alloys are added to give the steel the precise chemistry desired.

(American Iron and Steel Institute)

LADLE OF
MOLTEN STEEL

ALLOY
ADDITION

35

OPEN HEARTH STEELMAKING

Open hearth furnaces are so named because the limestone, scrap steel and molten iron charged into the shallow steelmaking area (the hearth) are exposed (open) to the sweep of flames. A furnace that will produce a fairly typical 350 tons of steel in five to eight hours may be about 90 feet long and 30 feet wide.

The cutaway drawing below shows several steps simultaneously that would normally occur in sequence. First the long-armed charging machine picks up boxes of limestone and steel scrap, thrusts them through the furnace doors and dumps the contents. The flame of burning fuel oil, tar, or gases partially melts the solid charge, after which molten iron (lower right) is poured into the furnace. High-temperature reactions cause several unwanted elements to combine with the limestone to form a slag.

When tests of samples show the steel to be of specified chemistry, the tap hole is opened by an explosive charge and the steel runs into a ladle. The slag, which is lighter than steel, floats on the metal and overflows into a slag thimble during pouring. Alloy additions are made to the steel in the ladle.

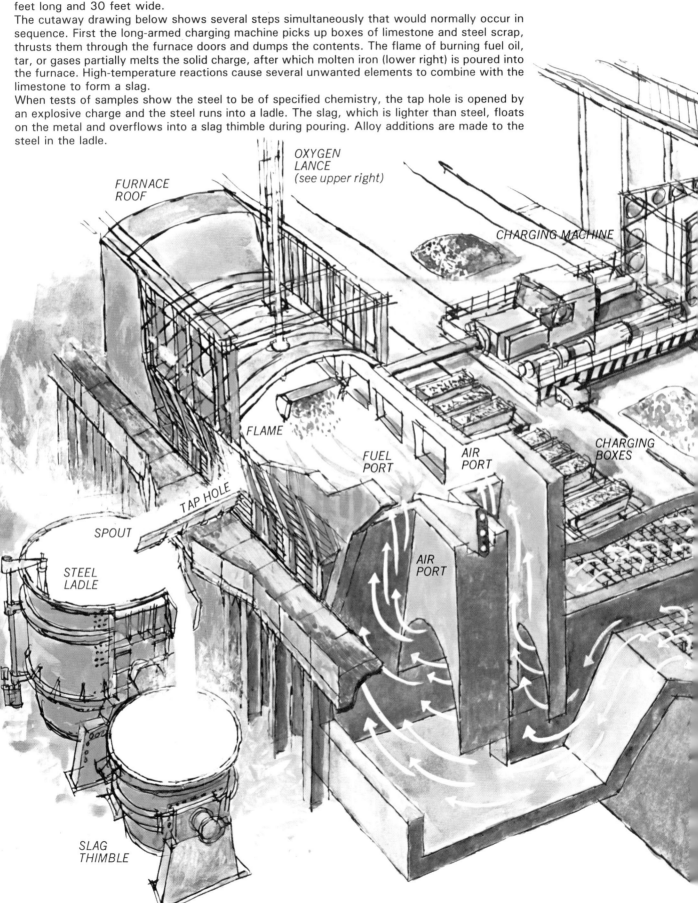

In recent years practically all open hearth furnaces have been converted to the use of oxygen. The gas is fed into the open hearth through the roof by means of retractable lances. The use of gaseous oxygen in the open hearth increases flame temperature, and thereby speeds the melting process.

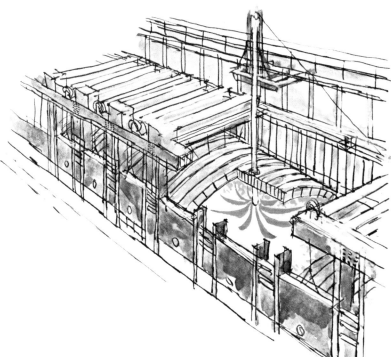

CONTROL PANELS

BRICK CHECKER CHAMBERS

Molten iron from a blast furnace is a major raw material for the open hearth furnaces. A massive "funnel" is wheeled to an open hearth door and the contents of a ladle or iron are poured through it into the furnace hearth. The principal addition of molten metal is made after the original scrap charge has begun to melt.

Brick checker chambers are located on both ends of the furnace. The bricks are arranged to leave a great number of passages through which the hot waste gases from the furnace pass and heat the brickwork prior to going through the cleaner and stack. Later on, the flow is reversed and the air for combustion passes through the heated bricks and is itself heated on its way to the hearth.

(American Iron and Steel Institute)

ELECTRIC FURNACE STEELMAKING

Traditionally used to produce alloy, stainless, tool, and specialty steels, electric furnaces have been developed in size and capability to become high-tonnage makers of carbon steel, too.

The heat within the furnace is precisely controlled as the electric current arcs from one electrode (of the three inserted through the furnace roof) to the metallic charge and back to another electrode.

ELECTRODES

At left, this cutaway drawing shows an electric furnace with its carbon electrodes attached to support arms and electrical cables and extending into the furnace. Molten steel and the rocker mounting on which the furnace may be tilted is also shown.

ELECTRIC FURNACE FACILITY

*CHARGING
BUCKET*

At right, the roof of a furnace is pivoted aside so that a charging bucket of scrap may be lowered into position for bottom-dumping. Alternatively, direct reduced pellets may be fed continuously during the meltdown.

Steel scrap is the principal metallic charge to electric furnaces. It is classified as "home scrap" (croppings originating in steel mills), "prompt industrial scrap" (trimmings returned by steel users), and "dormant scrap" (the materials collected and processed by dealers).

Direct reduction of iron ore produces pellets rich enough in iron to be used as a metallic charge, also.

SCRAP STEEL

FLUXES

CHARGING BOX

Alloying elements from many parts of the world are added to the molten metal, usually in the form of ferroalloys.

R

CROSS SECTION OF ELECTRIC FURNACE

When the roof of the furnace is in place, the three carbon electrodes are lowered until they approach the cold scrap. Electric arcs produce heat to melt the scrap.

TAPPING SPOUT

LADLE OF MOLTEN STEEL

SLAG

SLAG THIMBLE

Limestone and flux are charged after the scrap becomes molten. Impurities in the steel rise into a floating layer of slag, some or most of which can be poured off.

(American Iron and Steel Institute)

When the chemical composition of the steel meets specifications, the furnace is tilted backward. Molten steel pours out the spout into a ladle. The slag follows the steel and serves as an insulating layer.

FURNACE
LADLE

VACUUM PROCESS OF STEELMAKING

Steels for special applications are often processed in a vacuum to give them properties not otherwise obtainable. The primary purpose of vacuum processing is to remove such gases as oxygen, nitrogen, and hydrogen from molten metal to make higher-purity steel.

Many grades of steel are degassed by processes similar to those shown on this page. Even greater purity and uniformity of steel chemistry than available by degassing is obtained by subjecting the metal to vacuum melting processes.

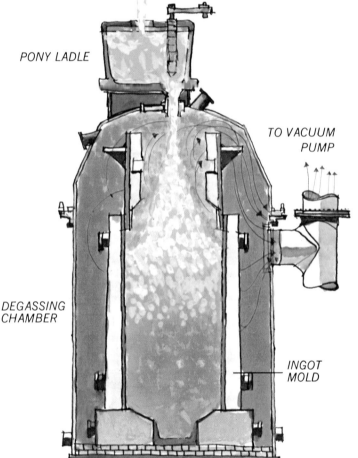

PONY LADLE

TO VACUUM PUMP

DEGASSING CHAMBER

INGOT MOLD

The Vacuum Degasses

In vacuum stream degassing (left), a ladle of molten steel from a conventional furnace is taken to a vacuum chamber. An ingot mold is shown within the chamber. Larger chambers designed to contain ladles are also used. The conventionally melted steel goes into a pony ladle and from there into the chamber. The stream of steel is broken up into droplets when it is exposed to vacuum within the chamber. During the droplet phase, undesirable gases escape from the steel and are drawn off before the metal solidifies in the mold.

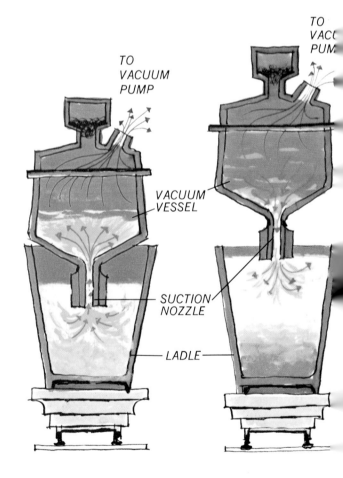

TO
VACUUM
PUMP

TO
VAC
PUM

VACUUM VESSEL

SUCTION NOZZLE

LADLE

Ladle degassing facilities (right) of several kinds are in current use. In the left-hand facility, molten steel is forced by atmospheric pressure into the heated vacuum chamber. Gases are removed in this pressure chamber, which is then raised so that the molten steel returns by gravity into the ladle. Since not all of the steel enters the vacuum chamber at one time, this process is repeated until essentially all the steel in the ladle has been processed.

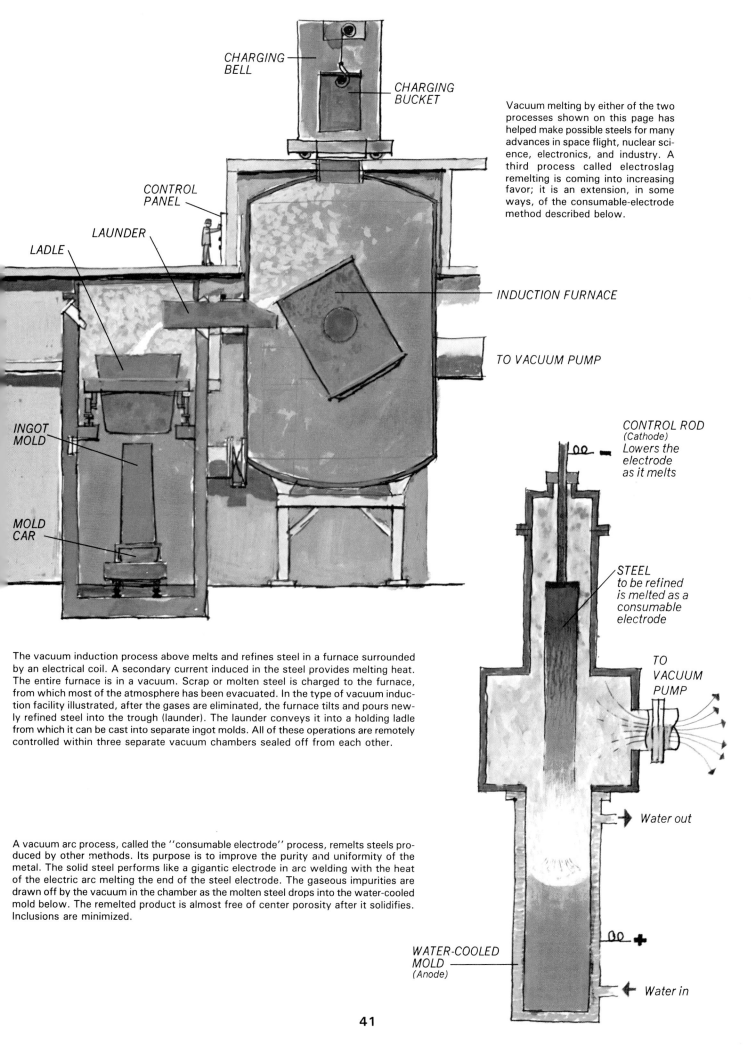

CHARGING BELL

CHARGING BUCKET

CONTROL PANEL

LAUNDER

LADLE

INGOT MOLD

MOLD CAR

INDUCTION FURNACE

TO VACUUM PUMP

Vacuum melting by either of the two processes shown on this page has helped make possible steels for many advances in space flight, nuclear science, electronics, and industry. A third process called electroslag remelting is coming into increasing favor; it is an extension, in some ways, of the consumable-electrode method described below.

CONTROL ROD
(Cathode)
Lowers the electrode as it melts

STEEL
to be refined is melted as a consumable electrode

TO VACUUM PUMP

Water out

WATER-COOLED MOLD
(Anode)

Water in

The vacuum induction process above melts and refines steel in a furnace surrounded by an electrical coil. A secondary current induced in the steel provides melting heat. The entire furnace is in a vacuum. Scrap or molten steel is charged to the furnace, from which most of the atmosphere has been evacuated. In the type of vacuum induction facility illustrated, after the gases are eliminated, the furnace tilts and pours newly refined steel into the trough (launder). The launder conveys it into a holding ladle from which it can be cast into separate ingot molds. All of these operations are remotely controlled within three separate vacuum chambers sealed off from each other.

A vacuum arc process, called the "consumable electrode" process, remelts steels produced by other methods. Its purpose is to improve the purity and uniformity of the metal. The solid steel performs like a gigantic electrode in arc welding with the heat of the electric arc melting the end of the steel electrode. The gaseous impurities are drawn off by the vacuum in the chamber as the molten steel drops into the water-cooled mold below. The remelted product is almost free of center porosity after it solidifies. Inclusions are minimized.

41

THE FIRST SOLID FORMS OF STEEL

Molten steel from basic oxygen, electric, and open hearth furnaces flows into ladles and then follows one or the other of two major routes to the rolling mills that form most of the industry's finished products. Both processes shown on these pages produce solid semifinished products—one, ingots (below); the other, cast slabs (far right).

SOAKING PIT

BUGGY

LADLE

Stripped ingots are taken to furnaces called "soaking pits." There they are "soaked" in heat until they reach uniform temperature throughout. Then the reheated ingots are lifted out of the pit and carried to the roughing mill on a buggy.

STRIPPER CRANE

INGOT MOLDS

The traditional method of handling molten steel is to position the ladle via an overhead crane above a line of ingot molds (left). Then the operator opens a stopper rod within the ladle, and a stream of steal flows through a hole in the bottom of the ladle to "teem" or fill the cast iron molds which rest on special ingot railroad cars.

Molten steel in an ingot mold cools and solidifies from the outside towards the center. When the steel is solid enough, a stripper crane lifts away the mold while a plunger holds the steel ingot down on the ingot car.

ROUGHING MILL

Roughing mills are the first stage in shaping the hot steel ingot into semifinished steel—usually blooms, billets, or slabs. Some roughing mills are the first in a series of continuous mills, feeding sequences of finishing rolls.

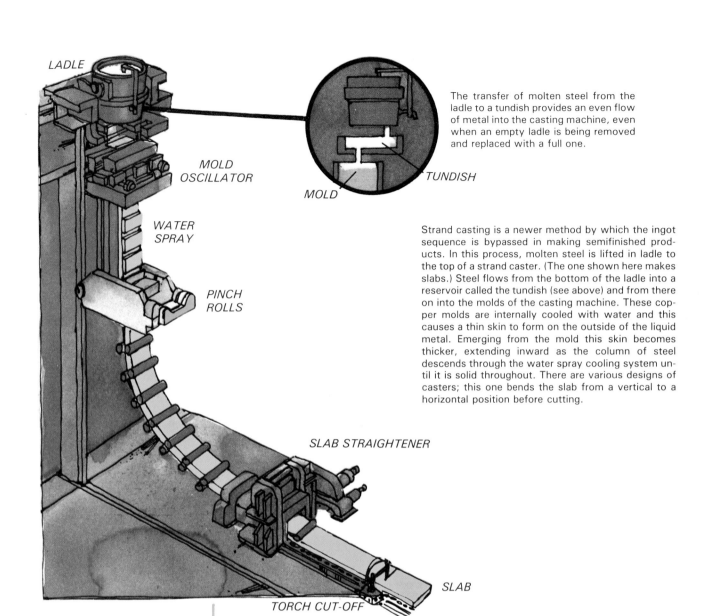

LADLE

MOLD
OSCILLATOR

WATER
SPRAY

PINCH
ROLLS

The transfer of molten steel from the ladle to a tundish provides an even flow of metal into the casting machine, even when an empty ladle is being removed and replaced with a full one.

MOLD   TUNDISH

Strand casting is a newer method by which the ingot sequence is bypassed in making semifinished products. In this process, molten steel is lifted in ladle to the top of a strand caster. (The one shown here makes slabs.) Steel flows from the bottom of the ladle into a reservoir called the tundish (see above) and from there on into the molds of the casting machine. These copper molds are internally cooled with water and this causes a thin skin to form on the outside of the liquid metal. Emerging from the mold this skin becomes thicker, extending inward as the column of steel descends through the water spray cooling system until it is solid throughout. There are various designs of casters; this one bends the slab from a vertical to a horizontal position before cutting.

SLAB STRAIGHTENER

SLAB

TORCH CUT-OFF

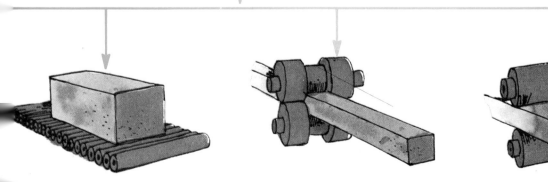

looms are large and mostly square in ross section; frequently used in manufac- ure of building beams and columns.

Billets—mostly also square—are produced from blooms and are smaller and longer than blooms. Bars, pipes, wire, and wire products are made from billets.

Slabs are the wide semifinished produce from which sheets, strip, plates, and other flat rolled steel products are made.

(American Iron and Steel Institute)

43

TEST YOUR KNOWLEDGE, Unit 2

Please do not write in the text. Place your answers on a separate sheet of paper.

1. Give two reasons why aluminum, magnesium, and titanium are used to manufacture airplanes.
2. Base metals are _____ metals.
3. Alloys are _____ of several metals.
4. Ferrous metals are those metals which contain _____ as the major element in their composition.
   a. Copper.
   b. Iron.
   c. Aluminum.
   d. Zinc.
5. What is the difference between ferrous and nonferrous metals?
6. How are carbon steels classified?
7. _____ _____ steel has a black coating. _____ _____ steel has a smooth surface.
8. Answer each of the following questions and also make drawings of the processes involved.
   a. How is metal in sheet or plate form made?
   b. Wire is made by _____ process.
   c. Seamless tubing is manufactured by _____ _____.

TECHNICAL TERMS TO LEARN

aluminum	nickel silver
alloy	nonferrous
base metal	oxide
brass	pewter
carbon steel	steel
cold finished steel	steerling silver
copper	tin
ferrous	tin plate
galvanized sheet	titanium
hot finished steel	tool steel
iron	uranium
magnesium	zinc
metals	

ACTIVITIES

1. How many applications can you name that need metals with special qualities? Classify them as base metals or alloys.
2. Secure samples of as many metals as you can. Mount them on hardboard and label each of the samples.

Steel mills are usually located on waterways to allow efficient delivery of iron ore and other materials by ship or barge. (Jack Klasey)

Unit 3 . . . .

Planning Your Project

This unit introduces the steps to follow when planning a project. You will learn the purpose of a working drawing, a Bill of Material, and a Plan of Procedure. You will be able to use these steps in planning your own project.

The experienced artisans plan their jobs carefully before starting. You should plan your projects with the same concern. Planning will save time, effort, and material.

If plans are not available for the project you want to make, your first task will be to prepare working drawings. These drawings may be sketched or made with drafting instruments, Fig. 3-1. The plans should be drawn full size if possible.

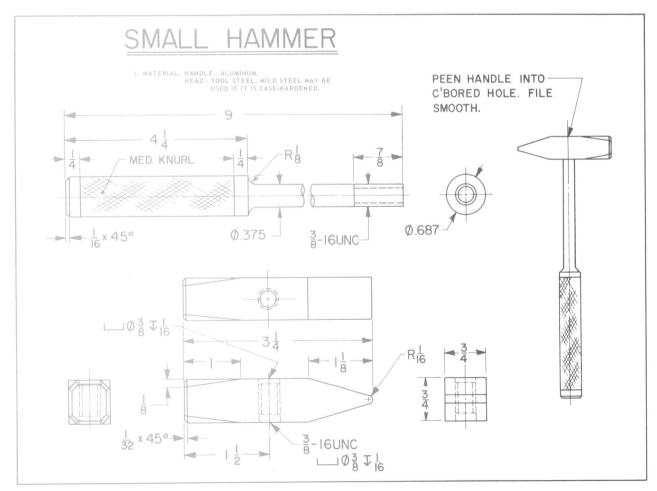

Fig. 3-1. Working drawing of the project that will be described in this unit.

While preparing the working drawings, you will need to decide on the methods of construction and fabrication you will use on your project.

The final steps in planning the project should be the preparation of a BILL OF MATERIAL and a PLAN OF PROCEDURE. A Bill of Material is a list of the materials needed to construct the project. A Plan of Procedure is a list of operations, in the order they will be done. These operations are those you will follow in the construction

of your project. You may want to combine both of them on the same sheet, Fig. 3-2.

PLANNING A PROJECT

Using the project plan sheet from Fig. 3-2, the following operations are necessary to manufacture the hammer shown in Fig. 3-1. The completed plan sheet is shown in Fig. 3-3. See Figs. 3-4 and 3-5 for a pictorial outline for making the hammer. The completed hammer is shown in Fig. 3-6.

PROJECT PLAN SHEET

Name _____ Period _____

Name of Project _____

Date Started _____ Date Completed _____

Source of Idea or Project _____

BILL OF MATERIAL

Part Name	No. of Pieces	Material	Size (T x W x L)	Unit Cost	Total Cost
				Total Cost	

PLAN OF PROCEDURE

List the operations to be performed in their sequential order.
Indicate the tool(s) and equipment needed to accomplish the job.

No.	Operation	Tools and Equipment

Fig. 3-2. A typical project plan sheet includes a Bill of Material and a Plan of Procedure.

PROJECT PLAN SHEET

Name RICHARD J. WALKER   Period 3 MON, WED, & FRI.

Name of Project MACHINIST'S HAMMER

Date Started SEPTEMBER 15   Date Completed DECEMBER 10

Source of Idea or Project EXPLORING METALWORKING

BILL OF MATERIAL

Part Name	No. of Pieces	Material	Size (T x W x L)	Unit Cost	Total Cost
HAMMER HEAD	1	C. F. STEEL	¾ x ¾ x 3 ¼		
HANDLE	1	ALUMINUM	¾ DIA. x 9 ¼		
				Total Cost	

PLAN OF PROCEDURE

List the operations to be performed in their sequential order.
Indicate the tool(s) and equipment needed to accomplish the job.

No.	Operation	Tools and Equipment
	HAMMER HEAD	
1.	CUT STOCK TO LENGTH AND REMOVE BURRS.	RULE, SCRIBE, HACK SAW AND FILE
2.	FILE HEAD SQUARE.	FILE AND SQUARE
3.	LAYOUT AS PER PLANS.	SCRIBE, RULE AND SQUARE
4.	FILE CHAMFERS AND BEVELS ON HEAD.	FILE
5.	CUT WEDGE END.	HACK SAW
6.	FILE WEDGE END TO SIZE.	FILE AND SQUARE
7.	DRILL ⅜ DIA. HOLE ¼ DEEP.	DRILL PRESS, VISE, PARALLELS, CENTER FINDER, CENTER DRILL AND ⅜ DIA. DRILL
8.	DRILL "F" DRILL THROUGH.	SAME SET UP BUT FINISH DRILLING WITH "F" DRILL
9.	TURN HEAD OVER IN VISE AND C'BORE ⅜" DIA. BY ⅛ DEEP.	SAME SET UP. ⅜ DIA. DRILL
10.	TAP HOLE ⅜-16 NC.	⅜-16 NC TAP, TAP HANDLE AND SQUARE
11.	CLEAN AND POLISH.	ABRASIVE CLOTH AND OIL
12.	CASE HARDEN.	FURNACE AND CASE HARDENING COMPOUND
13.	FINAL POLISH.	ABRASIVE CLOTH AND OIL
	HANDLE	
1.	CUT STOCK TO LENGTH.	RULE, SCRIBE AND HACK SAW
2.	FACE ENDS AND CENTER DRILL.	LATHE, 3-JAW UNIVERSAL CHUCK, JACOBS CHUCK, CENTER DRILL AND R.H. TOOL HOLDER
3.	TURN A SECTION 5 IN. LONG BY ¹¹/₁₆ IN. DIAMETER.	L.H. TOOL HOLDER, CALIPER AND RULE OR MICROMETER
4.	MARK OFF SECTION TO BE KNURLED AND KNURL.	HERMAPHRODITE CALIPER, RULE AND KNURLING TOOL
5.	MOVE HANDLE CLOSE INTO CHUCK AND MACHINE CHAMFER.	R.H. TOOL HOLDER AND RULE
6.	REVERSE WORK IN CHUCK AND TURN SHANK SECTION TO .375 IN. DIAMETER.	L.H. TOOL HOLDER, RULE AND MICROMETER
7.	THREAD SHANK ⅜-16 NC.	⅜-16 NC DIE AND DIE STOCK
8.	ASSEMBLE.	
9.	PEEN HANDLE. FILE SMOOTH.	BALL PEEN HAMMER AND SINGLE CUT FILE

Fig. 3-3. Completed project plan sheet for the hammer.

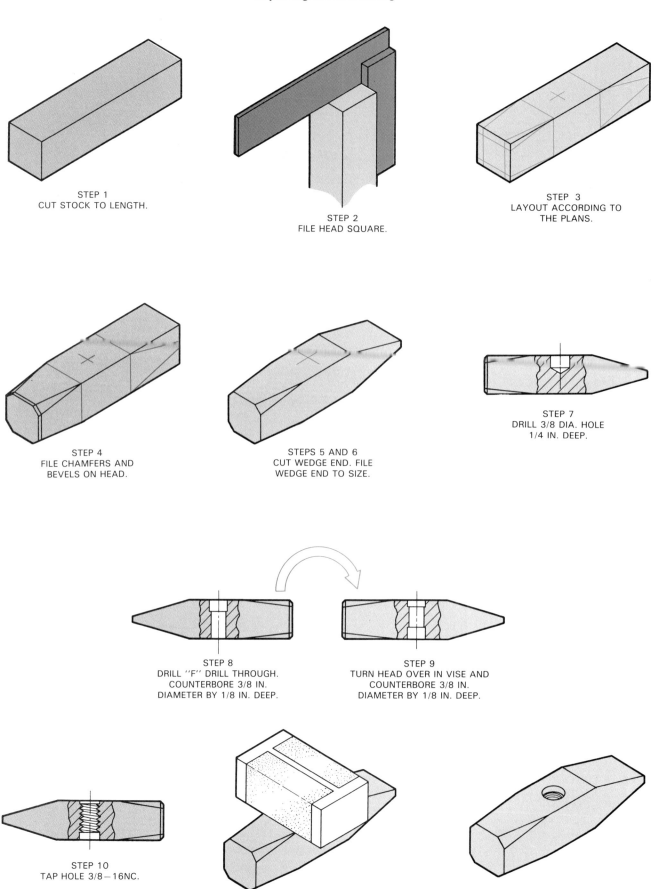

STEP 1
CUT STOCK TO LENGTH.

STEP 2
FILE HEAD SQUARE.

STEP 3
LAYOUT ACCORDING TO
THE PLANS.

STEP 4
FILE CHAMFERS AND
BEVELS ON HEAD.

STEPS 5 AND 6
CUT WEDGE END. FILE
WEDGE END TO SIZE.

STEP 7
DRILL 3/8 DIA. HOLE
1/4 IN. DEEP.

STEP 8
DRILL "F" DRILL THROUGH.
COUNTERBORE 3/8 IN.
DIAMETER BY 1/8 IN. DEEP.

STEP 9
TURN HEAD OVER IN VISE AND
COUNTERBORE 3/8 IN.
DIAMETER BY 1/8 IN. DEEP.

STEP 10
TAP HOLE 3/8 — 16NC.

STEP 11
CLEAN AND POLISH.

STEPS 12 AND 13
CASE HARDEN. FINAL POLISH.

Fig. 3-4. Steps in making the hammer head.

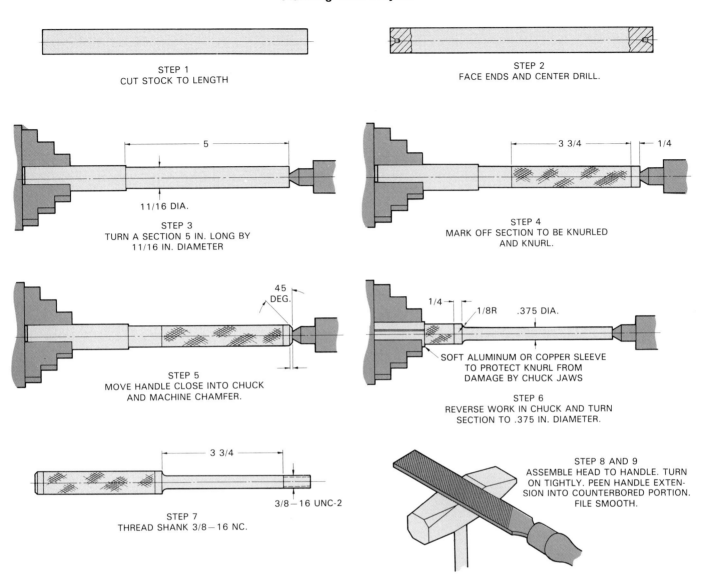

STEP 1
CUT STOCK TO LENGTH

STEP 2
FACE ENDS AND CENTER DRILL.

5

11/16 DIA.

STEP 3
TURN A SECTION 5 IN. LONG BY
11/16 IN. DIAMETER

3 3/4   1/4

STEP 4
MARK OFF SECTION TO BE KNURLED
AND KNURL.

45
DEG.

STEP 5
MOVE HANDLE CLOSE INTO CHUCK
AND MACHINE CHAMFER.

1/4   1/8R   .375 DIA.

SOFT ALUMINUM OR COPPER SLEEVE
TO PROTECT KNURL FROM
DAMAGE BY CHUCK JAWS

STEP 6
REVERSE WORK IN CHUCK AND TURN
SECTION TO .375 IN. DIAMETER.

3 3/4

3/8 — 16 UNC-2

STEP 7
THREAD SHANK 3/8 — 16 NC.

STEP 8 AND 9
ASSEMBLE HEAD TO HANDLE. TURN
ON TIGHTLY. PEEN HANDLE EXTEN-
SION INTO COUNTERBORED PORTION.
FILE SMOOTH.

Fig. 3-5. Steps in making the hammer handle.

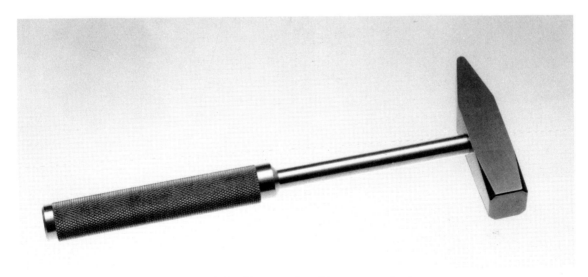

Fig. 3-6. The completed hammer project.

TEST YOUR KNOWLEDGE, Unit 3

Please do not write in the text. Place your answers on a separate sheet of paper.

1. Planning your work will save _____, _____, and _____.
2. When plans are not available, first prepare _____ _____.
3. A _____ _____ _____ is a list of items needed to construct a project.
4. What is a Plan of Procedure?
5. The following are steps recommended for planning a project. Put them in their correct order.
   a. Prepare a Plan of Procedure.
   b. Follow plans.
   c. Make working drawings.
   d. Prepare a Bill of Materials.

TECHNICAL TERMS TO LEARN

artisan
Bill of Material
construction
fabricate
fabrication

full size
manufacture
Plan of Procedure
project
working drawing

ACTIVITIES

1. Design a plan of procedure for use in your metals lab. Design it in such a way that it moves step-by-step through the schedule you follow during a typical class.
2. Secure samples of project plan sheets used by othe labs in your school. Review plan sheets done in other vocational departments in other schools. How do these plan sheets differ from those that you have done? Do the other plan sheets list steps that you may have forgotten?
3. Ask a local industry for a drawing of a simple assembly. If possible, also obtain a sample of this assembly. Based on the drawing and the sample, compile a sample project plan sheet that will allow the production of this piece.

The pilots of the U.S. Navy's BLUE ANGELS carefully plan their precision maneuvers before each flight. The more carefully *you* plan your work, the less chance there will be of *you* making a mistake.   (U.S. Navy)

Unit 4 . . . .

Designing a Project

After studying this unit, you will be able to identify the design guidelines to follow for making a good design. You will also be able to identify the elements of good design. And you will be able to explain how industry designs a project.

Good design is hard to define. Like most things, good design means different things to different people. What looks like good design to you may not appear so to a classmate. If good design cannot be defined and is different things to different people, then how do we know what is good design?

In many ways, good design may be thought of as a plan for a direct solution to a problem. Good design uses certain guidelines which point the way toward a well-designed product.

DESIGN GUIDELINES

Good design is characterized by the following guidelines.

FUNCTION. How well does the design fit the purpose for which it was planned? Does it fulfill a need?

ORGANIZATION. Do the individual parts of the design create interest when they are brought together? Are the proportions in balance? Do the parts seem to belong together? Does the basic shape look "chopped up," rather than blended together? Is the product pleasing in appearance?

QUALITY. Quality is also part of good design. A quality product is made well by people who know what they are doing. Quality must be built into the product. It cannot be added after the product is manufactured.

ELEMENTS OF GOOD DESIGN

Certain basic elements and principles are common to good designs.

LINES. Lines are used to define and give shape to an object, Fig. 4-1.

Fig. 4-1. Lines define and give shape to an object. Note how the straight lines show the unusual shape of these Lockheed F-117 aircraft.
(Lockheed Advanced Development Company)

Fig. 4-2. The shape of an object is often determined by its intended use. This arrangement of computer-controlled machining centers is known as the ''Doughnut'' system, because the units are arranged in a circle. Rather than the operator going to the machines, the machines come to the operator. This optimizes productivity. (Kurt Manufacturing Company)

Fig. 4-3. Form is the three-dimensional shape of the object. These candle holders illustrate how different shapes can be used.

SHAPE. The shape of an object may be detemined by the way it will be used. Refer to Fig. 4-2.

FORM. Form is the three-dimensional shape of the object. It may be round, square, or some other geometric shape, Fig. 4-3.

PROPORTION. Proportion is the balance between parts. Each part should be made the size that is best suited for its purpose, Fig. 4-4.

BALANCE. An object has balance when its parts appear to be of equal weight. The parts should be neither top-heavy nor lopsided. When the parts on each side of the centerline are alike in shape and size this is called SYMMETRICAL BALANCE, Fig. 4-5. INFORMAL BALANCE presents a design in such a manner that the balance cannot be measured. However, there is a feeling that the design is balanced, Fig. 4-6.

UNITY. A design with unity brings the various parts together as a whole. Each part of the object seems to have a relationship to another part.

Fig. 4-4. This camera is an example of a well-proportioned product. Its size and weight make it easy to handle and use.

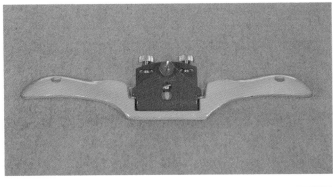

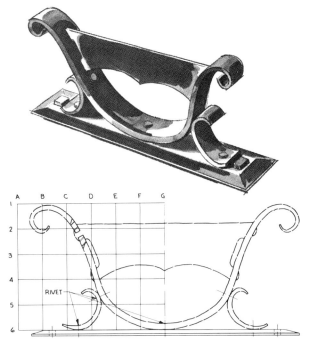

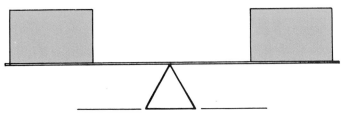

Fig. 4-5. An example of symmetrical balance.

Fig. 4-7. The curves of this foot scraper show rhythm.

EMPHASIS. This is where the design is given a point of interest.

RHYTHM. Rhythm is achieved by the repetition of lines, curves, forms, colors, and textures

within the design, Fig. 4-7. It gives an object a pleasing appearance.

TEXTURE. Texture is the condition of the surface of a material. Texture can be added by cutting, pressing, perforating, rolling, or expanding.

COLOR. All metals have a color of their own. Colors may also be added using chemicals, paints, lacquers, or other finishing materials. Selection of color is important.

HOW INDUSTRY DESIGNS A PRODUCT

How does industry go about developing a new product? Let us look at the automotive industry as an example.

New automobile designs are first developed as a series of sketches. These sketches are based on specifications made by management, Fig. 4-8. Specifications are usually based on market research.

A full size outline of the vehicle is prepared. This outline shows the placement of mechanical parts, Fig. 4-9. Line drawings and illustrations, while useful for early studies, do not provide the three-dimensions needed to test and prove design ideas. Therefore, a clay model is made, Fig. 4-10. After

Fig. 4-6. Example of informal balance. The front end of the truck is long to counteract or balance the weight of the big mixer located in the rear.

Fig. 4-8. New automobile designs start as a series of sketches in the company's design studio. (General Motors Design Studio)

Fig. 4-10. Clay model being formed. Clay is used because changes can be made quickly to check new design concepts. (General Motors Design Studio)

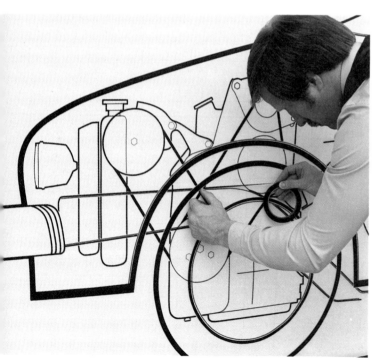

Fig. 4-9. A full-scale outline of the vehicle design is laid out. This will help in planning seating arrangement, placement of mechanical parts, and the general "look" of the car. Often, "tape-drawings," are used so that shapes and lines can be quickly changed as the design changes. (General Motors Design Studio)

further work, if the design is approved, a fiberglass model is constructed, Fig. 4-11.

Production planning uses precise, full-size wood die models to prepare permanent dies (to stamp out body panels), fabricate fixtures (devices to hold body panels while they are being welded together) and to check fixtures (measuring tools needed to maintain quality control). See Fig. 4-12. Finally the new model is made available to the public.

DESIGNING YOUR PROJECT

When designing your project, follow the pattern used by professional designers. Think of the project as a DESIGN PROBLEM. As such, there are often many ways to solve a particular design problem, Fig. 4-13. Never be afraid to experiment with new ideas that are different from the "usual" way of doing things.

SOLVING A DESIGN PROBLEM

1. STATE THE PROBLEM. What is the purpose for which the project is to be used?
2. THINK THROUGH THE PROBLEM. What must the project do? How can it be done? What

Fig. 4-11. Fiberglass model of an "idea" car. Only a few idea cars ever go into production but they are used for design studies. Many proposed changes are used on vehicles already being produced. (General Motors Corp.)

Fig. 4-12. Wood models are used to check seating and equipment placement. Similar models are used to check part fit and molding and trim design accuracy. (General Motors Corp.)

are the limitations, if any, that must be considered? How have others solved the problem?

3. DEVELOP YOUR IDEAS. Start with a simple design problem, such as a combination hat and coat hanger. The easiest solution might be to drive a nail into the door or wall. However, it would not be very neat and may damage the hat or coat.

After studying how other designers have done the job, make sketches of your ideas. See Fig. 4-14. Develop the ideas and discuss them with your teacher and fellow students. Determine the material(s) that will be most suitable.

4. PREPARE WORKING DRAWINGS. When you feel you have developed a good design, prepare working drawings, Fig. 4-15.

5. CONSTRUCT THE PROJECT. Make the project the best you are able. Do a job you will be proud to show others. See Fig. 4-16.

A

B

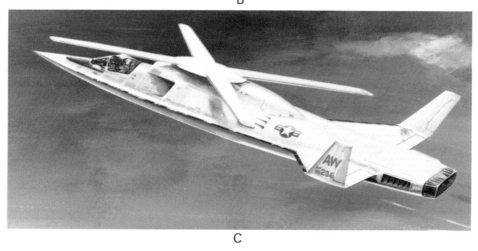

C

Fig. 4-13. There are many ways to solve a design problem. Shown are several ways aerospace designers have solved the problem of vertical take-off and landing (in addition to the familiar helicopter). A—Tilt-wing aircraft. Rotors fitted to the wing tilt vertically for take-off, as shown at left. When proper altitude is reached, right, they tilt forward for high-speed horizontal flight. (Bell Helicopter Textron/Boeing Helicopters) B—The jet engine outlets are tilted downward to lift the craft from the ground. The outlets are slowly pivoted as the craft climbs and goes into horizontal flight. The sequence is reversed for landing. The aircraft can hover like a helicopter, yet is able to attain near supersonic forward flight. (McDonnell-Douglas) C—The rotor/wing on this craft rotates for vertical takeoff. When sufficient altitude is reached, the rotor/wing is locked as shown and functions as a typical wing. This craft is also capable of high-speed forward flight. (Sikorsky Helicopter, Div. of United Technologies)

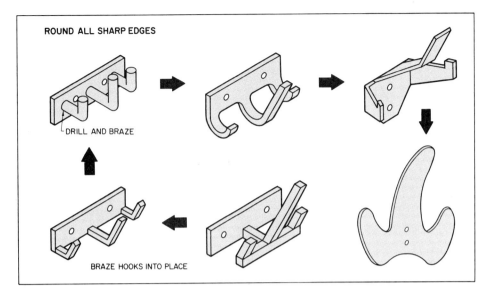

Fig. 4-14. PROBLEM: Design a simple hat and coat hanger. The first step is to study how others have solved the problem. Then, make sketches of your ideas.

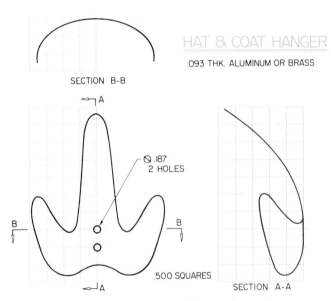

Fig. 4-15. Working drawing of hat and coat hanger.

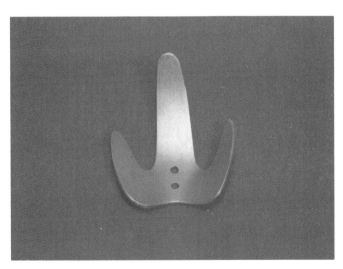

Fig. 4-16. Completed design project.

It takes time to acquire the skill to develop well-designed projects. YOU LEARN BY DOING. Keep a notebook of your ideas. Include photos of the projects you have designed and constructed. By reviewing your notebook it will be easy to see how your design skills improve.

TEST YOUR KNOWLEDGE, Unit 4

Please do not write in the text. Place your answers on a separate sheet of paper.

1. Use of _____ will help you on the way to a well-designed project.
2. Name three characteristics of good design.
3. Name four of the elements of good design and briefly explain each.
4. Design _____ are based on specifications made by management.
5. Which model is constructed first, the clay model or the fiberglass model?
6. List, in order, the steps to follow when solving a design problem.

ACTIVITIES

1. Develop and make plans for a wall rack to display model cars. Your design should hold at least three cars.
2. Prepare sketches of your ideas for a coffee table that can be made from wrought metal.
3. What are your ideas for book ends or a book rack? Prepare sketches of your ideas.
4. Design a model plane rack that is made from metal turned on the lathe.
5. Bird feeders that keep out squirrels are difficult to design. Prepare your ideas in sketch form. When you are satisfied that it will work, make a model of it.
6. Design a trivet (device used to prevent hot dishes and pots from scorching the table tops) that can be made from band iron. You may want to use ceramic tile on the top.
7. Prepare sketches for a post lamp made from copper. Include in your design the electrical fixtures.

TECHNICAL TERMS TO LEARN

balance	guidelines
characteristics	informal balance
color	organization
define	proportion
design	quality
elements	rhythm
emphasis	shape
form	solution
function	symmetrical

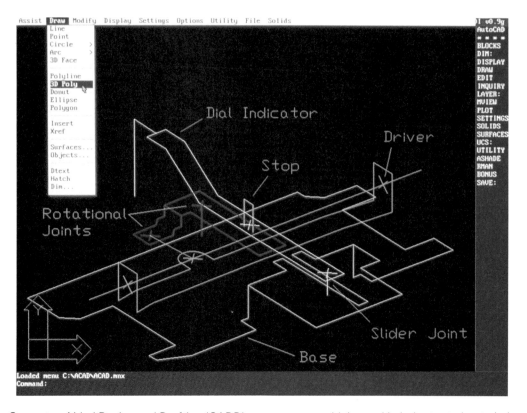

Computer-Aided Design and Drafting (CADD) programs are widely used in industry today to help designers develop new products and improve existing ones. (Autodesk, Inc.)

Unit 5

Metalworking Safety

After studying this unit, you will be able touse safe work habits in the metals lab. You will also be able to explain general safety rules and safety rules for hand tools.

The nature of metalworking makes safety necessary. You must exercise extreme care when working in the metals lab, Fig. 5-1. It can be a dangerous place for the careless.

Most accidents can be avoided. Develop safe work habits. ALWAYS BE ALERT. You are not a "sissy" if you wear goggles and follow safety rules. You are using good judgment. DON'T TAKE CHANCES.

Remember, IT HURTS WHEN YOU GET HURT. Become familiar with the safety rules shown and stressed by your teacher and become familiar with those included in this text. OBSERVE SAFETY AT ALL TIMES.

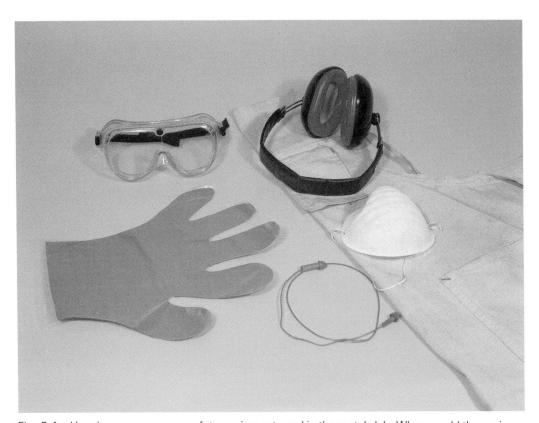

Fig. 5-1. Here is some common safety equipment used in the metals lab. When would these pieces of equipment be used?

GENERAL SAFETY RULES

Astronauts dress for the hazards of space flight, Fig. 5-2. The padding football players wear is designed to protect them from bumps and jolts on the playing field. When YOU work in the lab, dress for the job, Fig. 5-3.

The following are safety rules and guidelines to help you maintain safety in the lab.

1. Remove necklaces, scarves, or other dangling items that might be caught in machinery.
2. Roll up your sleeves, Fig. 5-4.
3. Wear approved safety goggles. Wear special goggles or use a shield when welding. Visitors must also obey this rule.
4. Remove wristwatches, rings, and other jewelry that might get caught in moving machinery. Also tie up or contain long hair with a cap or bandana.

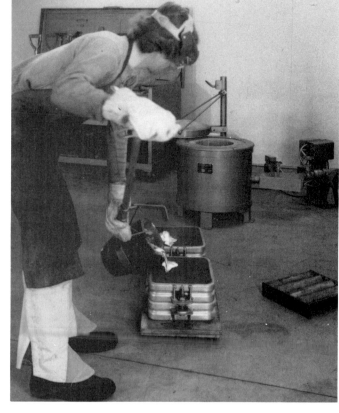

Fig. 5-3. This young person is dressed properly for pouring molten metal. What safety equipment can you identify? (McEnglevan Mfg. Co.)

Fig. 5-2. Always dress safely when working in the lab, Wear an apron or shop coat and remove rings, watch, or necklaces. Above all, WEAR APPROVED SAFETY GLASSES. (Millersville University)

Fig. 5-4. Roll your sleeves to or above your elbows. There will be no danger of them getting caught in moving parts of the machine.

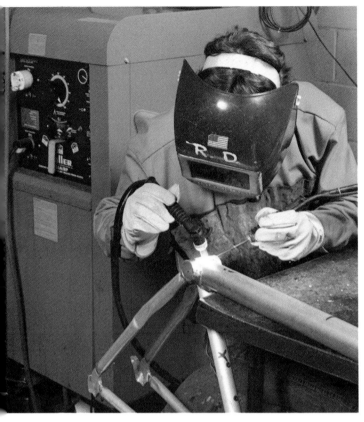

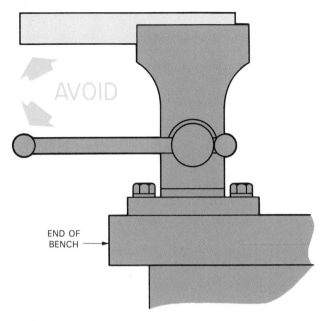

Fig. 5-6. Avoid this type of setup when working with a vise on the end of a bench.

Fig. 5-5. Wear special clothing when the job requires it. Note that this welder is wearing a face shield, leather jacket, and gloves.

Fig. 5-7. Be sure all guards and safety devices are installed on a machine before working with it. This machine should not be used until the guards are closed and locked in place.

5. Wear protective clothing when working in the foundry, forge, and welding areas. See Fig. 5-5.

6. An apron or shop coat will protect your school clothing.

7. The metals lab is no place for practical jokes or "horseplay." Tricks and pranks are dangerous to you and your fellow students.

8. Vise jaws should be left open slightly. The handle will then be in a vertical position when not in use. When working with a vise, avoid the setup shown in Fig. 5-6. Position the work and vise handle to the INSIDE of the bench.

9. Before starting any work, make certain all machines are fitted with guards and are in good working condition, Fig. 5-7.

10. Do not operate portable electric power tools in areas where thinners and solvents are used. A serious fire or explosion might result.

11. Always walk in the lab. Running is dangerous. You might stumble or collide with a fellow student who is operating a machine or pouring molten metal.

12. Get immediate medical attention for cuts, burns, bruises, and injuries no matter how minor. Report any accident to your teacher.

13. It is recommended that you NOT wear canvas shoes, sandals, or open footwear in the metals lab.

14. Place scrap metal and shavings in proper containers. Do not throw them on the floor.
15. Oil-soaked and greasy cleaning rags should be provided and placed in safety containers provided for them. DO NOT STORE THEM IN YOUR LOCKER.
16. Use care when handling long sections of metal. Watch for others who may be in your path. When removing or replacing long pieces from a vertical storage rack, be alert for people and objects that may be in your way, Fig. 5-8.
17. See your instructor before using any fluids in poorly-marked containers. Do not determine what is in a container by smelling the fumes.
18. Clean machines with brushes provided for that purpose. NEVER USE YOUR FINGERS OR HANDS TO REMOVE METAL CHIPS OR SHAVINGS FROM YOUR MACHINE.

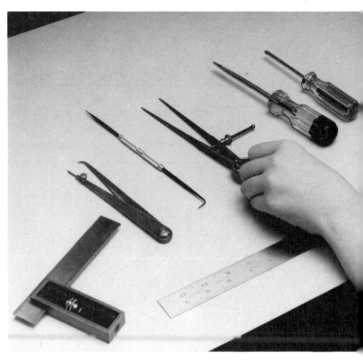

Fig. 5-9. Place sharp or pointed tools on the bench so there is no danger of being injured when you reach for them.

SAFETY WHEN USING HAND TOOLS

Painful accidents can result from using hand tools incorrectly or using tools not in good repair.

1. Avoid using a tool until you have received instruction in its proper use.

2. Keep tools sharp. Dull tools will not work properly and are dangerous.
3. Check each tool before use. Report defects such as loose or split handles on hammers. Grind mushroomed heads from chisels and punches.
4. A file without a handle should NEVER be used.
5. Use extreme care when carrying pointed hand tools or those with sharp edges. They should not be carried in your pockets.
6. When using dividers, scribes, etc., place them on the bench with the points and sharp edges directed AWAY from you, Fig. 5-9.
7. Tools should not be substituted for one another. For example, avoid using a wrench for a hammer, a screwdriver for a chisel, or pliers for wrenches.

There is very little chance of your being injured in the metals lab if you remember the ABCs of safety . . . ALWAYS BE CAREFUL.

TEST YOUR KNOWLEDGE, Unit 5

Please do not write in the text. Place your answers on a separate sheet of paper.

1. What hazard is avoided by rolling your sleeves up to or above your elbows?

Fig. 5-8. This safety poster stresses the importance of remaining alert at all times.

2. Leave vise jaws _____ (open, closed) when not in use so the handle will be in a vertical position.
3. Guards need not be in place when doing a "quick" job on a machine. True or False?
4. What is the danger in identifying liquids by smelling?
5. What are two causes of hand tool accidents?
6. The ABCs of safety are _____ _____ _____.
7. The same type of eye protection can be worn in all areas of the lab. True or False?

TECHNICAL TERMS TO LEARN

ABCs of safety   goggles
dangerous   protective clothing
eye protection   safety

ACTIVITIES

1. Design safety posters using one or more of the following themes.
   IT HURTS WHEN YOU GET HURT
   ALWAYS BE ALERT
   WEAR YOUR GOGGLES
   ALWAYS BE CAREFUL
   Or use your own idea. Then sketch your ideas on scrap paper. Draw your final design(s) in color on 8 1/2 in. by 11 in. poster board.
2. Design a bulletin board display on eye safety.
3. Using a tool catalog, calculate the cost of the safety equipment shown in Fig. 5-1.
4. Form a group to inspect the safety equipment in your lab. Prepare a report on the condition of this equipment and how much it will cost to replace damaged items. The report should also contain recommendations on how to improve the existing safety program.

No matter what you are doing in the metals lab, think *first* about safety. Wear proper protective clothing and equipment and follow all safety rules.

Unit 6 . . . .

Measurement and Layout Tools

After studying this unit, you will be able to identify common measuring and layout tools. You will also be able to use the measuring tools to correctly measure various objects. And you will be able to pick the correct layout tool for a certain job.

To do metalworking with accuracy, you must be able to correctly read and use basic measuring and layout tools, Fig. 6-1.

RULE

The STEEL RULE is the simplest of the measuring tools. Various styles and lengths are used in school labs, Fig. 6-2.

The rule usually has fractional divisions on all four edges. These divisions are in 1/8, 1/16, 1/32, and 1/64 in., Fig. 6-3. Lines representing the divisions are called GRADUATIONS.

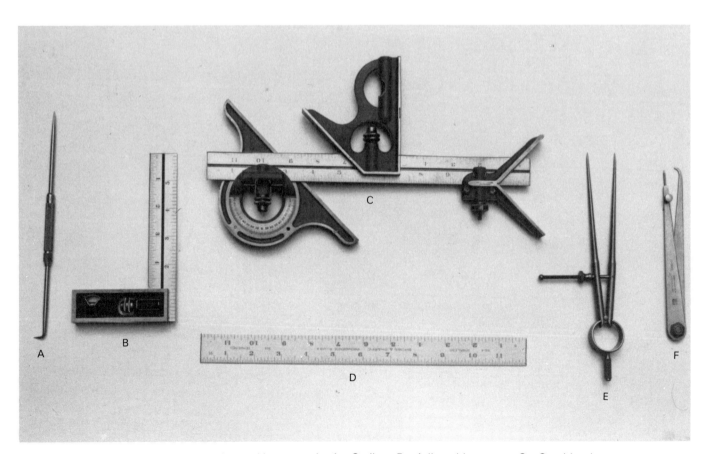

Fig. 6-1. Basic measuring and layout tools: A—Scriber. B—Adjustable square. C—Combination set. D—12 in. rule. E—Divider. F—Hermaphrodite caliper.

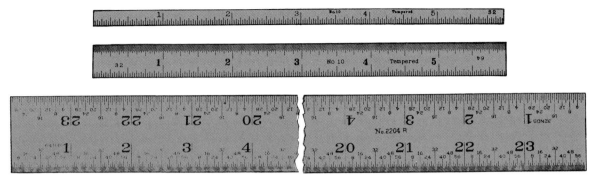

Fig. 6-2. A few of the many types of rules available to the metals student.

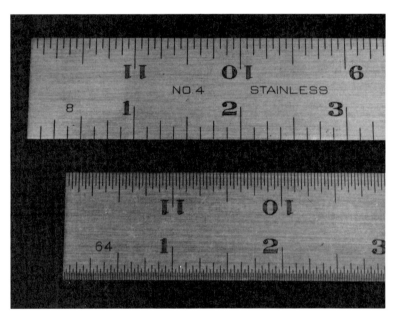

Fig. 6-3. The fractional divisions of the standard No. 4 steel rule.

The best way to learn to read a rule is to:

1. Practice making measurements with the 1/8 and 1/16 in. graduations until you are thoroughly familiar with them.
2. The same is then done with the 1/32 and 1/64 in. graduations.
3. Practice until the measurements can be made accurately and quickly.

How many measurements can you read correctly on the problem in Fig. 6-4?

Always reduce fractional measurements to their lowest terms. For example, a measurement of 6/8 reduces to 3/4, 6/16 reduces to 3/8.

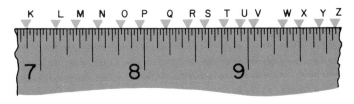

Fig. 6-4. How many of the divisions can you read correctly?

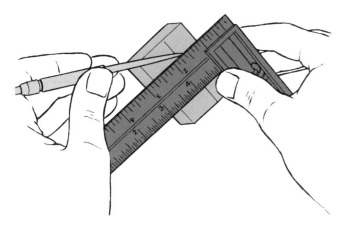

Fig. 6-5. In addition to being used to check the squareness of stock, the machinist's square can also be used for layout work.

SQUARES

The accuracy of a 90 deg. angle can be checked with a SQUARE, Fig. 6-5. The tool is also used for layout work and simple machine setups. Squares are manufactured in a variety of sizes and types.

COMBINATION SET

Many different measuring and layout operations can be performed with the COMBINATION SET, Fig. 6-6. The tool is composed of four parts: BLADE (rule), SQUARE HEAD, CENTER HEAD, and BEVEL PROTRACTOR. The blade fits all three heads.

The SQUARE HEAD, when fitted with the blade, will serve as a try square and miter square, Fig. 6-7. The tool can be used as a depth gauge by projecting the blade the desired distance beyond the edge of the unit. Simple leveling operations can be performed utilizing the SPIRIT LEVEL built into one edge.

The center of round stock can be located with the blade fitted in the CENTER HEAD, Fig. 6-8.

Various angles can be checked and/or laid out with the blade fitted in the PROTRACTOR HEAD. Refer to Fig. 6-9.

MICROMETER

The MICROMETER or "MIKE," is a precision measuring tool, Fig. 6-10. Study the major parts of the tool. A micrometer can be used to take measurements about one-thirtieth the thickness of the paper on which this is printed. The "mike" is made in many size and types, Fig. 6-11.

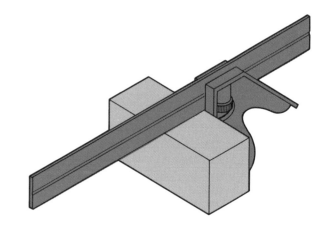

Fig. 6-6. The combination set. Left. Protractor head. Center. Square head. Right. Center head. These tools surround a 12 in. (300 mm) steel rule.

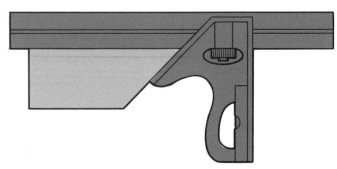

Fig. 6-7. In addition to being used for layout work, the square head of the combination set can be used to check squareness and accuracy of 45 deg. angle machined surfaces.

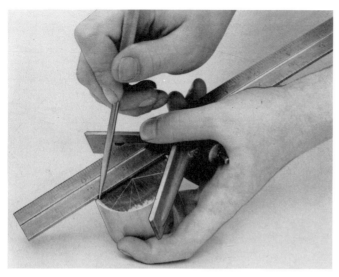

Fig. 6-8. Using center head to locate the center of round stock.

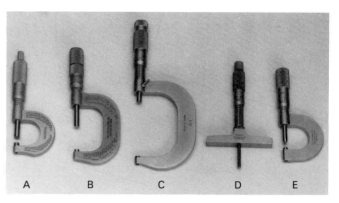

Fig. 6-11. A few of the many sizes and types of micrometers available: A—1 in. micrometer. B—2 in. micrometer. C—3 in. micrometer. D—Depth micrometer. E—Thread micrometer. Metric micrometers are similar in appearance but are sized in 25.0 mm increments.

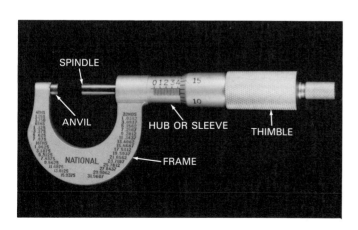

Fig. 6-9. Angular lines can be laid out using the protractor head of a combination set.

HOW TO READ AN INCH BASE MICROMETER

A micrometer has 40 precision threads per inch on its SPINDLE. When the THIMBLE (which is attached to the spindle) is rotated one complete turn, the spindle will move 1/40 in. (0.025 in.).

The line on the SLEEVE is divided into 40 equal parts per inch, Fig. 6-12. This corresponds to the number of threads on the spindle. Every fourth division is numbered 1, 2, 3, etc., representing 0.100 in., 0.200 in., 0.300 in., etc.

The THIMBLE has 25 equally spaced graduations. Each represents 1/1000 in. (0.001 in.). On some micrometers, each graduation is numbered. On others, every fifth graduation is numbered.

Fig. 6-10. The micrometer or "mike."

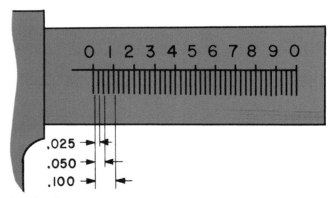

Fig. 6-12. The micrometer hub or sleeve is divided into 40 equal parts per inch. Each division is equal to 0.025 in. Every fourth division is numbered 1, 2, 3, etc., representing 0.100 in., 0.200 in., 0.300 in., etc.

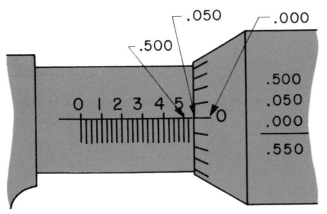

Fig. 6-13. The micrometer is read by recording the highest figure visible on the hub; 5 = 0.500 in. To this is added the number of vertical lines visible between the number and the thimble edge; 2 = 2 × 0.25 or 0.050 in. To this total add the number of thousandths indicated by the line on the thimble. This line coincides with the horizontal line on the hub.

To read the micrometer, do the following. Also, see Fig. 6-13.

1. Record the highest figure visible on the SLEEVE, such as 1 = 0.100 and 2 = 0.200.
2. To the above, add the number of vertical lines that can be seen between the number and the THIMBLE edge, 1 = 0.025, 2 = 0.050, and 3 = 0.075.
3. Finally, add the total number of thousandths indicated by the line on the THIMBLE that corresponds with the horizontal line on the SLEEVE.

Practice this sequence by reading the measurements seen in Figs. 6-14 and 6-15.

USING METRIC UNITS

Using metric units (meter, millimeter, etc.) as a basis for measurement is known as METRICA-

Fig. 6-14. Can you read this micrometer measurement?

Fig. 6-15. A section of sheet metal was measured with this micrometer. How thick is the metal?

TION. In metalworking, the millimeter (mm) is almost always used for measurement and layout work.

Over a period of years, the United States has slowly begun using the metric system along with the English (or standard) system for measurement. Because of this, it is to your advantage to learn to use metric-based measuring tools.

The best way to learn to use the metric system is to NOT compare metric measurements to English (fractional and decimal).

METRIC MEASURING TOOLS

The rule and micrometer are available graduated in metric units. The metric rule is compared with fractional and decimal rules in Fig. 6-16.

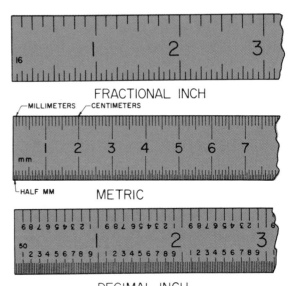

Fig. 6-16. A comparison of the metric rule with fractional and decimal rules.

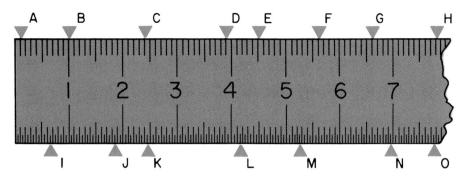

Fig. 6-17. How many of the dimensions marked can you read correctly?

How many of the dimensions marked on the metric rule, shown in Fig. 6-17, can you read? For example, measurement B would read 10.0 mm. Measurement J would be read 18.5 mm.

The metric micrometer, Fig. 6-18, is used in the same manner as the English type, except the graduations are in metric measures. The readings are obtained as follows:

1. Since the pitch of the spindle screw in a metric micrometer is 0.5 mm, one complete revolution of the thimble advances the spindle towards or away from the anvil exactly 0.5 mm.
2. The lengthwise line on the sleeve is graduated in millimeters from 0 to 25 mm. Each millimeter is subdivided in 0.5 mm. Therefore, two revolutions of the thimble are required to advance the spindle towards or away from the anvil a distance equal to 1.0 mm.
3. The beveled edge of the thimble is graduated into 50 divisions, with every fifth line numbered. Since a complete revolution of the thimble moves the spindle 0.5 mm, each graduation on the thimble is equal to 1/50 of 0.5 mm or 0.01 mm. Two graduations equal 0.02 mm, three equals 0.03 mm, and so on.

4. To read a metric micrometer, see Fig. 6-19. Add the total reading in millimeters (visible on the sleeve) to the reading in hundredths of a millimeter (indicated by the graduation on the thimble). The hundredths measurement lines up with the lengthwise line on the sleeve.

METRIC-DIMENSIONED DRAWINGS

Since 1960, the metric system has been referred to throughout the world as "Systeme International d'Unites" or the International Systems of Units. The abbreviation SI is universally used to indicate this system.

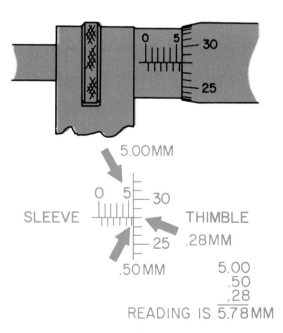

Fig. 6-19. Reading a metric micrometer. Find the total reading in millimeters shown on the sleeve. It is 5.5 mm. Add 5.5 to the reading in hundredths of a millimeter shown by the graduation on the thimble. In this case, it is .28 mm. This coincides with the lengthwise line on the sleeve.

Fig. 6-18. Metric-based micrometer.

69

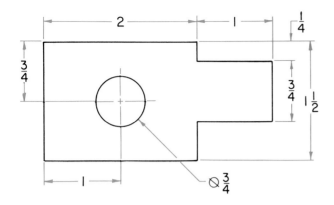

Fig. 6-20. A drawing dimensioned with the standard inch dimensioning system.

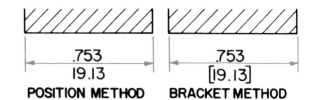

POSITION METHOD   **BRACKET METHOD**

Fig. 6-22. Current method of indicating inches and millimeters on a dual-dimensioned drawing.

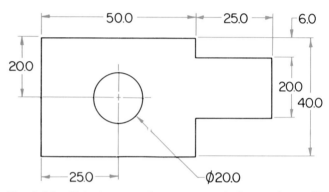

Fig. 6-23. This drawing shows a part similar to that in Fig. 6-21. This one, however, is designed for metric-sized materials. Note how the metric dimensions differ from those shown on the dual-dimensioned drawing, where metric values were exact conversions from inch dimensions.

You are familiar with drawings that use the inch dimensioning system, Fig. 6-20. DUAL DIMENSIONED drawings, Fig. 6-21, were the first step in the changeover to metric dimensioning. If the part was made in the United States, the inch dimension appeared as shown in Fig. 6-22. In metric countries, the millimeter dimension appear in the top position.

If the part is designed and dimensioned in the inch system, there is seldom any reason to convert inch dimensions to millimeters. However, if the product is designed using metric-sized material, metric dimensions must be used, Fig. 6-23. A comparison of inch sizes with the preferred metric-sized material is shown in Fig. 6-24.

HELPER MEASURING TOOLS

A helper measuring tool must be used with a steel rule or micrometer. A helper measuring tool cannot be used without one of these two tools as a guide.

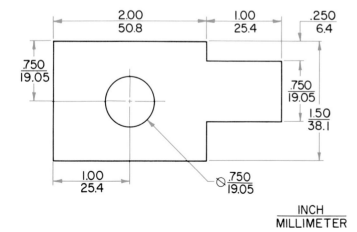

INCH
MILLIMETER

Fig. 6-21. A drawing based on dual dimensioning. Note how the location of the inch/millimeter dimensions are indicated. While many dual-dimensioned drawings are still in use, they are seldom drawn this way anymore.

INCH	mm
1/8	3.0
1/4	6.0
3/8	10.0
1/2	12.0
5/8	16.0
3/4	20.0
1	25.0
1 1/4	30.0
1 1/2	40.0
1 3/4	45.0
2	50.0

Fig. 6-24. This chart shows a comparison of inch sizes to metric sizes.

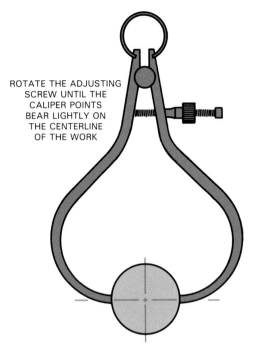

ROTATE THE ADJUSTING SCREW UNTIL THE CALIPER POINTS BEAR LIGHTLY ON THE CENTERLINE OF THE WORK

Fig. 6-25. Making a measurement with an outside caliper.

OUTSIDE CALIPER

External measurements can be made with an OUTSIDE CALIPER, Fig. 6-25, when a 1/64 in. (0.4 mm) tolerance is permitted. The 1/64 in. (0.4 mm) tolerance means that the part can be 1/64 in. (0.4 mm) larger or 1/64 in. (0.4 mm) smaller than the size shown on the plans and still be used.

Measurement of round stock is made by setting the caliper legs lightly on the centerline of the stock. Hold the caliper to the rule and read the size, Fig. 6-26.

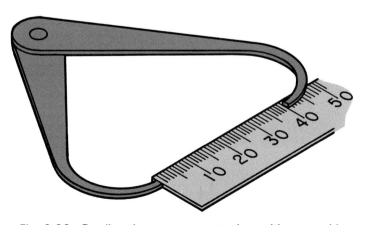

Fig. 6-26. Reading the measurement taken with an outside caliper.

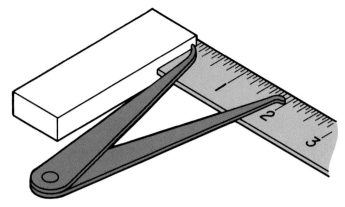

Fig. 6-27. Making a measurement with an inside caliper.

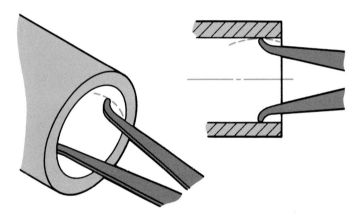

Fig. 6-28. Suggested way to read a measurement taken with an inside caliper.

Never force a caliper over the work. This will "spring" the caliper legs and give an inaccurate measurement.

INSIDE CALIPER

Interior dimensions are gauged with the INSIDE CALIPER, Fig. 6-27. Measurement is made by inserting the caliper legs into the opening. The legs are opened until they "drag" slightly when moved in or out, or from side to side. To read hole size, hold the caliper to the rule as shown in Fig. 6-28.

LAYOUT TOOLS

A LAYOUT is a series of reference points and lines that show the shape the material is to be cut or machined, Fig. 6-29. The layout may also include the location of openings and holes that must be made in the work.

71

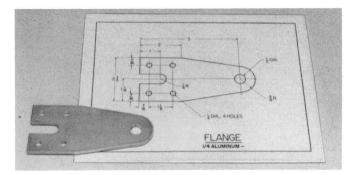

Fig. 6-29. A typical layout drawing. The part made using the drawing as a guide is also shown.

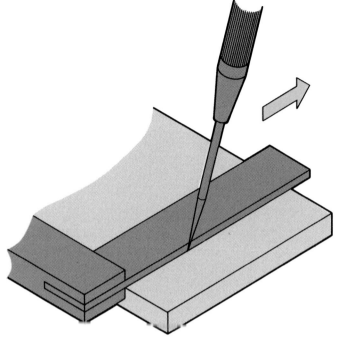

Fig. 6-31. Make sure the scriber is held firmly against the straightedge before making the layout line.

Accuracy depends, to a large extent, on your skill in properly using and caring for the layout tools.

MAKING LINES ON METAL

It is not easy to see layout lines on shiny metal. Therefore, a LAYOUT DYE, Fig. 6-30, is used. This coating is applied to the metal to provide contrast between the metal and the layout lines.

Chalk can be used on hot rolled steel as a layout background.

SCRIBER

Accurate layouts require scribing fine lines on metal surfaces. The lines may be made with a SCRIBER, Fig. 6-31. The tool point is made of hardened steel. It should be kept needle-sharp by frequent honing on a fine oilstone. There are many styles of scribers.

A pencil should never be used to make layout lines. The pencil line is too wide and rubs off easily.

CAUTION: NEVER CARRY OPEN SCRIBERS IN YOUR POCKET. PLACE THEM ON THE BENCH WITH THE POINT FACING AWAY FROM YOU.

DIVIDERS

Circles and arcs are drawn on metal with the DIVIDER, Fig. 6-32. The tool may also be employed to measure for equal distances.

To set a divider to the desired dimension, place one point on the inch/10.0 mm mark of a steel rule. Then open the divider until the other leg is set to the required size, Fig. 6-33.

Fig. 6-30. Layout dye is used to make scribed lines stand out on metal surfaces.

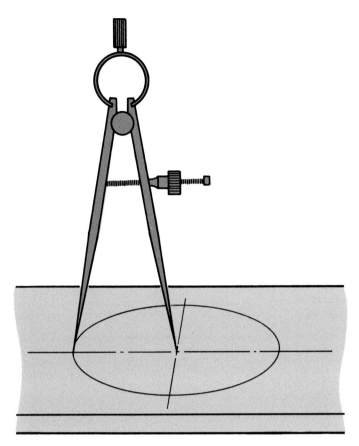

Fig. 6-32. Circles and arcs are drawn on metal with a divider.

CAUTION: NEVER CARRY DIVIDERS IN YOUR POCKET. PLACE THEM ON THE BENCH WITH THE POINTS FACING AWAY FROM YOU.

HERMAPHRODITE CALIPER

A HERMAPHRODITE CALIPER, Fig. 6-34, is a cross between an inside caliper and a divider.

A hermaphrodite caliper is used to lay out lines parallel to an edge. It is also used to locate the approximate center of irregularly shaped stock.

CAUTION: NEVER CARRY A HERMAPHRODITE CALIPER IN YOUR POCKET. ALSO PLACE THEM ON THE BENCH WITH THE POINT FACING AWAY FROM YOU.

PUNCHES

Two types of PUNCHES are commonly employed in making layouts. They are the following:

1. PRICK PUNCH, Fig. 6-35, top. A hardened, pointed steel rod is used to "spot" the point where centerlines intersect on a layout. The sharp point (60 deg.) makes it easy to locate points.

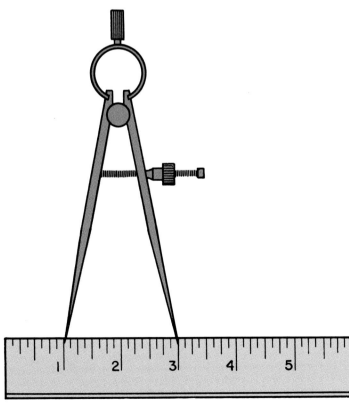

Fig. 6-33. Setting a divider to a required radius.

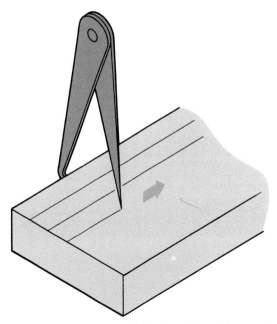

Fig. 6-34. Scribing a line parallel to the edge of the work with a hermaphrodite caliper.

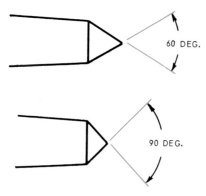

Fig. 6-35. Top. Prick punch. Bottom. Center punch.

2. CENTER PUNCH, Fig. 6-35, bottom. This is similar to a prick punch, but has a more blunt point (90 deg.). It is used to enlarge the prick punch mark after it has been checked and found to be on center.

HOW TO MAKE A LAYOUT

Each layout job will have its own problems. This will require careful planning before starting. The following sequence is recommended. Also refer to Figs. 6-36 and 6-37.

1. Carefully study the plans.
2. Cut the stock to size and remove all burrs and sharp edges.
3. Clean the metal and apply layout dye.

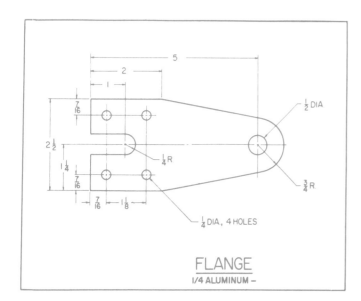

Fig. 6-36. This job requires layout in its manufacture.

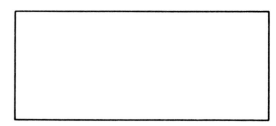

CUT METAL TO APPROXIMATE SIZE

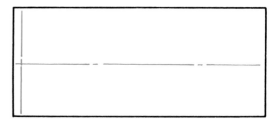

LOCATE CIRCLE AND ARC CENTERLINES

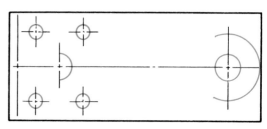

LOCATE AND SCRIBE ANGULAR LINES

LOCATE AND SCRIBE BASE LINES

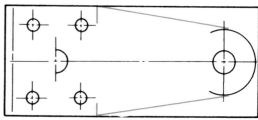

SCRIBE IN CIRCLES AND ARCS

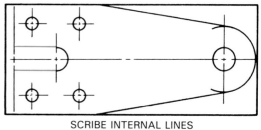

SCRIBE INTERNAL LINES

Fig. 6-37. Steps in laying out the job shown in Fig. 6-36.

4. Locate and scribe BASE or REFERENCE LINES. All measurements are made from these lines. If the material has one true edge, it can serve as one of the base or reference lines.
5. Locate all center and arc centerlines.
6. Locate and scribe angular lines.
7. Scribe in all other internal openings.

LAYOUT SAFETY

1. NEVER carry scribers, dividers, or other pointed tools in your pocket.
2. Cover sharp pointed tools with a cork when they are not being used.
3. When using sharp pointed tools, lay them on the bench with the pointed ends facing away from you. There will then be no danger of reaching into the points when you pick up the tool.
4. Wear goggles when repointing layout tools.
5. Remove burrs and sharp edges from the stock before starting to lay it out.
6. Secure prompt medical attention for any cut, scratch, or bruise, no matter how minor it may appear.

TEST YOUR KNOWLEDGE, Unit 6

Please do not write in the text. Place your answers on a separate sheet of paper.

1. The _____ _____ is the simplest and most widely used measuring tool.
2. The accuracy of 90 deg. angles can be checked with a _____.
3. The combination set is composed of four parts. Name them and briefly describe the use of each part.
4. Define metrication.
5. What is a dual dimensioned drawing?
6. A _____ is a series of reference points and lines that show the shape the material is to be cut or machined.
7. Straight layout lines are drawn using a _____.
8. To provide contrast between metal surfaces and layout lines, _____ _____ should be applied to the surface being laid out.
9. Make the readings on the micrometer drawings shown.

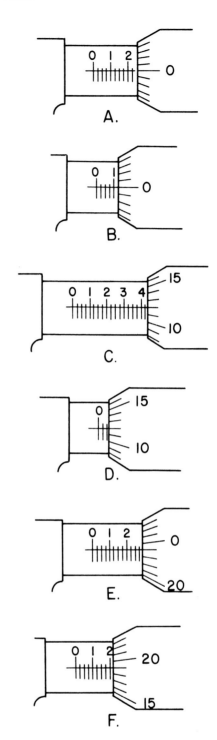

10. Determine the measurements on the metric rule section shown. Give your answers in millimeters.

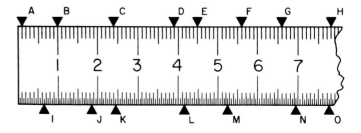

11. Make the readings on the metric micrometer drawings shown.

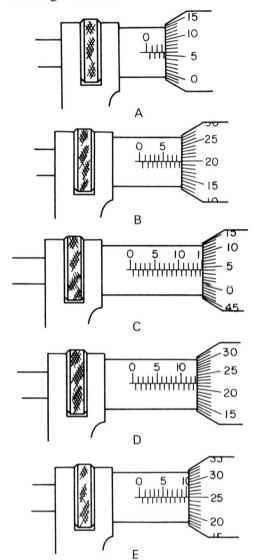

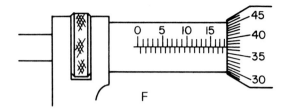

TECHNICAL TERMS TO LEARN

accuracy	layout tools
arc	measure
base line	metric
center head	metrication
center punch	micrometer
circle	millimeter
combination set	outside caliper
divider	protractor
dual-dimensioned	punch
fractional	reference line
graduation	rule
hermaphrodite caliper	scriber
inside caliper	square
layout	

ACTIVITIES

1. Secure a metric rule and micrometer from the science department at your school. Instruct the class in their use.
2. Make a drawing of a project to be made in the school shop. Use metric dimensioning.
3. Discuss the metric system with a representative of a nearby company. Find out whether the company would find the system an advantage or a disadvantage.

Unit 7 . . . .

Basic Metalworking Tools and Equipment

After studying this unit, you will be able to identify basic metalworking tools and equipment. You will be able to demonstrate the safe and proper use of these tools. You will also be able to safely use those machines that cut metal.

The proper and safe use of hand tools and machines is basic to all areas of metalworking.

VISE

Metal is normally held in a VISE while it is being worked, Fig. 7-1. There are many sizes and types of vises.

CAPS made of soft metal, Fig. 7-2, should be fitted over the vise jaws. These will protect the work from being damaged or marred by the jaw serrations (teeth).

HAMMERS

The BALL PEEN HAMMER, Fig. 7-3, is usually used in metalworking. Its size is usually determined by the weight of the head. For example, a ball peen hammer with a 4 oz. head is known as a 4 oz. hammer.

Commonly, the lightest hammer that will do the job easily and safely should be used.

SCREWDRIVERS

Select the screwdriver that fits the screw being driven, Fig. 7-4. Two types of screwdrivers that are commonly used in the metals lab are the

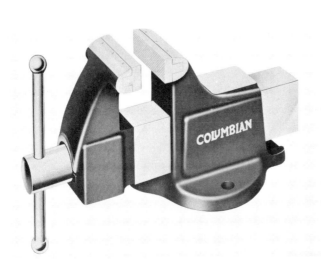

Fig. 7-1. Vise used in metalworking.

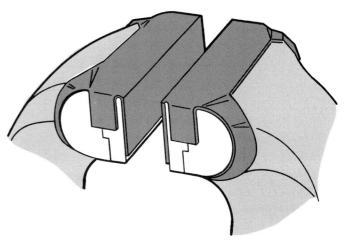

Fig. 7-2. Caps protect material from being damaged by the serrations on the vise jaws. The caps are made of soft metal.

77

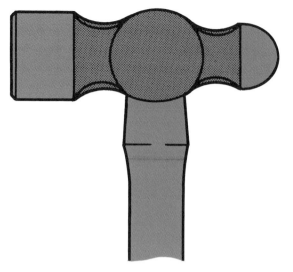

Fig. 7-3. Ball peen hammer.

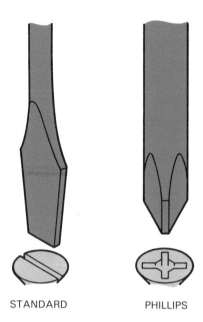

STANDARD   PHILLIPS

Fig. 7-5. Two types of widely used screwdrivers.

STANDARD TYPE for slotted heads, and the PHILLIPS TYPE for X-shaped recessed heads, Fig. 7-5.

PLIERS

Many holding, bending, and cutting jobs can be done with PLIERS, Fig. 7-6. Pliers are made in many sizes and styles to handle a variety of jobs. PLIERS SHOULD NEVER BE USED AS A SUBSTITUTE FOR A HAMMER OR A WRENCH.

Pliers commonly found in the metals lab include those listed in the next several paragraphs.

COMBINATION PLIERS (also known as SLIP-JOINT PLIERS) have many uses. The slip joint makes it possible to adjust the jaws and grip both large and small work. The jaws have serrations or teeth. On some slip-joint pliers, a short cutting edge for cutting wire is located near the hinge.

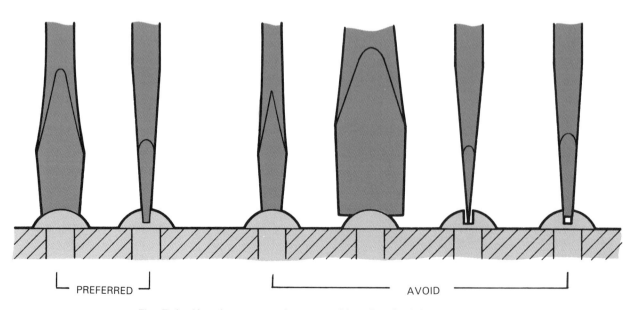

PREFERRED   AVOID

Fig. 7-4. Use the correct size screwdriver for the job to be done.

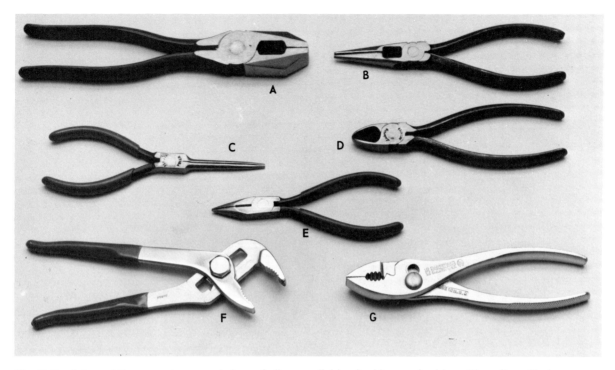

Fig. 7-6. A few of the many types and sizes of pliers available. A—Lineman's side cutting pliers. B—Long nose cutting pliers. C—Needle nose pliers. D—Diagonal cutting pliers. E—Short reach needle nose pliers. F—Groove joint pliers. G—Slip-joint or combination pliers.

The cutting edges of DIAGONAL PLIERS are at an angle. This angle makes cutting flush with the work surface possible.

Heavier wire and pins can be cut with SIDE-CUTTING PLIERS.

Wire and light metal can be bent and formed with ROUND NOSE PLIERS. The smooth jaws will not mar the work.

LONG or NEEDLE NOSE PLIERS are useful when space is limited, or where small work is to be held.

When using pliers keep your fingers clear of the cutting edges. When doing electrical work be sure to insulate the handles with rubber tape, or use specially manufactured rubber grips.

WRENCHES

Many types of wrenches are available to the metalworker. Each is designed for a specific use.

Many wrenches are adjustable to fit different sizes of nuts and bolts. However, the wrench shown in Fig. 7-7, is usually known as an AD-JUSTABLE WRENCH. It is made in a range of sizes. Use the smallest wrench that will fit the nut or bolt being worked.

The PIPE WRENCH, Fig. 7-8, is also adjustable. The movable jaw has a small amount of

Fig. 7-7. Adjustable wrench.   (Diamond Tool Co.)

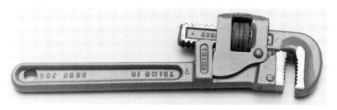

Fig. 7-8. Pipe wrench.

play built in it so that it can take a "bite" on round stock. A pipe wrench will leave marks on the stock. This wrench should not be used on nuts and bolts unless the corners have been so damaged a regular wrench cannot be used.

The size of the space between the jaws of the OPEN-END WRENCH, Fig. 7-9, determines its size. Open-end wrenches are made in many different sizes and styles.

The BOX-WRENCH, Fig. 7-10, completely surrounds the bolt head or nut. It is preferred over other wrenches because it will not slip. These wrenches are available in sizes to fit standard nuts and bolts.

The COMBINATION OPEN AND BOX-WRENCH, Fig. 7-11, has one open end and one box end.

SOCKET WRENCHES, Fig. 7-12, are like box-wrenches because they surround the bolt head or nut. However, they are made as detachable tools that fit many different types of handles. A typical socket wrench set contains various handles and a wide range of socket sizes and styles.

PULL, NEVER PUSH, on any wrench. Pushing is considered dangerous. If the nut loosens suddenly, you may strike your knuckles on the work (known as "knuckle dusting"). The movable jaw of a wrench should ALWAYS face the direction the fastener is being turned, Fig. 7-13.

FILES AND FILING

FILES are frequently used to remove extra metal.

FILE CLASSIFICATION

Files are classified by their shape, Fig. 7-14, by the cut of their teeth, Fig. 7-15, and by the coarseness of the teeth. Types of coarseness include rough, coarse, bastard, second-cut, smooth, and dead smooth.

Fig. 7-9. Open-end wrench.

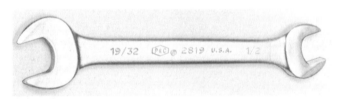

Fig. 7-10. Box wrench.

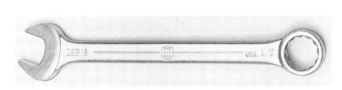

Fig. 7-11. Combination open and box wrench.

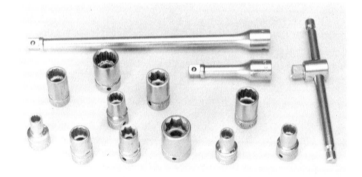

Fig. 7-12. Socket wrench set with extensions.

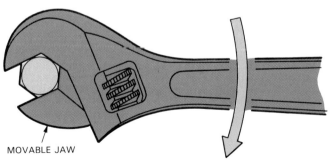

MOVABLE JAW

Fig. 7-13. The movable jaw of the wrench should ALWAYS face the direction the fastener is being turned.

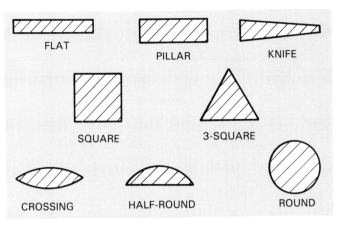

Fig. 7-14. File shapes.

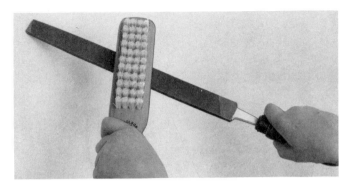

Fig. 7-16. Clean a file with a file card.

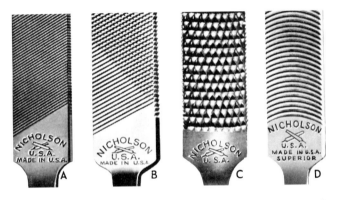

Fig. 7-15. These files are classified by the cut of their teeth.
A—Single-cut. B—Double-cut. C—Rasp. D—Curved-tooth.

Fig. 7-17. The proper way to hold the file for straight or cross filing.

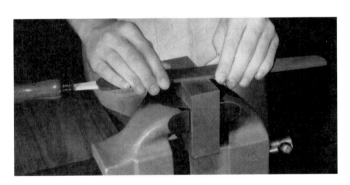

Fig. 7-18. When done properly, draw filing improves the surface finish.

FILE CARE

Your file should be cleaned frequently using a FILE CARD, Fig. 7-16. This will prevent PINNING. Pinning is a problem in which small slivers of metal clog the file and cause scratches on the work. DO NOT try to clean a file by striking it against the bench top or vise.

FILE SELECTION

The nature of the work will determine the size, shape, and cut of the file that should be used.

A SINGLE-CUT file is generally used to produce a smooth surface finish. DOUBLE-CUT files remove metal rapidly but produce a rougher surface finish. RASPS are used on wood and some plastics. Flat surfaces of steel and aluminum are worked with a CURVED-TOOTH file.

USING THE FILE

Most filing is done while the work is held in a vise. Mount the work at about elbow height for general filing. STRAIGHT or CROSS FILING is done by pushing the file lengthwise, straight ahead, or at a slight angle across the work, Fig. 7-17. DRAW FILING, Fig. 7-18, usually produces a finer finish than straight filing.

To avoid injury, NEVER USE A FILE WITHOUT A HANDLE. Avoid running your fingers over a newly filed surface. You might cut yourself on the sharp burr formed by the file.

CUTTING METAL BY HAND

Some metal cutting can be done easily and safely by hand using a chisel or hacksaw.

CHISELS

CHISELS are used to cut or shear metal. The four types shown in Fig. 7-19 are often used. These are usually referred to as COLD CHISELS.

NEVER USE A CHISEL WITH A MUSH-ROOMED HEAD, Fig. 7-20. Correct this dangerous condition by grinding.

Shearing is done with the stock held in a vise, Fig. 7-21. Flat stock should be cut on a soft steel backing plate. NEVER cut flat stock on the vise slide or on top of the anvil.

HACKSAWS

Most hacksaws can be adjusted to fit various blade lengths, Fig. 7-22. Some are made so the blade can be installed in either a vertical or horizontal position, Fig. 7-23.

A fine-tooth blade should be used to cut thin stock. Heavier work is cut with a coarse-tooth blade. When selecting a blade, keep in mind the THREE-TOOTH RULE. That rule says that at least three teeth of the blade should be in contact with the work at all times.

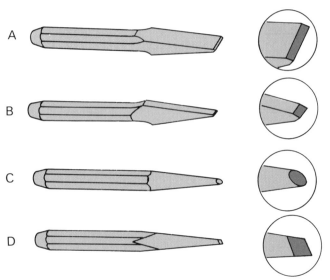

Fig. 7-19. COLD CHISELS. A—Flat chisel is used for general cutting. B—Cape chisel has a narrower cutting edge and is used to cut grooves. C—Round nose chisel is used to cut round grooves and radii. D—Diamond point chisel is used to square corners.

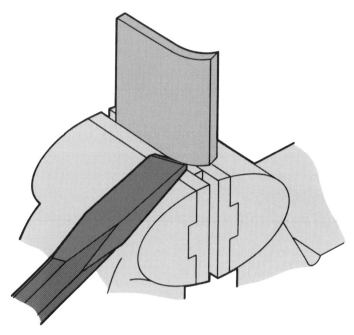

Fig. 7-21. Shearing work held in a vise with a chisel.

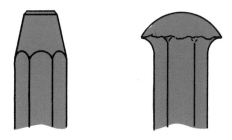

Fig. 7-20. Never use a chisel with a mushroomed head.

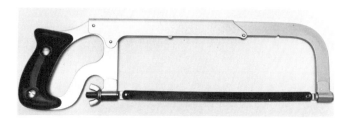

Fig. 7-22. The adjustable hacksaw.

82

Install blades with the teeth pointing AWAY from the handle, Fig. 7-24. Tighten until the blade "pings" when snapped with your finger.

HOLDING WORK FOR SAWING

Clamp the work so the cut to be made is close to the vise, Fig. 7-25. In this way, you can avoid "chatter" (vibration that dulls the teeth). Mount work so the cut is started on a flat side rather than on a corner or edge, Fig. 7-26. Start the cut using the thumb of your free hand to guide the blade. Methods for holding different metal shapes for cutting are shown in Fig. 7-27.

CUTTING METAL

Hold the saw firmly (but comfortably) by the handle and the front of the frame. Apply pressure on the cutting (forward) stroke. Lift the saw slightly on the return stroke. Make about 40 strokes per minute using the full length of the blade.

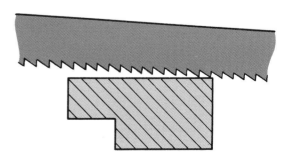

Fig. 7-24. Install a hacksaw blade with the teeth pointing away from the handle.

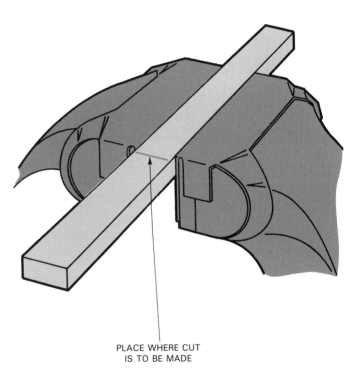

PLACE WHERE CUT
IS TO BE MADE

Fig. 7-25. Make cut as close to vise as possible to prevent chatter. Chatter can ruin the saw blade.

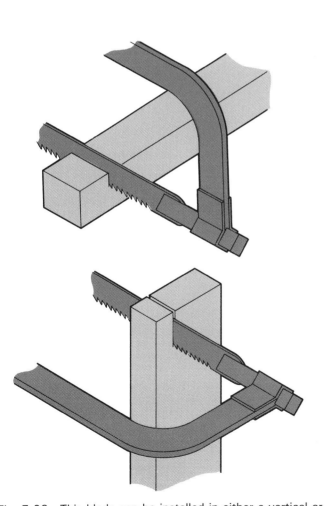

Fig. 7-23. This blade can be installed in either a vertical or horizontal position.

Fig. 7-26. Start the cut on a flat edge of the work rather than on a sharp corner.

83

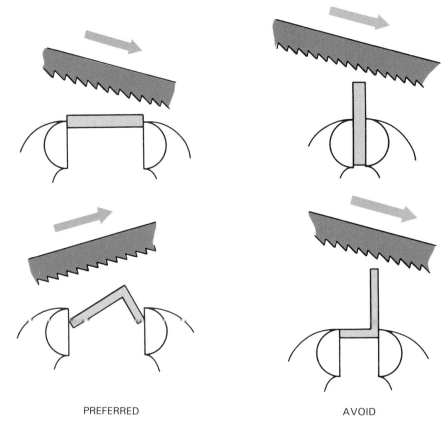

PREFERRED   AVOID

Fig. 7-27. Recommended ways to hold work of various shapes for sawing.

Saw slower when the blade has cut almost through the metal. Support the work so it will not drop when the cut is completed.

There may be times when a blade breaks or becomes dull. The blade must then be changed. After changing the blade, if possible, position the work so a new cut can be made. If a new cut is not made, the new blade will be pinched in the old cut, dulling quickly.

DO NOT TEST SAW BLADE SHARPNESS BY RUNNING YOUR FINGER ACROSS THE TEETH!

CUTTING METAL WITH MACHINES

Large metal sections can be cut quickly with a POWER HACKSAW. See Fig. 7-28.

As with hand sawing, the THREE-TOOTH RULE also applies to power sawing. In general, large pieces and soft material require saws with coarse teeth. Small or thin work, or hard materials, require a fine tooth blade.

Fig. 7-28. Top. Reciprocating type power hacksaw. Bottom. Band type power hacksaw.

Fig. 7-29. Sabre saw.

Mount the blade so it cuts on the power stroke. This is the back stroke on most reciprocating (back and forth) power saws.

Be sure the work is mounted solidly before starting the cut.

KEEP YOUR HANDS CLEAR OF THE MOVING BLADE. STOP THE MACHINE BEFORE MAKING ADJUSTMENTS. PULL THE PLUG WHEN CHANGING BLADES OR MAKING ADJUSTMENTS.

Thin material can be cut with a SABRE SAW, Fig. 7-29. The type and thickness of the metal determines the type of blade to use. If a cutting chart for a saw is available, use this as a guide.

DRILLING METAL

The DRILL PRESS, Fig. 7-30, is mostly used to cut round holes in metal. It operates by rotating a cutting tool (the drill) against material with

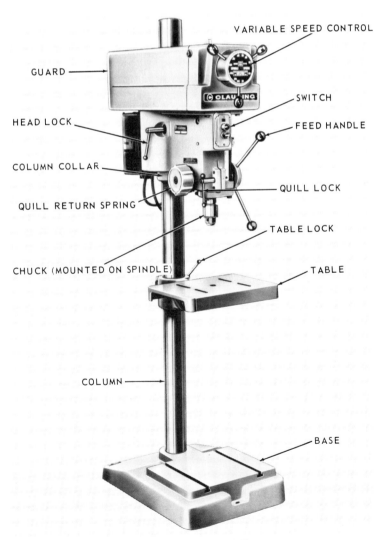

Fig. 7-30. Floor type drill press.

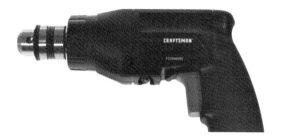

Fig. 7-31. The portable electric power drill has a built-in power source. The batteries are rechargeable; length of service with each charging will depend upon drill size and the material being drilled. ALWAYS WEAR SAFETY GLASSES WHEN USING POWER TOOLS.

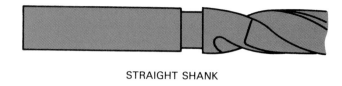

STRAIGHT SHANK

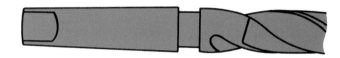

TAPER SHANK

Fig. 7-34. Types of drill shanks.

Fig. 7-32. Hand drill.

Drills are made of HIGH SPEED STEEL (HSS) or CARBON STEEL. High speed drills are costly when purchased. However, if used properly, they will cut faster and last longer than carbon steel drills. Proper use of drills includes following recommended cutting speeds. These are the speeds at which a certain drill should rotate. The speeds for several metals are given in Fig. 7-33.

enough pressure to cause the drill to cut into the material. The PORTABLE ELECTRIC DRILL, Fig. 7-31, and the HAND DRILL, Fig. 7-32, are also used to drill holes in all kinds of material.

STRAIGHT SHANK DRILLS, Fig. 7-34, top, must be held in a chuck. TAPER SHANK DRILLS, Fig. 7-34, bottom, mount directly in the drill press spindle.

CUTTING SPEEDS FOR HIGH SPEED DRILLS					
DRILL DIAMETER	ALUMINUM	BRASS	CAST IRON	MILD STEEL	TOOL STEEL
1/16	4500	4500	4500	4000	3500
1/8	2000	3000	1800	1800	1500
3/16	1800	2900	1500	1400	1200
1/4	1700	2300	1200	1100	1000
5/16	1500	1900	950	850	725
3/8	1200	1500	750	700	600
7/16	1100	1300	650	600	525
1/2	1000	1150	575	525	375
9/16	850	1000	500	525	350
5/8	750	900	450	425	300
3/4	600	750	375	350	250
7/8	550	650	325	300	225
1.000	450	575	280	265	185

PLEASE NOTE:

These cutting speeds are recommended. It may be necessary because of the characteristics of the material to increase or decrease the drill speed to do a satisfactory cutting job.
Use a cutting fluid on all metals EXCEPT cast iron.

Fig. 7-33. Suggested cutting speeds for drilling various types of metal.

DRILL SIZES

Drill sizes are expressed by one of the following drill series:

NUMBER DRILLS — No. 80 to No. 1 (0.0135 in. to 0.2280 in. diameter).

LETTER DRILLS — A to Z (0.234 in. to 0.413 in. diameter).

FRACTIONAL DRILLS — 1/64 in. to 3 1/2 in. diameter.

METRIC DRILLS — 3.0 mm to 76.0 mm diameter.

Number drills and letter drills are often needed for drilling holes that are to be tapped (threaded) or reamed.

The drill size, except on very small drills, is stamped on the drill shank. Should the size wear away, drill diameter can be checked using a DRILL GAUGE, Fig. 7-35, or a micrometer.

DRILLING PROCESS

The following steps should be followed when drilling a hole.

1. Lay out work to be drilled as shown on the layout plans.
2. Mount the work solidly on the drill press. If possible, use a vise, Fig. 7-36, or clamp the work to the drill press table. Be careful not to drill into the vise or table. SAFETY NOTE: When drilling, do not hold short pieces or thin stock by hand. A "merry-go-round" may result and cause a painful injury.
3. Center the work using a "wiggler" (center finder) or a center. See Fig. 7-37.
4. Select the proper size drill. Check it for size and sharpness. Mount it in the chuck. SAFETY NOTE: Be sure to remove the chuck key from the chuck.
5. Set the drill press to the correct speed. In general, use slow speeds for large drills and hard materials. Use faster speeds for small drills and soft materials. Check a DRILL SPEED

Fig. 7-36. Work mounted for drilling.

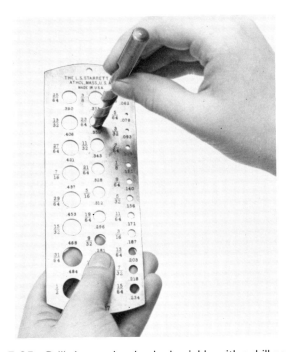

Fig. 7-35. Drill size can be checked quickly with a drill gauge.

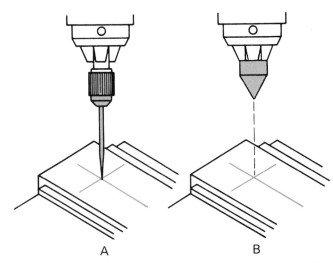

A   B

Fig. 7-37. Two techniques for locating the hole center when drilling. A—Wiggler or center finder. B—Small center.

CHART to determine the correct speed for the drill and material being used, Fig. 7-33.

6. Turn on the machine and bring the drill into contact with the work. Apply a few drops of cutting fluid (machine or lard oil) to the drill point from time to time to improve cutting action. Reduce pressure as the drill starts through the work. SAFETY NOTE: When using a drill press, be sure long hair is contained, sleeves are rolled up, hanging jewelry is removed, and safety goggles are worn.

7. Turn off the machine. Clean away chips. Unclamp the work and remove any burrs. SAFETY NOTE: Remove chips with a brush—NOT WITH YOUR HANDS.

8. Clean the drill press and drill. Return tools to their proper place.

When drilling holes larger than 1/2 in. (12 mm) in diameter, it is often best to first drill a smaller PILOT HOLE, Fig. 7-38.

Holes that will hold flat head fasteners should be COUNTERSUNK. This is done with a COUNTERSINK, Fig. 7-39. Countersink the hole deep enough so that the head of the fastener is flush with the work surface. See Fig. 7-40.

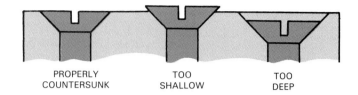

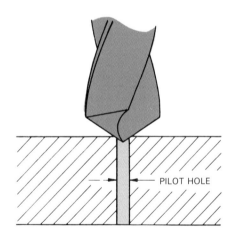

Fig. 7-38. Drilling large diameter holes is made easier by using a pilot hole.

Fig. 7-39. Countersink.

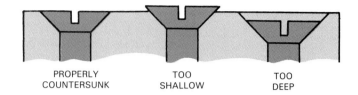

| PROPERLY COUNTERSUNK | TOO SHALLOW | TOO DEEP |

Fig. 7-40. Countersink deeply enough so that the screw head is flush with the work surface.

HAND THREADING

Spiral grooves found on nuts, bolts, and screws are called THREADS. The operation that cuts this groove in material is called THREADING.

Threads are cut by hand with either taps or dies, Fig. 7-41. INTERNAL THREADS (like those inside a nut) are cut with a TAP. EXTERNAL THREADS (like those on a bolt) are cut with a DIE.

THREAD SERIES

There are two widely used series of threads. The FINE THREAD SERIES, Fig. 7-42, left, has more threads per inch of length for a given thread diameter than the COARSE THREAD SERIES, Fig. 7-42, right. Both are part of the AMERICAN NATIONAL THREAD SYSTEM. The FINE THREAD SERIES is indicated by NF and the COARSE THREAD SERIES is indicated by NC.

Fig. 7-41. Tap and die sizes.

Fig. 7-42. Left. National Fine Thread (NF). Right. National Coarse Thread (NC).

In the late 1940s, Canada, Great Britain and the United States adopted a thread form (shape) that is very similar to the American National system. This new system is known as the UNIFIED SYSTEM. When used, the UNIFIED FINE THREAD SERIES is identified as UNF and the UNIFIED NATIONAL COARSE SERIES as UNC.

METRIC THREADS are now being used in some American-made products. Metric threads are made to standards set by the INTERNATIONAL ORGANIZATION FOR STANDARDIZATION (ISO). ISO is composed of 80 nations. The groups establish standards that define and allow measurements of length, volume, weight, and other values. Metric thread size is identified differently than in the Unified Thread System. See Fig. 7-43.

Metric threads have the same basic shape as UNF and UNC threads. While they may appear to be similar in diameter, ISO and UNF/UNC threads cannot be used in place of each other, however. See Fig. 7-44.

Because metric and UNF/UNC threads are similar in appearance, mismatching often occurs. To control this problem, metric fasteners can be identified as shown in Fig. 7-45.

CUTTING INTERNAL THREADS

A hole must be drilled before an internal thread can be cut. The diameter of the hole must be smaller than the tap size. The hole is made with a TAP DRILL. A tap drill is a number, letter,

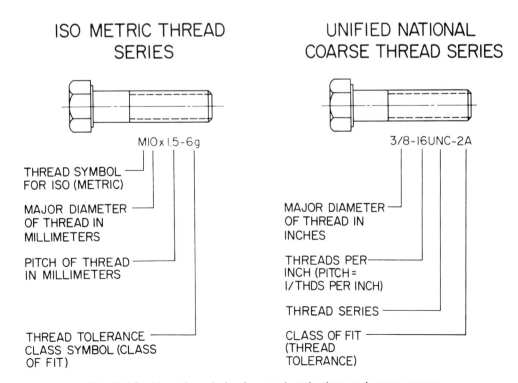

ISO METRIC THREAD SERIES

M10 x 1.5-6g

THREAD SYMBOL FOR ISO (METRIC)

MAJOR DIAMETER OF THREAD IN MILLIMETERS

PITCH OF THREAD IN MILLIMETERS

THREAD TOLERANCE CLASS SYMBOL (CLASS OF FIT)

UNIFIED NATIONAL COARSE THREAD SERIES

3/8-16UNC-2A

MAJOR DIAMETER OF THREAD IN INCHES

THREADS PER INCH (PITCH = 1/THDS PER INCH)

THREAD SERIES

CLASS OF FIT (THREAD TOLERANCE)

Fig. 7-43. How thread size is noted and what each term means.

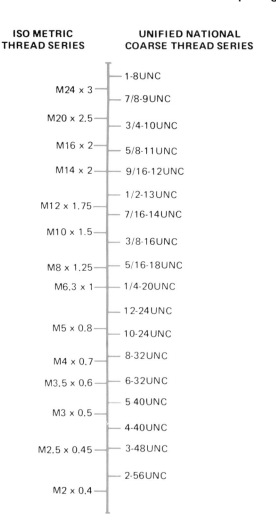

ISO METRIC THREAD SERIES | **UNIFIED NATIONAL COARSE THREAD SERIES**

1-8UNC
M24 x 3
7/8-9UNC
M20 x 2.5
3/4-10UNC
M16 x 2
5/8-11UNC
M14 x 2
9/16-12UNC
1/2-13UNC
M12 x 1.75
7/16-14UNC
M10 x 1.5
3/8-16UNC
M8 x 1.25
5/16-18UNC
M6.3 x 1
1/4-20UNC
12-24UNC
M5 x 0.8
10-24UNC
M4 x 0.7
8-32UNC
M3.5 x 0.6
6-32UNC
5 40UNC
M3 x 0.5
4-40UNC
M2.5 x 0.45
3-48UNC
2-56UNC
M2 x 0.4

ISO and Unified National Thread
Series ARE NOT INTERCHANGEABLE

Fig. 7-44. A comparison of ISO metric coarse pitch and Unified Coarse (UNC) inch based thread sizes. Even though several of them seem to be the same size, they are not switchable.

fractional, or metric drill. Using this drill, the diameter of the hole will be small enough to permit the tap to cut threads. A TAP DRILL CHART must be used to choose the proper drill size (tap drill) needed with a specified tap. You can find such a chart on page 260 of this text.

TAPS

Taps are made in sets of three, Fig. 7-46. In this set is a TAPER, PLUG, and BOTTOM TAP.

The TAPER TAP is so called because the point has a pronounced taper. This tool permits easy starting of holes. It is employed for tapping THROUGH HOLES. In through holes the threads are cut all of the way through the work.

The PLUG TAP is used to thread blind holes if the holes are drilled deeper than the threads are to be cut. Blind holes do not go all the way through the material.

The BOTTOM TAP is used when the thread must be cut to the bottom of a blind hole. Start the thread with a taper tap, cut with a plug tap, and complete with the bottom tap.

TAP HOLDERS

Taps are turned with a TAP HOLDER or TAP WRENCH. See Figs. 7-47 and 7-48. Tap size will determine which is to be used.

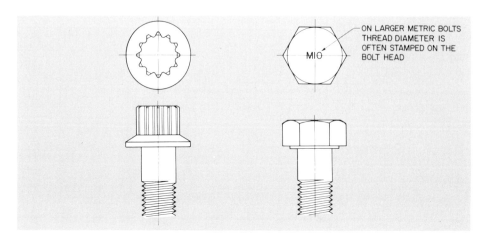

ON LARGER METRIC BOLTS THREAD DIAMETER IS OFTEN STAMPED ON THE BOLT HEAD

M10

Fig. 7-45. Much study is being done to find an easy way to identify metric-based fasteners from inch-based fasteners. The 12-element spline head and imprinted hex head (thread size is stamped on the head) are two methods being considered.

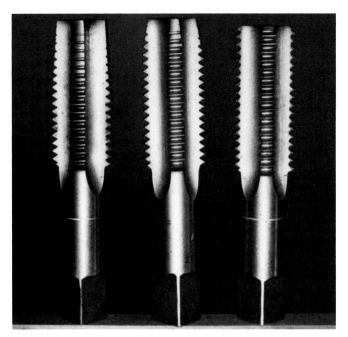

Fig. 7-46. Tap set. Left. Taper tap. Center. Plug tap. Right. Bottoming tap.

A T-HANDLE TAP WRENCH is used with small taps (under 1/4 in. or 6.5 mm). It allows a sensitive "feel" when tapping and reduces the danger of tap breakage.

More leverage is required with larger taps, so the HAND TAP WRENCH should be used.

NOTE: A conventional wrench is NEVER used to turn a tap when cutting threads.

TAPPING A HOLE

To keep tap breakage to a minimum, the following steps are recommended:

1. Drill the required size hole.
2. Start the tap square, Fig. 7-49. A drop of cutting oil will improve cutting ability.
3. Turn the tap into the work a partial turn. Back it off (counterclockwise) until you feel the chips break loose. DO NOT FORCE THE TAP. Continue this until the hole is tapped.
4. Use cutting oil for tap lubrication. If a blind hole is being threaded, back the tap out of the hole often to remove chips.
5. Use care. Broken taps are difficult to remove from work.

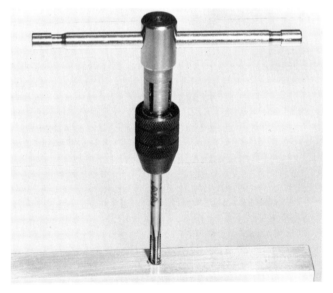

Fig. 7-47. T-handle tap wrench is used with small taps.

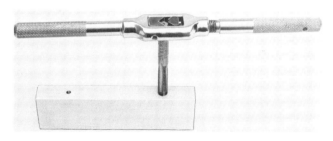

Fig. 7-48. Hand tap wrench.

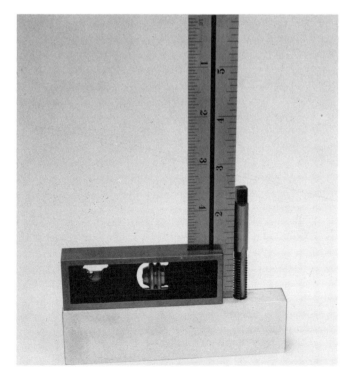

Fig. 7-49. The tap must be started square.

91

SAFETY NOTE: Use a brush to remove chips made by a tap. Also, avoid running your finger over a newly tapped hole. A burr is often present and can cause a painful cut.

CUTTING EXTERNAL THREADS

External threads are cut with a DIE, Fig. 7-50. A DIE STOCK, Fig. 7-51, holds the die and serves as a wrench for turning it.

When cutting external threads, remember the following rules.

1. Stock diameter is the same size as the required threads. That is, 3/8-16UNC threads would be cut on 3/8 in. diameter rod.
2. Grind a small chamfer on the end of the stock, Fig. 7-52. This makes it easier to start the die.
3. Mount the work solidly in a vise.
4. Start the cut with the tapered end of the die. Again, see Fig. 7-52.
5. If an adjustable die is used, make trial cuts on scrap stock to see if the die is properly adjusted.

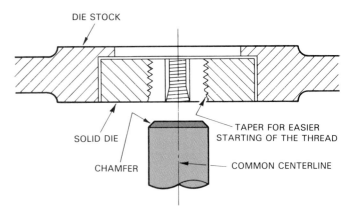

Fig. 7-52. A small chamfer ground or turned on the end of the stock will permit the die to be started easier.

6. Back off the die every turn or two to break the chips and to allow them to fall free.
7. Apply liberal amounts of cutting fluid. Be careful not to spill any on the floor.
    SAFETY NOTE: Do not remove chips from newly cut threads with your fingers. A brush will do it better and more safely.

REAMERS

Drilled holes may be enlarged to the desired size with a REAMER. A HAND REAMER, Fig. 7-53, is turned with a tap wrench. Like the machine reamer that is used with the drill press, it is available with STRAIGHT or SPIRAL FLUTES, Fig. 7-54.

EXPANSION REAMERS, Fig. 7-55, permit slight size adjustment.

Fig. 7-50. Two types of adjustable dies.

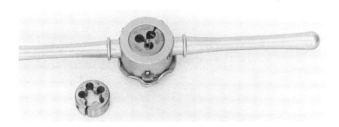

Fig. 7-51. Die stock.

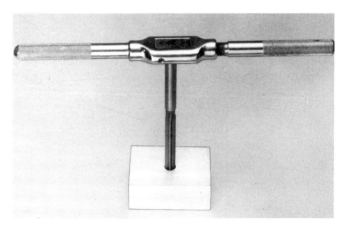

Fig. 7-53. Hand reamer mounted in tap wrench.

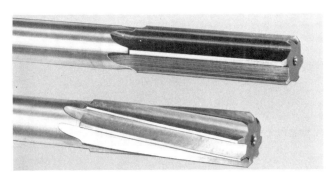

Fig. 7-54. Cutting portion of machine reamers.

Fig. 7-55. Adjustable reamer.

These allowances (how much smaller the hole must be drilled) are recommended for reaming:

a. To 1/4 in. diameter allow 0.010 in.

b. 1/4 to 1/2 in. diameter allow 0.015 in.

c. 1/2 to 1.0 in. diameter allow 0.020 in.

d. 1.0 to 1 1/2 in. diameter allow 0.025 in.

Use sharp reamers.

Fig. 7-56. Reaming table.

After drilling a hole to the correct size for reaming, the following steps are suggested to hand ream a hole. See Fig. 7-56 for recommended allowances.

1. Mount the work solidly in a vise.
2. Position the reamer in the hole. The end of the tool is tapered slightly so it will fit easily into the hole. If proper alignment is a problem, use a square.
3. Slowly turn the reamer CLOCKWISE until it is centered in the hole.
4. After the reamer is centered, keep turning the wrench clockwise with a firm, steady pressure

until the reamer is through the work. Lubricate the reamer with cutting or machine oil. Remove the tool from the hole by turning the wrench CLOCKWISE and raising the reamer at the same time.

CAUTION: Do not turn the reamer counterclockwise at any time. This will dull the tool.

TEST YOUR KNOWLEDGE, Unit 7

Please do not write in the text. Place your answers on a separate sheet of paper.

MATCHING QUESTIONS: Match the following sentences with the words listed below.

a. Hacksaw.   h. Die.
b. Double-cut.   i. Countersink.
c. Standard.   j. UNC.
d. Vise caps.   k. Tap.
e. File card.   l. Straight shank.
f. Single-cut.   m. UNF.
g. Phillips.   n. Reamer.

1. ____ The soft covers used to protect work held in a vise.
2. ____ The screwdriver used to drive slotted head screws.
3. ____ The screwdriver used to drive "X" slotted head screws.
4. ____ The file cut used to produce a smooth surface finish.
5. ____ The file cut that removes metal quickly but makes a rough surface finish.
6. ____ Used to clean files.
7. ____ Tool used to cut metal.
8. ____ Enlarges drilled holes.
9. ____ Drill held in a drill chuck.
10. ____ Cuts internal threads.
11. ____ Cuts external threads.
12. ____ Tool used to permit flat head screws to be mounted flush with the work surface.
13. ____ Used to indicate Unified National Coarse Thread Series.
14. ____ Used to indicate Unified National Fine Thread Series.

15. Name the four commonly used drill series.
16. A _____ tap is used to start the thread.
17. The _____ tap is used to cut threads to the bottom of the hole.

18. Identify the taps shown below.

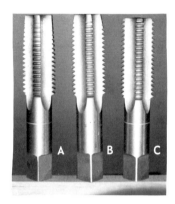

TECHNICAL TERMS TO LEARN

adjustable wrench
ball peen hammer
bottom tap
box wrench
burr
center finder/wiggler
chisel
clockwise
combination set
combination pliers

combination wrench
counterclockwise
cross filing
diagonal pliers
die
die stock
double-cut
draw filing
drill
drill press

file
file card
hacksaw
needle-nose pliers
open-end wrench
Phillips screwdriver
pilot hole
pipe wrench
pliers
plug tap
reamer
round nose pliers
sabre saw

screwdriver
side cutting pliers
single-cut
socket wrench
straight shank
tap
tap drill
taper shank
taper tap
tap wrench
threads
vise

ACTIVITIES

1. Example the tools in your metals lab. Repair those that are damaged.
2. Prepare a series of safety posters on the proper way to use tools.
3. Inventory the hand tools in your lab. Using tool catalogs, determine how much it would cost if they had to be replaced.
4. Design a new tool panel and storage facility for your lab.
5. Devise a method for quickly checking whether all tools were returned to their proper place at the end of a work period.

Unit 8 · · · · · · · · · ·

Wrought Metal

After studying this unit, you will be able to identify the hand tools and specially designed tools used for bending metals. In addition, you will demonstrate how to twist metal and shape curves in metal. And, finally, you will be able to create your own piece of wrought metalwork.

In Colonial America, wrought metalwork was hammered and worked into shape by BLACK-SMITHS, Fig. 8-1. Their products were not only useful, but also decorative, Fig. 8-2.

Today, wrought metalwork is also known as ornamental ironwork and bench metal.

The metal most commonly used is wrought iron. It is almost pure iron and contains very little carbon (carbon makes iron harder and tougher).

Fig. 8-1. In Colonial America, blacksmiths hammered and worked metal into useful shapes.
(Colonial Williamsburg)

Fig. 8-2. Reproductions of hand wrought work made by Colonial blacksmiths are not only useful, but also decorative. (Old Guilford Forge)

Wrought iron is easy to bend (either hot or cold) and weld, but is expensive. Standard hot rolled steel shapes are often used as substitutes.

BENDING WITH HAND TOOLS

Metal up to 1/4 in. in thickness can be bent cold. Heavier metal bends easier when heated.

Cut the metal to length. This can be done with a hacksaw or a ROD PARTER, Fig. 8-3.

In working with wrought iron, the length of the metal is reduced slightly with each bend. To make up for this, add one-half the metal thickness to the length of the piece for each bend.

Some projects require that several bends be made in the same piece of metal. The bending sequence must be planned carefully. If it is poorly planned, it may be difficult to make all the bends with accuracy, Fig. 8-4.

Many bends in wrought ironwork can be made using a heavy vise and a ball peen hammer. Make the necessary layout. Place the metal in the vise, with the extra material allowed for the bend, projecting above the jaws, Fig. 8-5. Start the bend by striking the metal near the vise, with the flat of the hammer, Fig. 8-6.

Right angle bends are squared by using one corner of the vise jaw as a form, Fig. 8-7. Strike the metal near the bend.

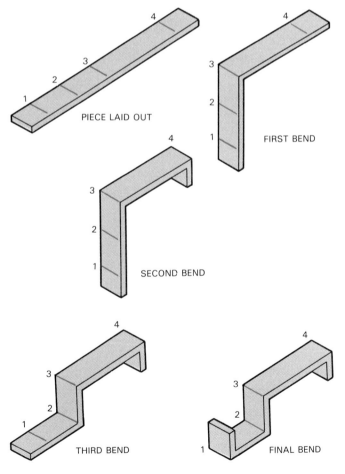

Fig. 8-4. Recommended bending sequence.

Fig. 8-3. Bar and rod stock can be easily sheared to length by using a ROD PARTER. (Di-Acro)

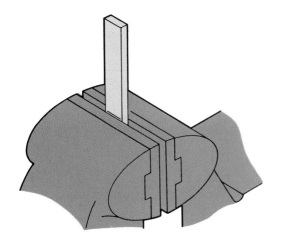

Fig. 8-5. Add one-half the thickness of the metal to the total length of the piece, for each bend. Place the section with this extra metal above the vise.

ACUTE ANGLES (angles less than 90 deg.) can also be made in the vise. However, this is done after the first bend has been made, Fig. 8-8.

OBTUSE ANGLES (angles more than 90 deg.) may be made using a MONKEY WRENCH (an adjustable wrench that resembles a pipe wrench, but has smooth jaws) as a bending tool, Fig. 8-9. It is also called a SPUD WRENCH.

Thin stock can be bent in a vise using two pieces of angle iron or wood to position the metal. Make the bend with a mallet, Fig. 8-10.

Fig. 8-6. Many bends can be made using a vise with a hammer.

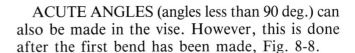

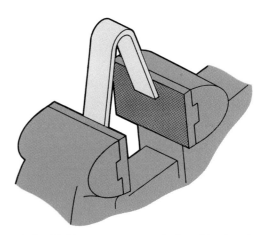

Fig. 8-8. Making an acute angle bend in the vise.

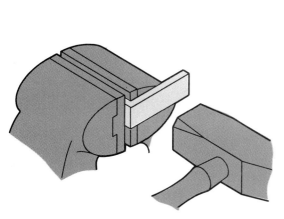

Fig. 8-7. Making a right angle bend using the vise.

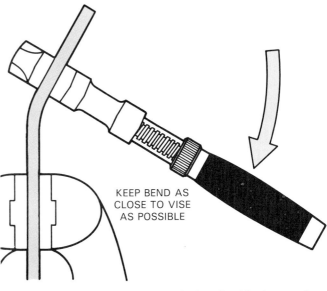

KEEP BEND AS CLOSE TO VISE AS POSSIBLE

Fig. 8-9. Making an obtuse angle bend with the monkey wrench.

Fig. 8-10. Thin stock can be bent by placing it between two pieces of angle iron and making the bend with a mallet.

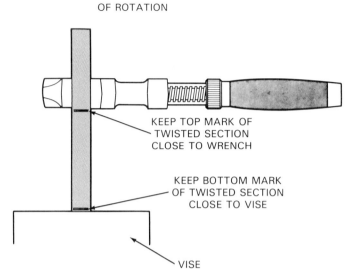

SAFETY NOTE:
THE MOVABLE JAW SHOULD
ALWAYS FACE THE DIRECTION
OF ROTATION

KEEP TOP MARK OF
TWISTED SECTION
CLOSE TO WRENCH

KEEP BOTTOM MARK
OF TWISTED SECTION
CLOSE TO VISE

VISE

Fig. 8-12. Making a twisted section. Place a monkey wrench at the top mark and make the required number of turns.

TWISTING METAL

Wrought metal may be twisted for increased strength and rigidity, for decorative purposes, or to alter the look of long flat sections. See Fig. 8-11.

Lay out the section to be twisted. Allow extra material because twisting shortens the metal slightly.

Short sections may be twisted in a vise. Place the metal in the vise. Place the bottom layout mark flush with the jaws. Place a monkey wrench at the top mark and make the required number of turns. See Fig. 8-12.

Long sections of metal often bend out of line when twisted. To avoid this problem, slide a section of snug fitting pipe over the portion to be twisted. When you have finished twisting, remove the pipe. Minor bends can be straightened with a mallet.

BENDING CIRCULAR SHAPES

Some wrought ironwork makes use of curved sections for decorative purposes, Fig. 8-13. The

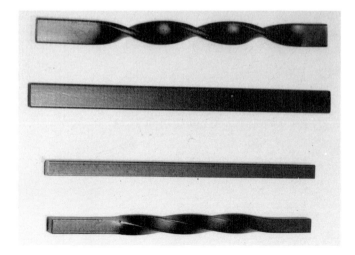

Fig. 8-11. Twisted sections have extra strength and rigidity. They are also more decorative than long, flat pieces.

Fig. 8-13. A wrought iron trivet that makes use of curved sections.

curves can be made over the anvil horn or with a BENDING JIG, Fig. 8-14. For best results, make a full size pattern of the proposed curve.

Stock length can be found by forming a piece of wire over the pattern. Straighten the wire and measure its length.

The SCROLL, Fig. 8-15, is frequently used. It is a curved section with a constantly expanding radius that looks like a loose clock spring.

The scroll is formed with the aid of a bending jig. One section is formed at a time, Fig. 8-16. Check the curve against the pattern during the forming operation to insure accuracy.

Often, a scroll is required on both ends of the piece, Fig. 8-17. One curve should blend smoothly into the other curve.

Scroll ends are often flared or decorated, Fig. 8-18. This is done before the scroll is formed.

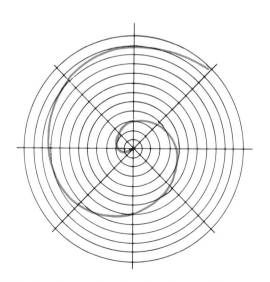

Fig. 8-14. One type of bending jig.

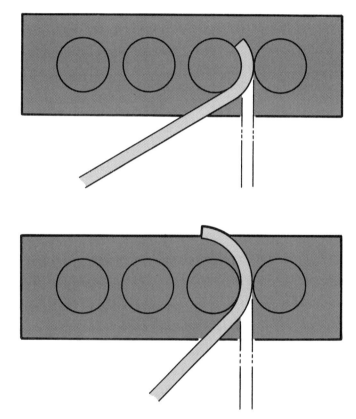

Fig. 8-16. Making a scroll on a bending jig.

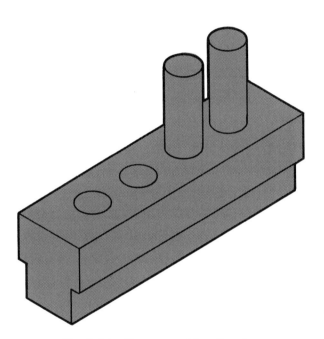

Fig. 8-15. Scrolls may be developed using this technique.

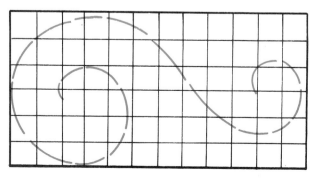

Fig. 8-17. A pattern for a double end scroll.

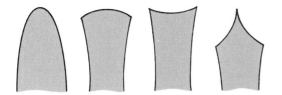

Fig. 8-18. Typical scroll ends.

Curves of a given radius can be formed using a vise and a piece of pipe or rod. The diameter of the pipe must equal the inside diameter of the required curve.

Clamp the metal in the vise as shown in Fig. 8-19. Pull the metal forward. As the curve takes shape, move the work farther in and around the pipe.

Curves can also be formed using a hammer and a rod clamped in the vise, Fig. 8-20.

BENDING WITH SPECIAL TOOLS

Bending can be done by using special machine. See Figs. 8-21, 8-22, and 8-23. The machines provide additional leverage for bending heavier metal. In addition, special attachments permit complex shapes to be formed easily.

The bending sequence must be planned BEFORE cutting the metal. Do not forget to make allowances for the bends.

Metal formed in a bending machine has some "springback" (the metal tries to return to its original shape). Problems caused by this can be avoided by using a bending form with a radius slightly smaller than the required radius.

Springback varies with metal thickness. It may be helpful to make a sample bend. Use scrap metal of the required size to determine the correct form to use.

Be sure to study the instruction book supplied by the manufacturer of the machine being used.

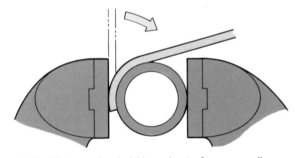

Fig. 8-19. Using a pipe held in a vise to form a scroll or curved section.

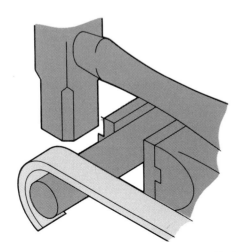

Fig. 8-20. Making a curved section over a rod held in a vise.

Fig. 8-21. The Di-Acro bender can be used to mechanically form rod and bar stock. (Di-Acro)

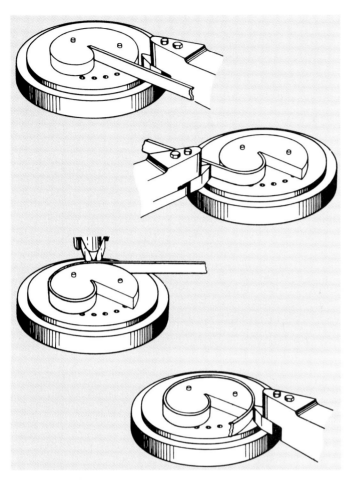

Fig. 8-22. Scrolls and other shapes of irregular radii can be formed with a bender. Use a collar having the same contour as the shape to be formed.

ASSEMBLY

Wrought ironwork may be assembled by riveting or welding.

FINISHING WROUGHT IRONWORK

Early wrought ironwork acquired a pleasing surface texture (finish) when the metal was forged to usable size. Today, with a large range of standard metal sizes available, it is no longer necessary to forge the material to size. In order to achieve the same surface look as forged metal, however, peening was developed. In PEENING, the work is struck over and over with the ball end of the hammer, Fig. 8-24. Today, peening is widely used. However, the "real" artisan still takes the time to forge the metal to size, Fig. 8-25.

Flat black lacquer or paint is applied for the final surface finish. It is easier to apply than the scorched linseed oil finish used by Colonial artisans.

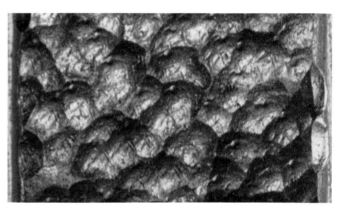

Fig. 8-24. Close-up of a peened surface.

Fig. 8-23. The Metl-Former. (Swayne, Robinson and Co.)

Fig. 8-25. An attractive surface is made when metal is forged to size. It is not an artificial surface finish like a peened surface.

SAFETY

1. Remove all burrs and sharp edges from the metal before shaping it.
2. Wear your safety glasses when cutting, chiseling or grinding metal.
3. Have any cuts, bruises, or burns treated promptly.
4. Handle long sections of metal with extreme care so that persons working nearby will not be injured.
5. Keep your fingers clear of the moving parts of the bending machine.
6. Do not use a bending machine unless you know how to operate it safely. When in doubt, consult your instructor.
7. Do not use finishing materials near an open flame or in an area that is not properly ventilated. Store oily and solvent soaked rags in an approved closed container.

TEST YOUR KNOWLEDGE, Unit 8

Please do not write in the text. Place your answers on a separate sheet of paper.

1. The first wrought ironwork in America was made by _____.
2. Give two other names by which wrought iron-work is known.
3. Metal up to 1/4 in. thick can be bent _____. Heavier metal bends easier when it is _____.
4. There are many ways metal can be bent. List four of them.
5. Which two of the following points must be considered when making a bend in metal? (Choose all that apply.)
   a. Heavier metals must be used to allow extra metal for the bend.
   b. The length of the metal is reduced slightly by each bend and allowances must be made for this reduction.
   c. Bends should be made heated.
   d. Bends should be made with a hammer of the proper size.
   e. If several bends are to be made in the piece, the bending sequence must be planned very carefully.
6. What are some reasons for twisting metal?
7. The _____ is a curved section that looks like a loose clock spring.
8. What is springback?
9. How much will 25 feet of wrought iron cost if it is priced at 18.75 cents a foot?

TECHNICAL TERMS TO LEARN

acute angle	ornamental ironwork
bending jig	rod parter
blacksmith	scroll
carbon	sequence
circular	springback
decorative	wrought
obtuse angle	

ACTIVITIES

1. Make a collection of illustrations showing wrought ironwork.
2. Secure catalogs from historic developments (Williamsburg, Cooperstown, Greenfield Village, Old Sturbridge Village, Mystic Seaport, etc.). Develop wrought iron projects that can be made in the school lab.
3. Demonstrate the proper and safe way to make bends on the Di-Acro bender.

Unit 9 . . . .

Fasteners

After studying this unit, you will be able to identify various types of fasteners. You will also be able to explain several uses for each type of fastener. And you will be able to demonstrate the safe use of epoxy adhesives.

FASTENERS (nuts, bolts, screws, rivets, etc.) may be thought of as small clamps that hold manufactured products together. They are made in many shapes, sizes, and styles, Fig. 9-1.

RIVETS

RIVETS are used for permanent assemblies. They cannot be removed without damaging the product. Rivets are made from many materials: soft iron, aluminum, copper, and brass, to name a few. And rivets come in many shapes and sizes, Fig. 9-2.

Fig. 9-1. Common fasteners found in the metals lab.

103

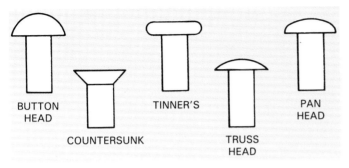

Fig. 9-2. Rivet styles. Many others are available.

Fig. 9-4. Rivet set.

SETTING A SOLID RIVET

Solid rivets can be set by hand or machine. The following steps should be followed when hand setting a rivet:

1. Select the type and length of rivet you will use. To find the proper rivet length for your work, add the total thickness of the material being joined to one and one-half times the rivet diameter. Wrought iron projects should be joined with soft iron rivets, aluminum projects with aluminum rivets, and so on.
2. Locate the point to be riveted. Drill or punch a hole of the proper size for the rivet. Countersink the hole if a countersunk flat head rivet is to be used. Remove all burrs and sharp edges.
3. Seat the rivet and draw the pieces together, Fig. 9-3A.
4. Flatten the rivet, Fig. 9-3B.
5. Form the rivet head, Fig. 9-3C, with a RIVET SET, Fig. 9-4.

If a rivet must be set flush with both work surfaces, each side of the hole must be countersunk. Place the work on a steel plate and flatten the rivet shank to fill the countersunk holes.

Button or round head rivets are held in the cup of a rivet set, while the head is formed on the shank.

BLIND RIVETS

BLIND RIVETS are used when joints are reachable from one side only. Special tools are used to put the rivets in place.

One type of blind rivet, and the tool needed to set it, are shown in Fig. 9-5. This set can be found in any hardware store. This rivet is set as shown in Fig. 9-6.

THREADED FASTENERS

Threaded fasteners permit the work to be taken apart and put back together without damage.

MACHINE SCREWS

MACHINE SCREWS, Fig. 9-7, are widely used in the metals lab. Many head styles are available with slotted or recessed heads.

Machine screws clamp parts together by screwing them into tapped holes. Square or hexagonal (six-sided) nuts may be used with the screws.

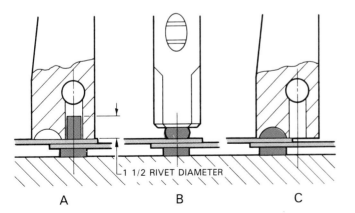

Fig. 9-3. Setting a rivet. A—Drawing the pieces together. B—Flattening the rivet. C—Forming the rivet head with a rivet set.

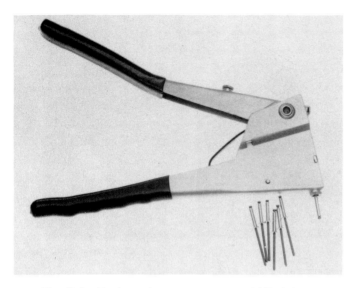

Fig. 9-5. Tool used to set one type of blind rivet.

MACHINE BOLTS

MACHINE BOLTS, Fig. 9-8, are used to assemble products that do not need close tolerance fasteners.

CAP SCREWS

CAP SCREWS, Fig. 9-9, are much like machine bolts. However, they are made more exactly than machine bolts. And, they are used in projects that require a higher quality fastener. Cap screws are available in a wide variety of head styles.

Nuts may be used with cap screws. However, common use of cap screws involves passing them through a CLEARANCE HOLE (a hole slightly larger than the screw) in one of the pieces. Then they are screwed into a threaded hole in the other piece, Fig. 9-10.

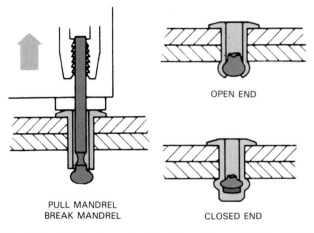

OPEN END

CLOSED END

PULL MANDREL
BREAK MANDREL

Fig. 9-6. This is how the blind rivet shown in Fig. 9-5 is set in place.

Fig. 9-8. Machine bolts.

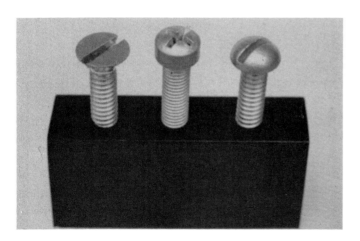

Fig. 9-7. Three types of machine screw heads.

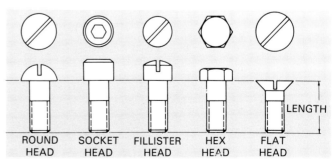

ROUND HEAD | SOCKET HEAD | FILLISTER HEAD | HEX HEAD | FLAT HEAD

LENGTH

Fig. 9-9. Cap screws.

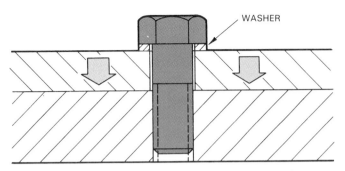

Fig. 9-10. This is how a cap screw joins work.

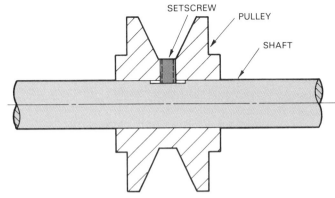

Fig. 9-12. Setscrew in use.

STUD BOLTS

STUD BOLTS, Fig. 9-11, are threaded at both ends. One end is screwed into a tapped hole, the piece to be clamped is fitted into place over the stud. A nut is screwed on the other end of the bolt, to clamp the two pieces together.

SETSCREWS

SETSCREWS, Fig. 9-12, have several uses. They are used to prevent pulleys from slipping on a shaft. They are used to hold collars in place on a shaft. And they are used to hold shafts in place on assemblies. Many types of setscrews are made, Fig. 9-13.

NUTS

NUTS may be standard square or hexagonal in shape. They are used with bolts having the same shape heads. They are also made for decorative and special applications, Fig. 9-14.

WASHERS

WASHERS permit a bolt or nut to be tightened without damage to the work surface.

STANDARD and LOCK WASHERS, Fig. 9-15, are commonly found in the metals lab.

KEYS

Keys prevent gears and pulleys from moving on shafts. Several key styles are shown in Fig. 9-16.

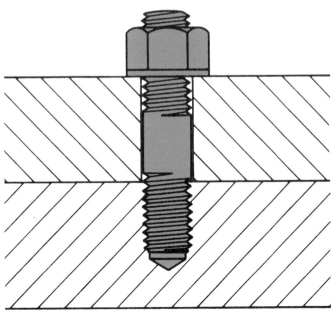

Fig. 9-11. Stud bolt. Note that it is threaded on both ends.

Fig. 9-13. Typical setscrews. These are only a few of the many types made.

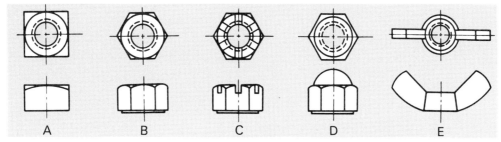

Fig. 9-14. Commonly used nuts. A—Square nut. B—Hex nut. C—Slotted nut. D—Acorn or cap nut. E—Wing nut.

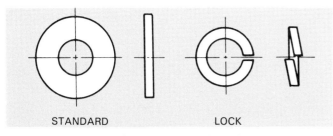

Fig. 9-15. Two of the many steel washers available.

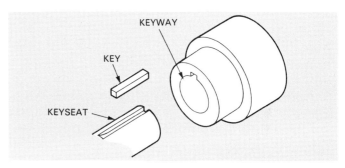

Fig. 9-17. Key, keyway, and keyseat.

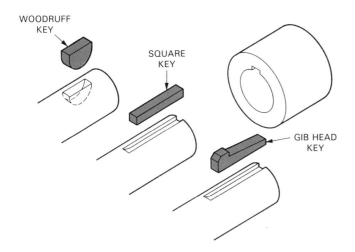

Fig. 9-16. Types of keys.

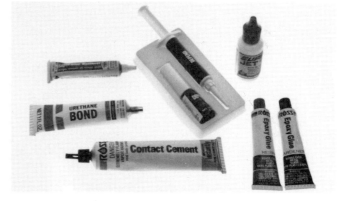

Fig. 9-18. Many types of adhesives are available that will bond metal to metal and metal to other materials. They are safe to use, if reasonable precautions are taken and manufacturer's instructions are strictly followed.

One-half of the key fits into a KEYSEAT on the shaft. The rest of the key fits into a KEYWAY in the hub of the gear or pulley. See Fig. 9-17.

EPOXY ADHESIVES

There are many adhesives used in metalworking. Many can be bought at any good hardware store, Fig. 9-18.

When using adhesives in metalworking, it is very important that the surfaces to be joined are cleaned correctly. Clean them with a fine abrasive paper. Then wipe with a solvent to remove all oil, grease, and dirt.

Before using an adhesive, carefully read the manufacturer's instructions on the container AND

FOLLOW THEM. If an adhesive must be mixed, blend the parts EXACTLY as specified.

CAUTION: ALL ADHESIVES CAN IMPAIR, OR CAUSE LOSS OF, SIGHT. SKIN IRRITATIONS MAY ALSO RESULT IF SKIN COMES IN CONTACT WITH SOME TYPES OF ADHESIVES. WEAR SAFETY GLASSES. KEEP ADHESIVES AWAY FROM YOUR EYES. WEAR DISPOSABLE PLASTIC GLOVES WHEN PREPARING AND USING ADHESIVES. WASH YOUR HANDS THOROUGHLY AFTER USING AN ADHESIVE. READ AND STRICTLY FOLLOW ALL MANUFACTURER'S INSTRUCTIONS BEFORE USING ANY ADHESIVE.

Adhesives are a good way to join metal to metal, or metal to other materials. They are safe to use if the manufacturer's instructions are closely followed, and safety precautions taken.

TEST YOUR KNOWLEDGE, Unit 9

Please do not write in the text. Place your answer on another sheet of paper.

1. Permanent assemblies are made with _____.
2. What can be done with threaded fasteners that cannot be done with rivets?
3. Which of the following are fasteners?
   a. Bolts.
   b. Nuts.
   c. Screws.
   d. All of the above.
4. What is similar to a machine bolt, but made to more exacting standards?

MATCHING QUESTIONS: Match each of the following terms with their correct definitions.
   a. Washer.   d. Stud bolt.
   b. Key.   e. Nut.
   c. Setscrew.

5. ____ Has several uses, one of which is to prevent a pulley from slipping on a shaft.
6. ____ Used with bolt that has the same shape head.
7. ____ Permits a bolt or nut to be tightened without damage to work surface.
8. ____ Is threaded on both ends.
9. ____ Prevents a gear or pulley from moving on a shaft.

TECHNICAL TERMS TO LEARN

acorn nut	lock washer
adhesive	machine bolt
blind rivet	machine screw
bolt	nut
cap screw	rivet
clearance hole	screws
epoxy	set screw
fasteners	solid rivet
key	washer
keyseat	wing nut
keyway	

ACTIVITIES

1. Prepare a collection of fasteners. Mount them on a display panel.
2. Research the manufacturing process used for threaded fasteners.
3. Obtain samples of several fasteners in common use.

Unit 10 . . . .

Sheet Metal

After studying this unit, you will be able to use the different methods of pattern development. You will also be able to cut and bend sheet metal using a number of tools. You will be able to demonstrate soldering procedure. And, you will be able to work safely with sheet metal and when soldering.

Great amounts of sheet metal are used in the manufacturer of metal objects such as aircraft, automobiles, furniture, and household appliances.

See Fig. 10-1. Sheet metal is also used by the building trades (air conditioning, heating, roofing, and prefabricated structures), Fig. 10-2.

Products made from sheet metal are given three-dimensional shape and rigidity. This is done by bending and forming the metal sheet into the required shape.

In many manufacturing jobs metal is cut to shape using a pattern as a guide. A PATTERN is a full-size drawing of the surfaces of the object.

Fig. 10-1. The auto industry uses millions of tons of various sheet metals. Many hundreds of pounds will be needed to manufacture each unit of this sports-utility vehicle. The metal will be given additional strength and ridigity when it is formed into 3-dimensional shape. The vehicle shown is a concept model used to study the best way to manufacture production models.   (Isuzu)

Fig. 10-2. A building made from sheet metal.   (Stran-Steel)

It is stretched out as a single surface, Fig. 10-3. The pattern drawing is often called a STRETCH-OUT. It is made using a form of drafting called PATTERN DEVELOPMENT.

PATTERN DEVELOPMENT

There are two basic types of pattern development: parallel line development and radial line development.

PARALLEL LINE DEVELOPMENT is a technique used to make patterns of prisms and cylinders, Fig. 10-4.

RADIAL LINE DEVELOPMENT is used to make patterns of regular tapering forms such as cones and pryamids, Fig. 10-5.

Patterns developed from more complex geometric shapes are drawn using variations and combinations of basic pattern development techniques.

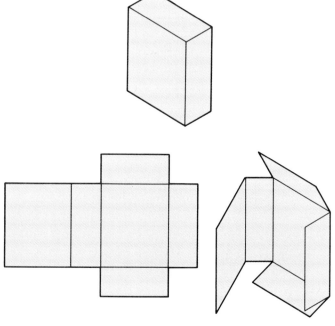

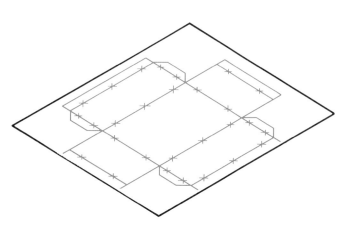

Fig. 10-3. A sheet metal layout or pattern. Folds are to be made as shown by the letter ''X.''

Fig. 10-4. A pattern made by parallel line development.

110

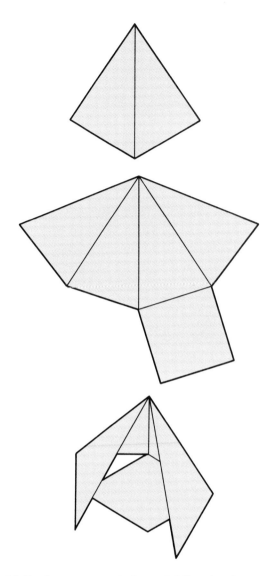

Fig. 10-5. A pattern made by radial line development.

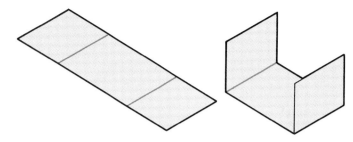

Fig. 10-6. A heavy solid line indicates a sharp fold.

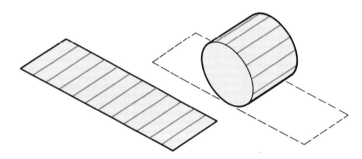

Fig. 10-7. Construction (light) lines or centerlines indicate a curved or circular surface.

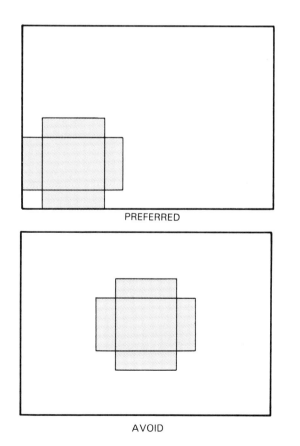

Fig. 10-8. Locate the pattern on the metal so there will be a minimum of waste.

Lines used in pattern development give additional meaning to the drawing. A heavy solid line (visible object line) indicates a sharp fold or bend, Fig. 10-6. Curved surfaces are shown on the pattern by construction lines or centerlines, Fig. 10-7.

A word of caution. Be sure to allow enough material to make the various joints, hems, and seams. These are needed to join metal together and to add rigidity to thin metal sheets. This will be explained later in the unit.

Patterns may be developed on paper and transferred to the metal, or they can be drawn directly onto the metal. Carefully plan layouts made directly on metal so there will be a minimum of waste, Fig. 10-8.

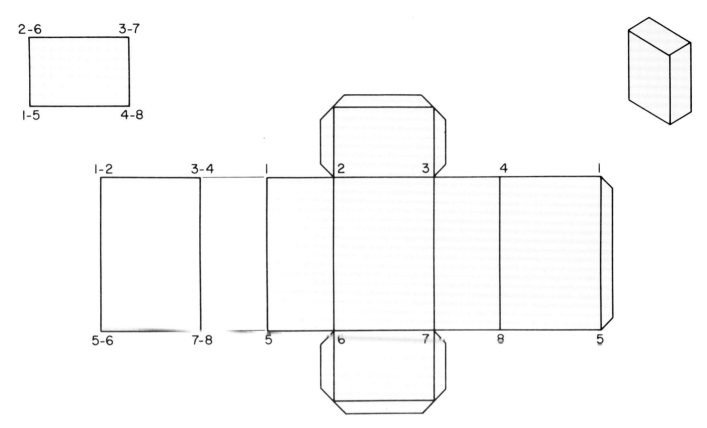

Fig. 10-9. Developing a pattern for a rectangular or square object.

PATTERN DEVELOPMENT OF A RECTANGULAR OBJECT

To develop rectangular or square objects, see Fig. 10-9. The steps to follow for this method are explained in the next section.

1. Draw front and top views.
2. The height of the pattern is the same as the height of the front view. Project light lines from the top and bottom of the front view. Number as shown.
3. Measure about 1 in. from the front view. Then draw a vertical line between the extended lines to locate 1 - 5.
4. Set the compass or divider from 1 to 2 on the top view. Transfer this distance to the extended lines to locate 2 - 6. Locate the other distances in the same manner.
5. Using 2 - 3 and 6 - 7 as one side draw the top and bottom.
6. Allow about 1/4 in. for seams. (This amount may vary, depending on the size of the object). Go over all outlines and folds with heavy lines (object lines).

PATTERN DEVELOPMENT OF CYLINDRICAL OBJECTS

Cylindrical objects, Fig. 10-10, are developed using the following method.

1. Draw the front and top views. Divide the top view into twelve equal parts and number as shown.
2. The height of the pattern is the same as the height of the front view. Project light lines from the top and bottom of the front view.
3. Measure about 1 in. from the front view. Draw a vertical line between the extended lines to locate 1.
4. Set the compass or divider from 1 to 2 on the top view. Transfer this distance to the extended lines to locate points 1, 2, 3, etc., as shown. Draw light vertical lines at each point.
5. Draw the top and bottom tangent to the extended lines.
6. Allow material for the seams. Go over all outlines with heavy lines (object lines). The lines that depict curves or circular lines may be drawn in color, or left as light lines.

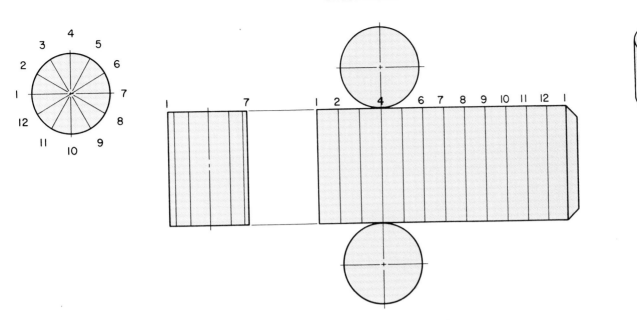

Fig. 10-10. Pattern development for a cylinder.

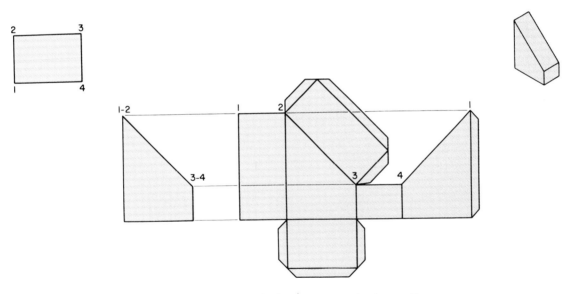

Fig. 10-11. Developing a truncated prism pattern.

PATTERN DEVELOPMENT OF A TRUNCATED PRISM

A truncated prism is cut off at an angle to its base, Fig. 10-11. Development of this shape is made as follows.

1. Draw front and top views. Number views as shown.
2. Proceed as in the previous examples of parallel line development.
3. Mark off and number the folding points. Project point 1 on the front view, to line 1 of the stretchout. Repeat with points 2, 3, and 4.
4. Connect the points 1 to 2, 2 to 3, 3 to 4, and 4 to 1.
5. Draw the top and bottom (if needed) in position.
6. Allow material for seams. Go over the outline and folds with visible object lines.

113

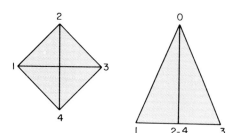
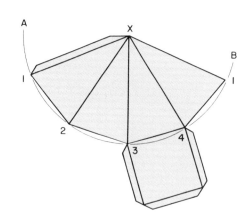
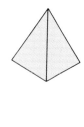

Fig. 10-12. Developing a pattern for a pyramid.

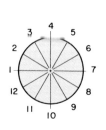

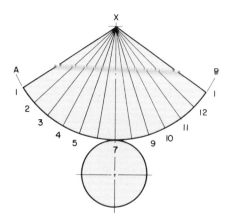

Fig. 10-13. Developing a pattern for a cone.

PATTERN DEVELOPMENT OF A PYRAMID

The pattern for a pyramid, Fig. 10-12, is developed as follows.

1. Draw front and top. Number as shown.
2. Locate centerline X of the stretchout.
3. Set the compass to a radius equal to 0 - 1 on the front view. Using X of the stretchout as the center, draw arc AB.
4. Draw a vertical line through centerline X and arc AB.
5. Set the compass from 1 to 2 on the top view. Then, using the place where the vertical line intersects the arc as the starting point, step off two divisions on each side of the line (points 1-2-3-4-1 on the stretchout).
6. Connect the points and draw the bottom in place (if needed). Go over the outline and folds with object lines.

PATTERN DEVELOPMENT OF A CONE

Developing the pattern for a cone, Fig. 10-13, is done as follows.

1. Draw front and top views. Divide the top view into twelve equal parts and number as shown.
2. Locate centerline X of the stretchout.
3. Set the compass from 0 to 1 on the front view. Using X as the centerline, draw arc AB.
4. Draw vertical construction line through centerline X and the arc.
5. Set the compass from 1 to 2 on the top view. Using the place where the vertical line intersects the arc as the starting point, step off six divisions on both sides of the line (points 1-2-3-4 etc. on the pattern).
6. Go over the outline with object lines. The lines that represent the curved portion are drawn in color, or are left as construction lines.

114

WORKING WITH SHEET METAL

METALS USED IN SHEET METAL

TIN PLATE (a mild steel with a tin coating), GALVANIZED STEEL (a mild steel with a zinc coating), and COLD FINISHED STEEL SHEET are most often used in sheet metal work in the school shop.

These metals are available in standard thicknesses and sizes. The thickness can be measured with a micrometer or SHEET METAL GAUGE. See Fig. 10-14.

CUTTING SHEET METAL

SNIPS are used a great deal for cutting metal sheets. They are made in a number of sizes and styles, Fig. 10-15.

Large sheet metal sections are cut on SQUAR-ING SHEARS, Fig. 10-16. When a quantity of sheet metal must be cut on the job, smooth, clean cuts can be made with an electric tool, Fig. 10-17.

Do not cut wire, band iron, or steel rod with snips or squaring shears. This will damage the cutting edges.

KEEP YOUR HANDS CLEAR OF THE BLADE AND YOUR FOOT FROM BENEATH THE FOOT PETAL WHEN USING SQUARING SHEARS.

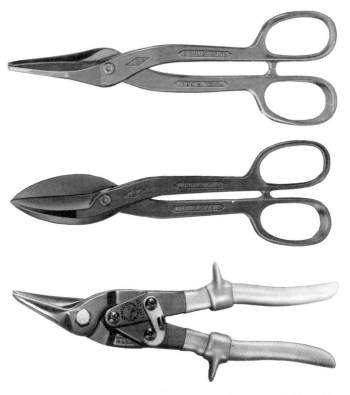

Fig. 10-15. Typical snips used to cut sheet metal. Top. Circular pattern snips. Center. Straight pattern snips. Bottom. Aviation snips, left cut. (Diamond Tool Co.)

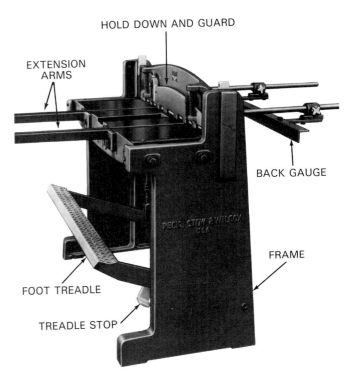

Fig. 10-16. Foot powered squaring shears.

Fig. 10-14. Measuring sheet metal thickness with a sheet metal gauge.

MAKING SMALL DIAMETER HOLES IN SHEET METAL

In addition to drilling, small holes can be made in sheet metal with a HOLLOW PUNCH, Fig. 10-18, and a SOLID PUNCH, Fig. 10-19.

BENDING SHEET METAL

Sheet metal is often bent into three-dimensional shapes. The bending makes thin metal rigid.

Some hand and machine bending techniques are described in the following paragraphs.

BENDING METAL BY HAND

Sheet metal may be bent by fitting it between two blocks of hardwood or pieces of angle iron, Fig. 10-20. Press the metal over by hand. Square up the bend with a wooden mallet.

USE EXTREME CARE WHEN HANDLING SHEET METAL TO AVOID PAINFUL CUTS FROM THE SHARP EDGES OF THE MATERIAL.

Bending can also be done using a STAKE, Fig. 10-21.

Fig. 10-18. Using a hollow punch to cut holes in sheet metal.

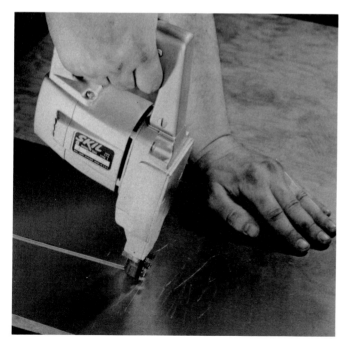

Fig. 10-17. The nibbler cuts sheet metal cleanly and smoothly, with neither cut edge bending. (Skil Corp.)

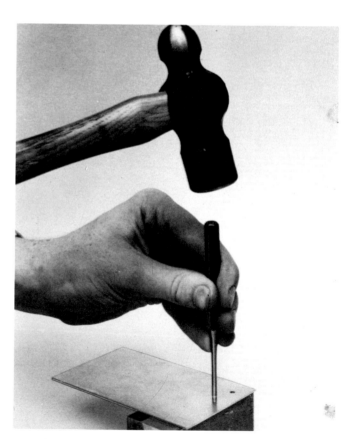

Fig. 10-19. Small diameter holes can be made in sheet metal with a solid punch. Use a bar of lead or end-grain wood block to support the work while making the hole.

116

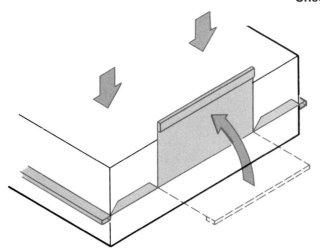

Fig. 10-20. Using blocks of wood to make a bend in sheet metal.

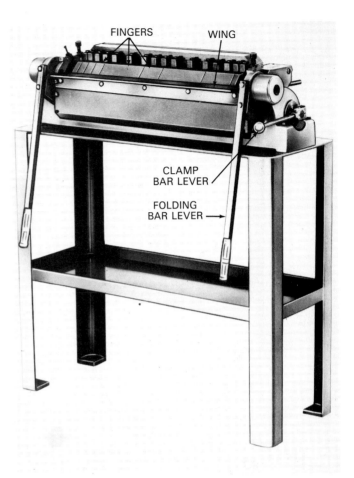

FINGERS   WING

CLAMP
BAR LEVER

FOLDING
BAR LEVER

Fig. 10-22. Box and pan brake.   (Di-Acro)

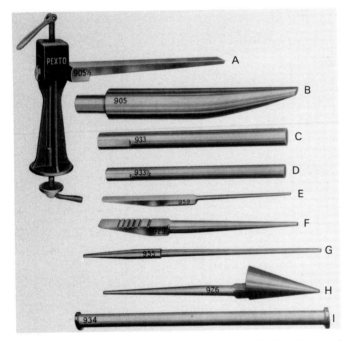

Fig. 10-21. A few of the many stakes available. A—Universal stake holder fitted with the rectangular end of a beakhorn stake. B—Beakhorn stake. C—Conductor stake, large end. D—Conductor stake, small end. E—Needle case stake. F—Creasing stake with horn. G—Candle mould stake. H—Blowhorn stake. I—Double seaming stake.   (Pexto)

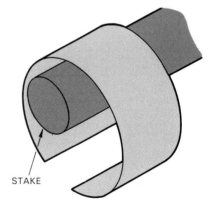

STAKE

Fig. 10-23. Circular shapes can be formed by hand, over a stake or metal rod.

BENDING SHEET METAL ON BOX AND PAN BRAKE

The BOX AND PAN BRAKE, Fig. 10-22, makes accurate bends mechanically. Its upper jaw is made of a number of blocks that are of different widths. These can be positioned or removed to permit all four sides of a box to be formed.

MAKING CIRCULAR AND CONICAL SHAPES

Circular and conical shapes can be made by hand, over a stake, Fig. 10-23. However, it is difficult to make the curves smooth and accurate.

Most cylindrical shapes can be formed quickly and accurately on a SLIP ROLL FORMING MACHINE, Fig. 10-24. The rolls can be adjusted to fit different thicknesses of metal and to form the desired curve, See Fig. 10-25.

COMMON SHEET METAL SEAMS, HEMS, AND EDGES

Various SEAMS are used to join sheet metal sections, Fig. 10-26. Sheet metal seams are often finished by soldering.

HEMS, Fig. 10-27, are used to straighten lips of sheet metal objects. These are made in standard fractional sizes — 3/16, 1/4, etc.

The WIRE EDGE, Fig. 10-28, gives additional strength and rigidity to sheet metal edges.

FOLDS are basic to the making of seams, edges, and hems. Folds are made on a BAR FOLDER, Fig. 10-29.

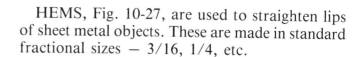

LAP SEAM   COUNTERSUNK LAP SEAM

FLAT LOCK SEAM   GROOVED FLAT LOCK SEAM

Fig. 10-26. Typical sheet metal seams.

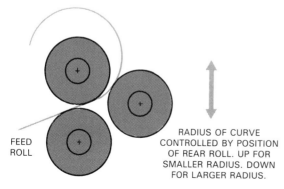

Fig. 10-24. Slip roll forming machine.

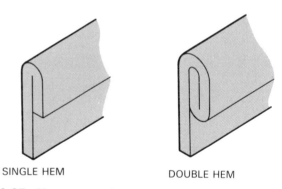

SINGLE HEM   DOUBLE HEM

Fig. 10-27. Hems are made on sheet metal to provide added strength to the metal.

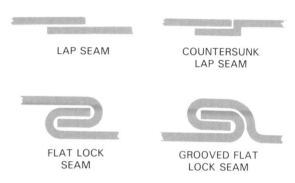

FEED ROLL

RADIUS OF CURVE CONTROLLED BY POSITION OF REAR ROLL. UP FOR SMALLER RADIUS. DOWN FOR LARGER RADIUS.

Fig. 10-25. The rolls can be adjusted to fit sheet metal of different thicknesses and to form various curvatures.

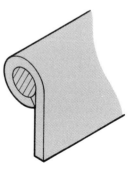

Fig. 10-28. Wire edge.

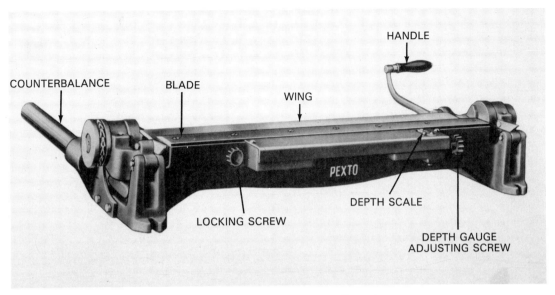

Fig. 10-29. Bar folder. (Pexto)

The width of the folded edge is set on the DEPTH GAUGE of the machine. The sharpness of the folded edge can vary. It will be sharp for a hem or seam, and rounded for a wire edge. This sharpness is determined by the position of the WING, Fig. 10-30. The machine can also be adjusted to make bends of 45 deg. and 90 deg.

Folds for seams are made on a bar folder. After the sections are fitted together, the seams may be locked with a HAND GROOVER, Fig. 10-31.

A COMBINATION ROTARY MACHINE, Fig. 10-32, can be used to make a wire edge. See Fig. 10-33. The machine can be fitted with a variety of rolls to perform operations such as CRIMPING, Fig. 10-34.

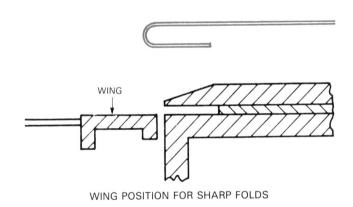

WING POSITION FOR SHARP FOLDS

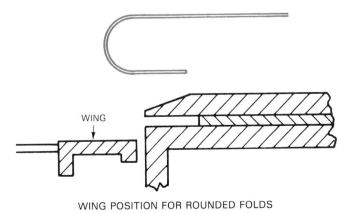

WING POSITION FOR ROUNDED FOLDS

Fig. 10-30. Setting the wing of the bar folder to make different size folds.

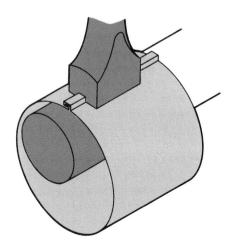

Fig. 10-31. Using a hand groover.

SHEET METAL SAFETY

1. Treat cuts and bruises immediately, no matter how minor.
2. Remove all burrs formed during the cutting operation, before doing further work on the metal.
3. Clean the work area with a brush. NEVER brush metal with your hands.
4. Use sharp tools.
5. Keep your hands clear of the blade on the squaring shears.
6. Do not run your hand over metal that has just been cut or drilled. Painful cuts from the burrs may result.
7. Place scrap pieces of sheet metal in the scrap box.
8. Do not use tools that are not in first-class condition — hammer heads should be tight, files should have handles, machines should have guards.
9. Always wear goggles when working in the shop.

SOLDERING

To SOLDER properly the steps outlined here should be followed.

1. A 50-50 solder alloy (50 percent tin-50 percent lead) is most commonly used.
2. The correct FLUX must be applied. A NON-CORROSIVE flux such as RESIN works best on tin plate and brass.

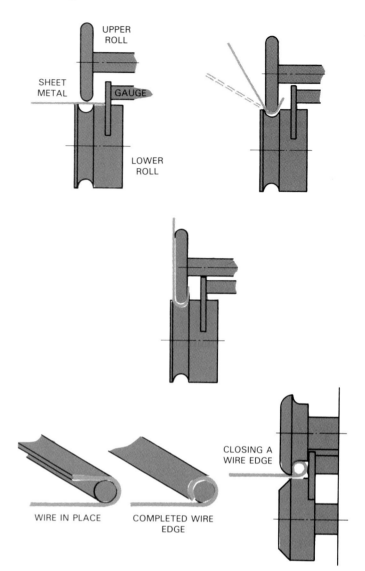

Fig. 10-33. Top. Turning a wire edge with a rotary machine. Bottom. Closing the wire edge.

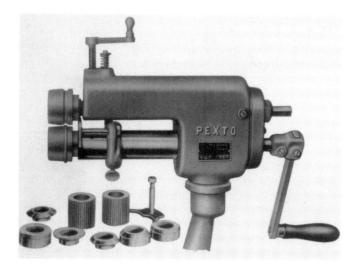

Fig. 10-32. Combination rotary machine with extra forming rolls.

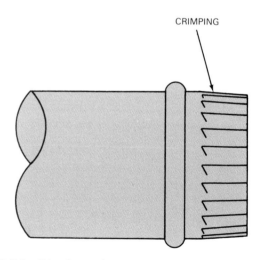

Fig. 10-34. Crimping makes one end of the metal pipe smaller. It will fit easily into the end of another pipe of the same diameter.

3. The SOLDERING COPPER must furnish sufficient heat for the job.
4. The surfaces being soldered must be clean.

SOLDERING DEVICES

Heat for soldering is often applied with an ELECTRIC SOLDERING COPPER, Fig. 10-35. Also used is a SOLID SOLDERING COPPER, Fig. 10-36, that is heated in a SOLDERING FURNACE.

Fig. 10-35. Electric soldering copper. (American Electrical Heater Co.)

Fig. 10-36. Solid soldering copper.

Fig. 10-37. Properly tinned soldering copper.

A soldering copper must be TINNED, Fig. 10-37, before it will solder properly. TINNING (coating the tip of the soldering copper with solder) is done by first cleaning the copper tip with a file. Heat the tip until it will melt solder freely. Rub it on a sal ammoniac block on which a few drops of solder have been melted, Fig. 10-38. This will clean the tip and cause the solder to adhere. Remove excess solder by rubbing the tip over a clean cloth.

SOLDERING SHEET METAL

Clean the area to be soldered and apply flux. Place the pieces on a heat-proof surface.

Heat and tin the soldering copper. Hold the seam together with the tang of the file or stick of wood, Fig. 10-39. Tack it with small amounts of solder. Apply the solder directly in front of the soldering copper tip rather than on it.

Keep the seam pressed together with a file tang. Lay the soldering copper FLAT on the work. Start moving the copper slowly toward the far end of the joint, as the solder melts and begins to flow.

Clean the soldered seam with hot water to remove all traces of flux.

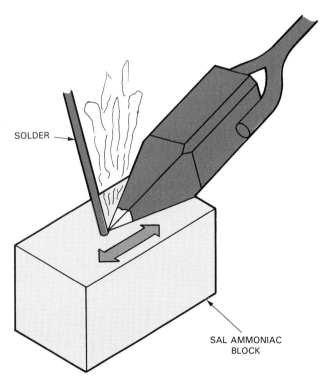

SOLDER

SAL AMMONIAC BLOCK

Fig. 10-38. Tinning soldering copper on a sal ammoniac block.

121

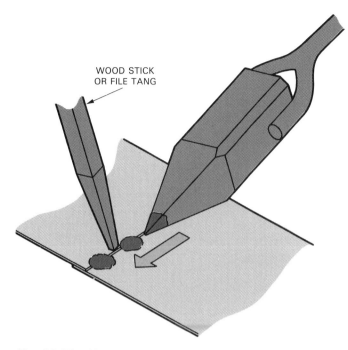

WOOD STICK
OR FILE TANG

Fig. 10-39. Hold sheet metal pieces together with a wooden stick or file tang until the molten solder "freezes."

SOLDERING SAFETY

1. Wear safety glasses when soldering.
2. Wash your hands carefully after soldering to remove all traces of flux.
3. Have burns treated promptly.
4. Avoid touching just-soldered joints.
5. Use care when storing the soldering copper after use. Improper or careless storage can result in serious burns or a fire.

TEST YOUR KNOWLEDGE, Unit 10

Please do not write in the text. Place your answers on a separate sheet of paper.

1. Sheet metal is cut to shape using a _____ as a guide.
2. Name the two basic types of pattern development.
3. A heavy, solid line on a pattern indicates a:
   a. Fold or bend.
   b. Flat surface.
   c. Curve.
   d. Cut.

4. What three steels are most often used for sheet metal work in the school shop?

MATCHING QUESTIONS: Match each of the following terms with their correct definitions.
   a. Hollow punch.   c. Squaring shears.
   b. Sheet metal gauge.   d. Snips.

5. ____ Used to cut large sheet metal sections.
6. ____ Used to make small holes in sheet metal.
7. ____ Used to cut sheet metal.
8. ____ Used to measure sheet metal thickness.
9. What is the purpose of a hem, a seam, and a fold?
10. A soldering copper must be _____ before it will solder properly.

TECHNICAL TERMS TO LEARN

bar folder
bending
box and pan brake
cone
crimping
curved
cylindrical
flux
forming
hand groover
hem
parallel
pattern
prism
punch
pyramid

radial
rectangular
rigidity
rotary machine
sal ammoniac
seam
shape
sheet metal
sheet metal gauge
ships
squaring shears
stake
stretchout
three-dimensional
tinning
truncated

ACTIVITIES

1. Collect illustrations that show objects made from sheet metal. Prepare a bulletin board using the pictures.
2. Use an empty cereal box to demonstrate how a pattern is used.
3. Prepare posters on sheet metal safety.
4. Demonstrate the correct way to use tin snips.
5. Demonstrate the correct way to use the box and pan brake.
6. Prepare examples of hems, folds, and a wire edge.
7. Demonstrate how to tin a soldering copper.
8. Prepare examples of properly soldered seams.

Unit 11 . . . .

Art Metal

After studying this unit, you will be able to demonstrate the annealing and the pickling processes. You will also be able to form bowls and trays using the beating down and raising methods. In addition, you will be able to explain how to hard solder joints and demonstrate how to safely work with art metal.

Hand skills can easily be developed in art metal since most of the work is done by hand, Fig. 11-1. Machines are seldom used.

There are four classifications of art metal. They are hollow ware, Fig. 11-2; flatware, Fig. 11-3; strip work, Fig. 11-4, and jewelry making, Fig. 11-5.

Fig. 11-1. Artisans in the James Geddy Silversmith Shop. They use 18th century methods to pound out colonial design articles from silver bars.   (Colonial Williamsburg)

Fig. 11-2. This beautiful bowl is an example of hollow ware. (Shirley Pewter Shop, Williamsburg, VA)

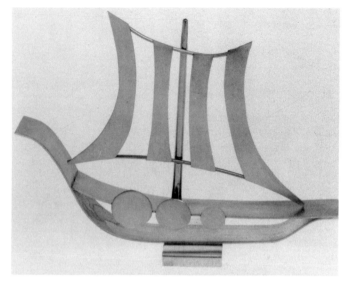
Fig. 11-4. Strip work model of early Norse ship.

Fig. 11-3. This salad server set is typical of flatware work.

Fig. 11-5. Jewelry making is one type of art metalwork.

ANNEALING AND PICKLING METAL

As metal is worked, it becomes hard and brittle. Therefore, it must be ANNEALED (softened by heating) from time to time. Then further shaping and forming can be done. Without annealing, the metal may crack.

PICKLING is closely related to the annealing process. Annealing causes an oxide (a coating like rust) to form on the metal. The oxide must be removed or it will mar the surface of the metal when any other work is done on it.

Abrasives can be used to remove this oxide. However, it is a time-consuming job. A simpler method is to heat the piece and plunge it into a dilute solution of sulphuric acid. HAVE YOUR INSTRUCTOR DEMONSTRATE THIS OPERATION FOR YOU. WHEN YOU DO IT YOURSELF, WEAR A FACE SHIELD.

Anneal copper and sterling silver by heating to a dull red. Quench the hot metal in water or pickling solution.

Brass, bronze, and German silver are heated to a dull red. Then they are allowed to cool slightly before plunging into water or pickling solution.

The metal may be heated with a torch or soldering furnace.

CAUTION: ASK YOUR INSTRUCTOR TO MIX THE PICKLING SOLUTION. THE ACID IT CONTAINS IS DANGEROUS. IT CAN CAUSE SERIOUS BURNS IF NOT PROPERLY HANDLED.

CUTTING AND PIERCING METAL

The metals used in art metal can be cut using hacksaws, snips, squaring shears, etc. However, these tools are not useful for cutting the decorative, internal designs often used in art metal. These cuts should be done with a JEWELER'S SAW, Fig. 11-6. The operation is known as PIERCING. Use a solid support when sawing, Fig. 11-7. The openings made with a jeweler's saw are cleaned with JEWELER'S FILES, Fig. 11-8.

HAMMERS AND MALLETS

Many different HAMMERS, Fig. 11-9, are used to shape and form metal. They are made of steel. The hammer faces should be kept polished.

MALLETS, Fig. 11-10, are made of hardwood, plastic, rawhide, and rubber. They are used to form softer metals. After forming with a mallet, the piece is finished with a hammer.

Fig. 11-8. Jeweler's files.

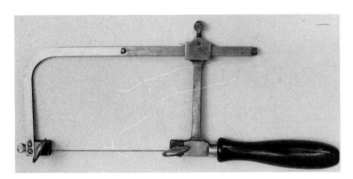
Fig. 11-6. Jeweler's saw.

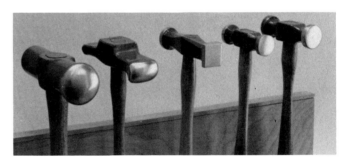
Fig. 11-9. Common types of art metal hammers.

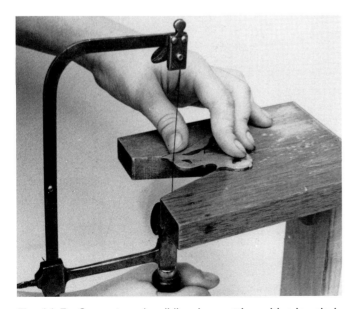
Fig. 11-7. Support work solidly when cutting with a jeweler's saw.

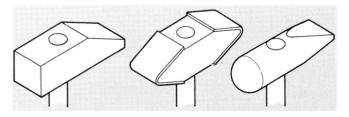
Fig. 11-10. Art metal mallets. Left. Hardwood forming mallet. Center. Leather faced forming mallet. Right. Round end forming mallet.

FORMING BY BEATING DOWN

Shallow trays and plates are often formed by beating down portions of the metal. They are beat over either a hardwood stake or form.

Both methods for beating down require a pattern, Fig. 11-11. Guide lines indicate the part to be beat down.

Hold the metal over the stake with the guide lines about 1/8 in. from the edge of the stake, Fig. 11-12. Use a forming hammer to beat down the metal. Rotate the blank slightly after each blow until the correct depth is reached. A template may be used to check the progress of the forming operation.

A wooden form block, Fig. 11-13, may also be used to shape the piece.

Position the metal over the block. Fasten it at the corners with small nails or screws. Use a mallet when working on soft metals (pewter and soft aluminum). For use on other metals, select a hammer with about the same contour (shape) as the form block sides.

Start working at the outer edges and slowly work toward the center.

The work will have a tendency to warp slightly and must be flattened. This is done on a flat, clean surface. Use a wooden block and a mallet to hammer the surface flat, Fig. 11-14.

Trim, planish (smooth by hammering lightly), and polish the piece.

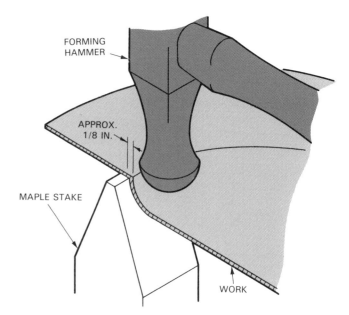

Fig. 11-12. Hold the metal on the stake.

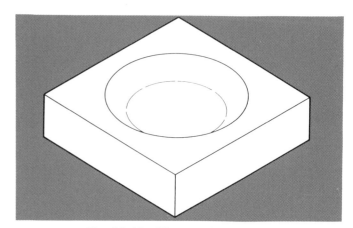

Fig. 11-13. Wooden form block.

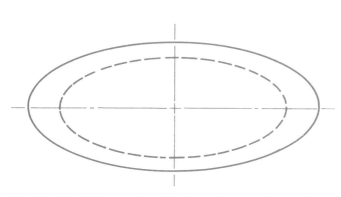

Fig. 11-11. Pattern with guide lines showing the portion to be formed.

Fig. 11-14. One method that may be used to flatten work that has been warped in the forming operation.

126

PLANISHING

PLANISHING is an operation done to make a metal surface smooth. See Fig. 11-15. It is done with a planishing hammer. Only a hammer with a mirror smooth face should be used.

Lay the hammer blows on evenly. Rotate the piece so that no two blows fall in the same place. Use a stake with a shape that is near to the desired shape.

FORMING BY RAISING METAL

A bowl may be raised by one of several methods. The design of the project will determine the method to be used.

Shallow pieces can be raised using a block of hardwood that has a shallow depression in one of the end grain sides, Fig. 11-16.

Slowly form the metal into the depression. When the desired depth has been reached, clean the piece and planish it on a MUSHROOM STAKE, Fig. 11-17. Trim, Fig. 11-18, smooth the edges, and polish.

Fig. 11-19 shows how to determine the diameter of the metal blank.

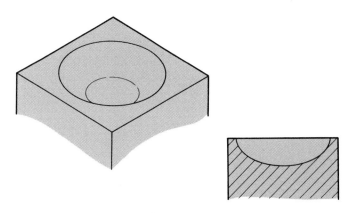

Fig. 11-16. A forming block.

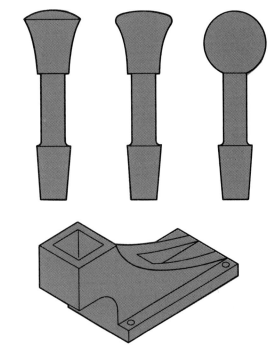

Fig. 11-17. Mushroom stakes with stake holder.

Fig. 11-15. Note how the planish marks enhance the appearance of this brass mug.   (Henry Kauffman)

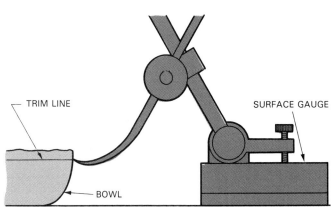

Fig. 11-18. Using a surface gauge to mark a line for trimming.

TRIM LINE

SURFACE GAUGE

BOWL

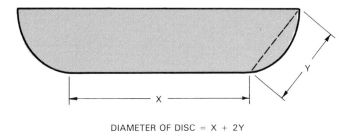

DIAMETER OF DISC = X + 2Y

Fig. 11-19. Calculating the diameter of the metal disc.

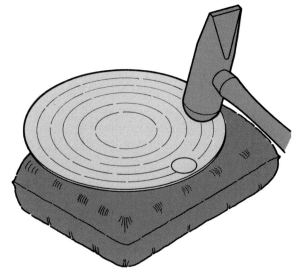

Fig. 11-21. Starting to shape a bowl on a sandbag.

Bowls can be raised using a sandbag and mallet. Scribe concentric circles (several circles having the same center) on a disc of the proper size, Fig. 11-20. Place the disc on the sandbag. Raise the edge opposite the one to be struck with the mallet, Fig. 11-21. Shape the bowl by striking the disc a series of blows around the outer circle. Continue working toward the center until the desired depth is obtained. Planish on a stake, trim to height, and polish.

A form can also be raised over a stake. Forms of considerable height can be obtained using this method, Fig. 11-22.

Cut the disc and scribe the concentric circles. Start the raising on the sandbag. Anneal the piece and place it on a RAISING STAKE, Fig. 11-23. Begin hammering by going around the scribed circles.

To continue the raising operation, hold the work on the stake. The hammer blows must land just ABOVE the point where the metal touches the stake, Fig. 11-24.

Fig. 11-22. Forms of varying heights can be raised over a stake.

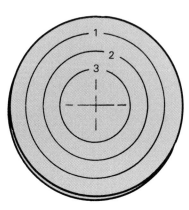

Fig. 11-20. Concentric circles on metal disc.

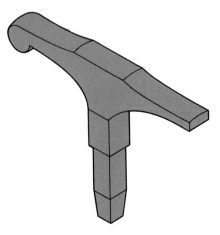

Fig. 11-23. Stake used for raising work.

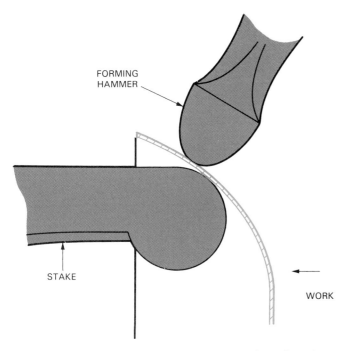

Fig. 11-24. Land hammer blows just above the point where the bowl rests on the stake.

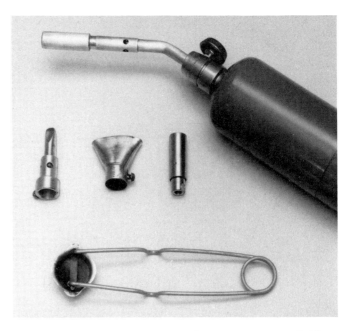

Fig. 11-25. A gas torch with a few of the tips available.

Continue the operation. Anneal when needed, until the desired height is reached.

Pickle, trim, planish, and polish.

HARD SOLDERING

HARD SOLDERING, or SILVER SOLDER-ING, produces a joint much stronger than soft solder. It is often used in art metal. A torch, Fig. 11-25, must be used to reach the temperatures needed. These range from 800 to 1400°F (430 to 760°C), depending on the silver solder used. The solder is available in sheet and wire form.

Most nonferrous metals (copper, brass, and silver) can be joined by this method.

When silver soldering, follow these steps:

1. Carefully fit the pieces together, Fig. 11-26.
2. Clean the metal. This may be done with abrasive cloth or by pickling.
3. Fluxing the metal. A proper flux can be made by mixing borax and water to form a thick paste.
4. Support the joint, Fig. 11-27. The pieces must not slip during the heating. Use clamps or binding wire.

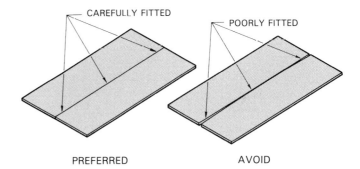

Fig. 11-26. The pieces to be hard soldered (silver soldered) must be carefully fitted together.

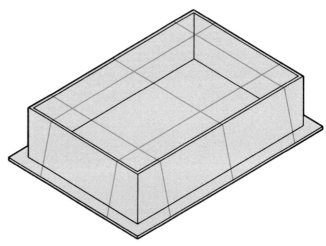

Fig. 11-27. Support the joints to be soldered. This can often be done by wiring them together with soft iron wire.

129

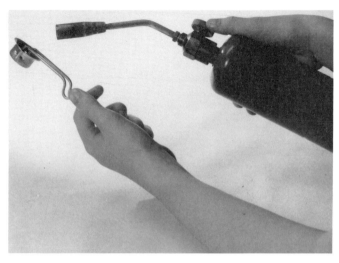

Fig. 11-28. The recommended way to light the torch. NEVER USE MATCHES!

5. Cut the solder into pieces about 1/16 in. long. Dip them in flux and place them on the joint with a small brush or tweezers. CAUTION: WHEN LIGHTING THE TORCH HOLD IT SO IT IS POINTING AWAY FROM YOU. USE A SPARK LIGHTER, Fig. 11-28.

Keep the torch in motion while heating the joint. This will assure a uniform heat. As the solder melts, it will be drawn into the joint.

If different size pieces are to be soldered, apply more heat to the larger section.

6. Remove all traces of flux and oxides from the joint using abrasive cloth or pickling.

SAFETY

1. Remove all burrs and sharp edges from metal before attempting to work with it.
2. Use caution when handling hot metal. Do not place it where it can start a fire.
3. Have your instructor mix the pickling solution. It contains acid and may cause serious and painful burns.
4. Wear a face shield when using the pickling solution. Wear your regular goggles when working in the lab.
5. Use the pickling solution in a well ventilated area. Do not breathe the fumes.
6. Stand to one side when plunging hot metal into the pickling solution.

7. Clear the soldering area of solvents and other flammable material before soldering.
8. Have cuts, bruises, and burns treated promptly.

TEST YOUR KNOWLEDGE, Unit 11

Please do not write in the text. Place your answers on a separate sheet of paper.

1. List the four classifications of art metal.
2. Why must metal be annealed?
3. Cleaning metal by heating it and then plunging it into a dilute solution of acid is called _____.
4. Name two methods used to form bowls and trays.
5. _____ is the name of the operation done to make a metal surface smooth.
6. _____ soldering produced a stronger joint than _____ soldering.
7. List several safety rules that must be observed when working with art metal.

TECHNICAL TERMS TO LEARN

annealing	mallet
art metal	pickling
beating down	piercing
borax	planish
flatware	raising
gas torch	silver soldering
hard soldering	stake
hollow ware	strip work
jewelry making	surface gauge

ACTIVITIES

1. Collect illustrations from magazines, newspapers, and catalogs to use for art metal project.
2. Visit a museum to study examples of art metal made by well-known artisans.
3. Demonstrate hard soldering.
4. Design and craft an outstanding artisan award for the Industrial Arts department of your school.
5. Prepare posters on art metal safety.
6. Secure samples of the various types of art metalwork. Describe them to your class. Stress what you consider to be their good points of design.

Unit 12
Metal Finishes

After studying this unit, you will be able to discuss various types of abrasives and identify the best uses for each type. You will also learn about several types of finishing techniques and how they are done.

Finishes are applied to metal for two reasons. They protect surfaces from corrosion and enhance surface appearance, Fig. 12-1. Many types of finishes are available.

No matter what type of finish is applied, the surface of the metal must be clean.

HAND POLISHING WITH ABRASIVES

Any hard, sharp material that can be used to wear away another material is an abrasive. For many purposes, manufactured abrasives (aluminum oxide, silicon carbide, etc.) are superior to natural abrasives (emery and iron oxide).

Fig. 12-1. Aircraft is painted to enhance its appearance and make it easier to see in the air. The top of the fuselage is painted white, or any light color tint, to reflect the heat of the sun.   (Canadair Limited)

Abrasive grains are bonded to a cloth or paper backing. The coarseness (grain size) of an abrasive is identified by number. The higher the number, the smaller the grain and the finer the finish it will produce. Aluminum oxide and silicon carbide abrasive sheets used in the metals lab usually range from 1 extra coarse to 8/0 extra fine.

Properly filed work can be polished using only a fine-grain abrasive cloth. However, if there are deep scratches, it is best to start with coarse-grain cloth. Change to medium-grain cloth, then finish with a fine-grain abrasive. A few drops of machine oil will speed the operation.

Support the abrasive cloth by wrapping it around a wood block or using a sanding block, Fig. 12-2. Applying pressure, move the abrasive back and forth in a straight line. Rub it parallel to the long edge of the work, if possible.

DO NOT POLISH MACHINED SURFACES.

BUFFING

BUFFING, Fig. 12-3, provides a bright mechanical finish. It is commonly applied to nonferrous metals like aluminum, copper, brass, pewter, and silver. Copper base alloys then must

Fig. 12-3. Buffing produces a highly polished surface on metal.

be covered by a clear plastic or lacquer coating to protect the polished surface. Buffing is done on a BUFFER-POLISHER, Fig. 12-4

Remove all scratches with an abrasive before buffing.

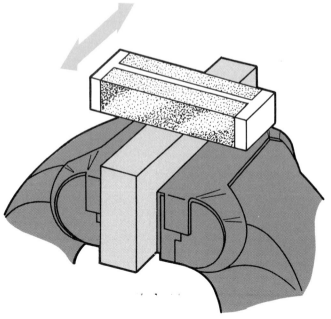

Fig. 12-2. When polishing, wrap the abrasive cloth around a block of metal or wood, or use a sanding block.

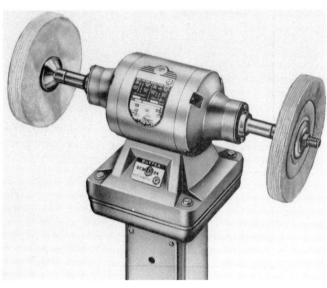

Fig. 12-4. This buffing machine is typical of those found in the school metal shop. (Delta-Rockwell)

To buff, use a fairly stiff wheel. Charge it with tripoli or pumice. This will remove the small scratches formed by the abrasive cloth.

Final polishing is done with a loose flannel wheel and polishing compound.

Buffing should be done with the work held below the centerline of the wheel, Fig. 12-5.

WIRE BRUSHING

WIRE BRUSHING produces a smooth, satin sheen on the metal. Wire size will determine the smoothness of the finish: the finer the wire the smoother the finish.

PAINTING

PAINTING, Fig. 12-6, is another finishing technique. Many colors and finishes are available. They can be applied to the project by spraying, Figs. 12-7 and 12-8, brushing, rolling, or dipping.

MACHINED SURFACES SHOULD NOT BE PAINTED.

COLORING WITH HEAT

This type of finish may be applied to steel. Clean the metal and slowly heat it. Watch the colors as they appear. Plunge the metal into cool water when the correct color is reached. Protect the resulting finish with clear lacquer.

Fig. 12-6. The painted finish on this factory-built structure is attractive and also reduces maintenance and repair costs. (Stran-Steel)

Fig. 12-7. A wide selection of paint colors are available in pressurized spray cans. Project being finished is a barrel for a model cannon.

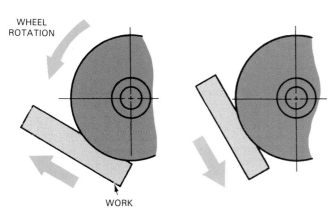

Fig. 12-5. Work below the centerline of the buffing wheel. Left. Pull the metal toward you when starting the operation. If the work is pulled from your grasp, your hands will not be pulled into the wheel. Right. For the final high polish, pass the work lightly into the wheel.

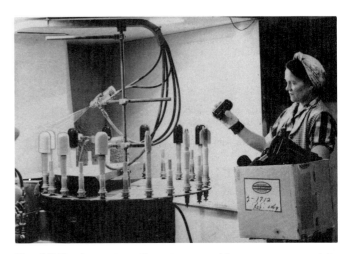

Fig. 12-8. An automatic rotary machine sprays porcelain enamel on metal parts for lighting fixtures. The machine boosted production 300 percent over hand spraying and had fewer rejects. (DeVilbiss Co.)

Fig. 12-9. Metal parts being hot dipped to produce a zinc (galvanized) coating on the parts.
(American Hot Dip Galvanized Assoc., Inc.)

OTHER METAL FINISHES

There are several other finishes that can be applied to metal. However, some of these finishes require special equipment for application. This equipment is not readily available in a school lab.

HOT DIPPING, Fig. 12-9, is applied to steel by dipping the metal into molten aluminum, zinc, tin, or lead. GALVANIZED STEEL is an example of this finishing technique.

ANODIZING is a process used to form a protective layer of aluminum oxide on aluminum parts. The anodized coating can be dyed a wide range of colors. The color becomes a part of the surface of the metal.

ELECTROPLATING is a finishing technique in which a metal coating is applied to or deposited on a metal surface by an electrical current, Fig. 12-10.

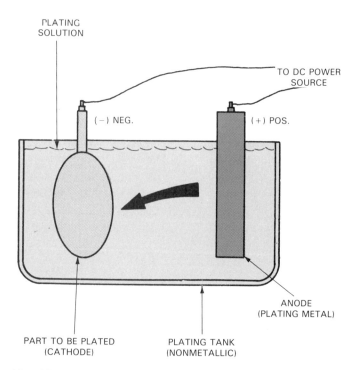

PLATING SOLUTION

TO DC POWER SOURCE

(−) NEG.

(+) POS.

PART TO BE PLATED (CATHODE)

PLATING TANK (NONMETALLIC)

ANODE (PLATING METAL)

Fig. 12-10. Electroplating is the process by which one metal is coated with another by electricity.

TEST YOUR KNOWLEDGE, Unit 12

Please do not write in the text. Place your answers on a separate sheet of paper.
1. Finishes are applied to:
   a. Protect surfaces from corrosion.
   b. Enhance surface appearance.
   c. Both a and b.
   d. None of the above.
2. Hard, sharp material that can be used to wear away another material is an _____.
3. Aluminum oxide and silicon carbide are examples of _____ _____.
4. Name two types of natural abrasives.

MATCHING QUESTIONS: Match each of the following terms with their correct definitions.
   a. Painting.   c. Buffing.
   b. Wire brushing.
5. ____ Produces a smooth, satin sheen.
6. ____ Technique in which finishes are applied by spraying, rolling, brushing, or dipping.
7. ____ Produces a bright mechanical finish.
8. Galvanized steel is an example of a finish applied by the _____ _____ finishing technique.
9. Finishing technique in which a metal coating is applied to a metal surface.
   a. Electroplating.
   b. Anodizing.
   c. Hot dipping.
   d. None of the above.

TECHNICAL TERMS TO LEARN

abrasive
aluminum oxide
anodizing
appearance
application
buffer-polisher
buffing
corrosion
electroplating
emery
hot dipping
iron oxide
painting
polish
silicon carbide
surface finish
wire brushing

ACTIVITIES

1. Collect samples of metals with different types of finishes. Why was each finish used?
2. Look around your metals lab. Note the different types of finishes used on the tools and machinery. How many types can you identify?
3. Prepare samples of metal sheet with different kinds of painted finishes. Devise a method for testing the durability of each finish.
4. Demonstrate electroplating. SAFETY NOTE: Before attempting to demonstrate electroplating, have your instructor check over the equipment and its wiring harness. Be sure they are in safe operating condition. Wear safety glasses and rubber or disposable plastic gloves when electroplating.

Unit 13 . . . .

Hand Forging

After studying this unit, you will be able to explain and demonstrate various forging processes. You will be able to identify various forging tools and demonstrate their use.

Metal is forged by heating it to less than the melting point, then using pressure to shape the hot metal. Heating makes the metal PLASTIC (more easily shaped).

In HAND FORGING, pressure is applied by using a hammer, Fig. 13-1. Forging improves the physical characteristics (strength, toughness) of the metal.

Fig. 13-1. Master blacksmith hand forges useful ironwork articles at the Deane Forge at Colonial Williamsburg, just as his 18th century predecessors did. (Colonial Williamsburg)

EQUIPMENT FOR HAND FORGING

FORGE

Metal is heated in a FORGE, Fig. 13-2. The forge may be gas- or coal-fired. Gas is preferred because it is cleaner to use.

Lighting a gas forge

1. Open the forge door. Check to be sure the gas valve is closed.
2. Start the air blower and open the air valve slightly.
3. Apply the lighter and slowly turn on the gas. CAUTION: STAND TO ONE SIDE AND DO NOT LOOK INTO THE FORGE WHEN YOU LIGHT IT.
4. After the gas has ignited, adjust the gas and air valves for the best combination.

ANVIL

Heated metal is shaped on an ANVIL, Fig. 13-3. The HORN, which is conical in shape, is used to form circular sections.

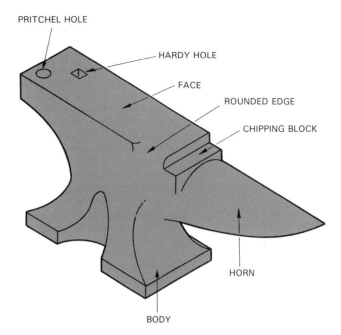

Fig. 13-3. The parts of an anvil.

Various anvil tools can be mounted in the HARDY HOLE. The PRITCHEL HOLE is used to punch holes or to bend small diameter rods.

ANVIL TOOLS

Many anvil tools are available. You will probably use the HARDY, Fig. 13-4, to cut metal. It is inserted in the Hardy hole. The metal to be cut is placed on the cutter and struck with a hammer, Fig. 13-5, until it is cut. If metal thicker than 1/2 in. is to be cut, it should be cut hot.

Fig. 13-2. A gas-fired forge. (Johnson Gas Appliance Co.)

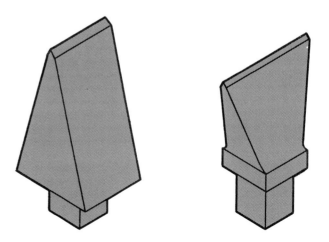

Fig. 13-4. Hardies.

137

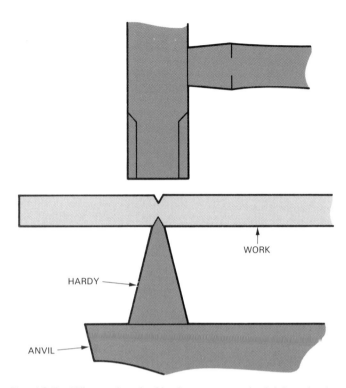

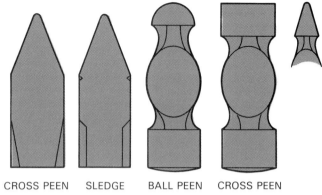

Fig. 13-6. Forging hammers.

CROSS PEEN   SLEDGE   BALL PEEN   CROSS PEEN

Fig. 13-5. When using the Hardy to cut metal, nick it on both sides. Then bend it back and forth until it breaks. Metal thicker than 1/2 in. should be cut while hot.

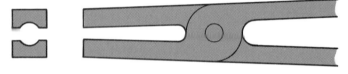

STRAIGHT LIP

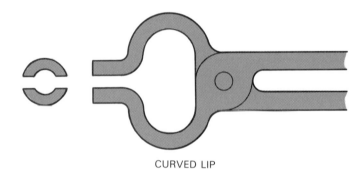

CURVED LIP

Fig. 13-7. Typical forging tongs.

HAMMERS

Many different types of HAMMERS are available for hand forging. See Fig. 13-6. Use a 1 1/2 - 2 lb. hammer for light work. A 3 lb. hammer will be satisfactory for heavy work. Do not "choke-up" on the hammer handle — you may injure yourself.

TONGS

Tongs are used to hold the hot metal while it is being forged, Fig. 13-7. Use tongs that are best suited for the work being done, Fig. 13-8.

FORGING

It is necessary to heat metal to the correct temperature before it can be forged. Mild steel should be heated to a BRIGHT RED. Carbon steel should not be heated beyond a DULL RED. Avoid WHITE HEAT, where sparks fly from the piece.

CAUTION: WEAR A FACE SHIELD WHEN FORGING. THE SCALE THAT FLIES ABOUT IS HOT. GLOVES SHOULD BE WORN, TOO.

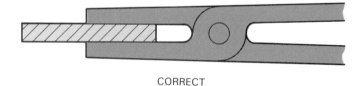

CORRECT

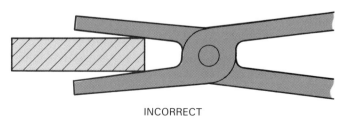

INCORRECT

Fig. 13-8. Use the correct tongs for the work to be forged.

DRAWING OUT METAL

The forging operation employed to stretch or lengthen metal is called DRAWING OUT. Fig. 13-9 shows the sequence recommended for drawing out round stock. Square stock is drawn out in much the same way. Round stock can be pointed as shown in Fig. 13-10.

BENDING METAL

There are several ways to make a bend in stock. Unless a small size rod is to be bent, all require the metal to be heated to a red heat.

1. Bend the metal over the anvil face and edge, Fig. 13-11.
2. Place the stock in the Hardy or Pritchel hole and bend it over, Fig. 13-12. Square the bend over the anvil edge.
3. Curved sections are made on the anvil horn, Fig. 13-13.

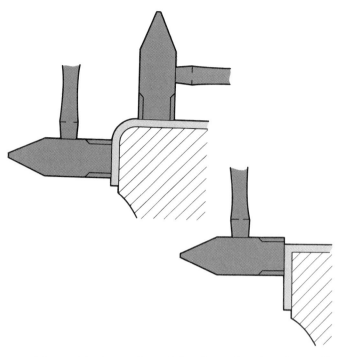

Fig. 13-11. Making a right angle bend over the edge of an anvil.

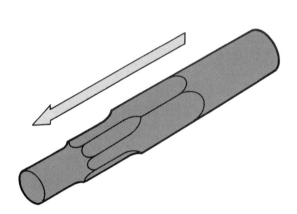

Fig. 13-9. Drawing out sequence.

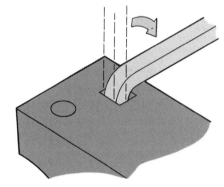

Fig. 13-12. Making a bend using the Hardy hole.

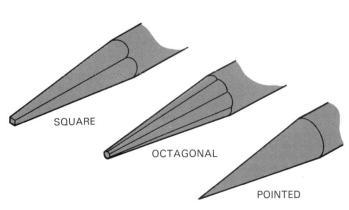

SQUARE

OCTAGONAL

POINTED

Fig. 13-10. Steps in drawing out a point.

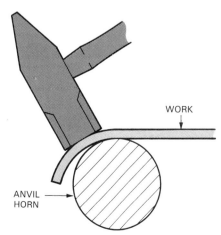

WORK

ANVIL HORN

Fig. 13-13. Circular shapes can be made over the anvil horn.

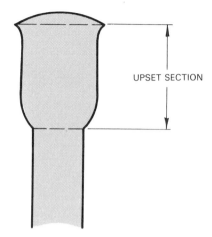

Fig. 13-14. Upsetting decreases the length of the metal but increases the thickness.

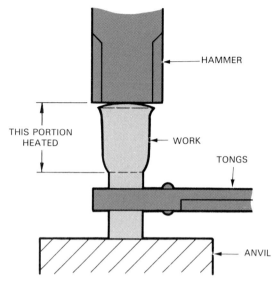

Fig. 13-15. Short pieces can be upset on the face of the anvil.

UPSETTING METAL

UPSETTING is an operation that increases the thickness of the metal at a given point, Fig. 13-14. This also shortens the metal.

1. Heat the metal to a red heat.
2. Short work is upset using the anvil face. See Fig. 13-15.
3. Mount the work in a vise if it is short enough. The heated end extends above the vise jaws and is hammered to increase its size.

If the metal becomes hard to work because of cooling, reheat it and continue the operation.

TEST YOUR KNOWLEDGE, Unit 13

Please do not write in the text. Place your answers on a separate sheet of paper.

1. Explain how metal is forged.
2. Heating makes the metal _____.
3. Where is metal heated?

MATCHING QUESTIONS: Match the following terms with their correct definitions.
a. Tongs.   d. Pritchel hole.
b. Anvil.   e. Hardy hole.
c. Horn.
4. ____ Used to punch holes or to bend small diameter rods.

5. ____ Used to shape heated metal.
6. ____ Used to mount various anvil tools.
7. ____ Used to hold hot metal while it is being forged.
8. ____ Conical shape used to form circular sections of metal.
9. _____ _____ is an operation that lengthens or stretches metal.

TECHNICAL TERMS TO LEARN

anvil	horn
drawing out	physical characteristics
forge	plastic
forging	pressure
gas forge	Pritchel hole
Hardy	tongs
Hardy hole	upsetting

ACTIVITIES

1. Prepare posters on forging safety.
2. Demonstrate the proper way to light a gas forge.
3. Hand-forge a cold chisel.
4. Secure products that have been forged.

Unit 14 . . . .

Casting Metals

After studying this unit, you will be able to explain various casting processes. You will also be able to demonstrate the proper way to make a sand mold. Finally, you will be able to demonstrate safety in the foundry area.

Casting metals is one of the oldest processes in metalworking. Objects are made by pouring molten metal into a mold. The mold is a cavity the shape and size of the object to be cast. It is made of material suitable for holding the molten metal until it cools. The part made by this process is called a CASTING. In industry, castings are made in a FOUNDRY.

PERMANENT MOLD CASTING

Permanent mold castings are made in metal molds. These molds are not destroyed when removing the casting. That is why they are called permanent molds. The process creates accurate parts with fine surface finishes. Many nonferrous metals (metals other than iron) can be cast this way.

The molds used to cast fishing sinkers and toy soldiers are examples of castings made in permanent molds, Fig. 14-1. Many of the pistons that are used in automobiles are made by this technique.

Fig. 14-1. Familiar items made by the permanent mold casting process.

141

Fig. 14-2. Die casting machines are the most complex equipment used in any major casting procedure. They provide economical production of large quantities at very high output rates. Die casting develops superior finish quality and surface detail. Shown is a crane setting die in machine.
(Aluminum Company of America)

DIE CASTING

Die casting is a variation of the permanent mold process. It is very useful in the metalworking industry. The metal is forced into the mold or die under pressure, Figs. 14-2 and 14-3. Castings produced have smoother finishes, finer details, and are more accurate than regular sand castings, Fig. 14-4. Large quantities of die castings can be produced quickly on automatic casting machines.

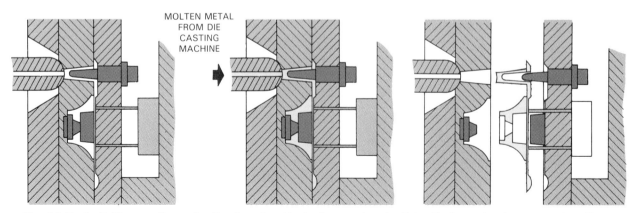

Fig. 14-3. Left. Two sections of a die, closed and locked to receive the "shot" of metal to form a casting. Center. The cavity of the die is now completely filled. Note the metal in the overflow well at the bottom of the cavity. This provides an outlet for the air trapped in the die cavity. Right. The die is opened to permit ejection of the casting. Note the two pins which free the casting from the die.

Fig. 14-4. Typical items made by the die casting method.

INVESTMENT OR LOST WAX CASTING

Investment or lost wax casting is a foundry process used when very accurate castings of complex shapes or detailed designs must be produced, Figs. 14-5 and 14-6.

In the investment casting process, Fig. 14-7, patterns of wax or plastic are placed (invested) in a refractory mold. A refractory mold will withstand high heat. When the mold has hardened, it is placed in an oven. Then the mold is heated until the wax or plastic pattern is burned out (lost). This leaves a cavity in the mold the shape of the pattern. Molten metal is forced into the mold. It is allowed to cool and the mold is broken apart to remove the casting.

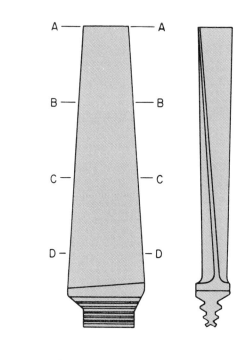

Fig. 14-5. Jet engine turbine blade made by the investment or lost wax casting process.

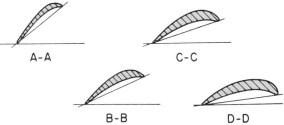

Fig. 14-6. Note the complex shape of the turbine blade. This made it expensive to manufacture by any other method.

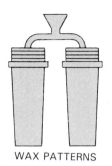
WAX PATTERNS

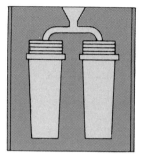
PATTERNS INVESTED IN
REFRACTORY MOLD

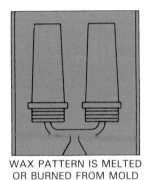
WAX PATTERN IS MELTED
OR BURNED FROM MOLD

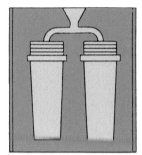
MOLD IS POURED

Fig. 14-7. The investment casting process.

Fig. 14-9. Pattern halves are ready to receive the specially prepared mix used in shell molding.

SHELL MOLDING

Shell molding, a fairly new foundry process, is a variation of sand casting. The molds are made in the form of thin sand shells, Fig. 14-8.

A metal pattern attached to a steel plate is fitted into the molding machine. Then the pattern is heated to the required temperature. A measured amount of mix is deposited on the pattern, Fig. 14-9. The mix consists of thermosetting resin and sand. The heat causes the thermosetting resin to take a permanent shape. The thin soft shells are then cured until the desired hardness is obtained.

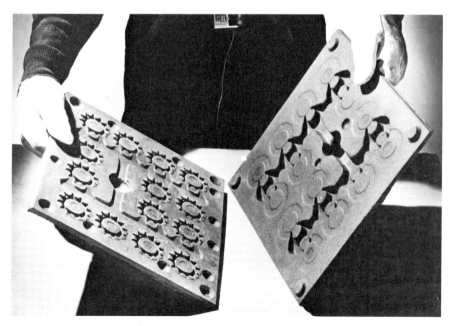
Fig. 14-8. A shell mold.   (Link-Belt)

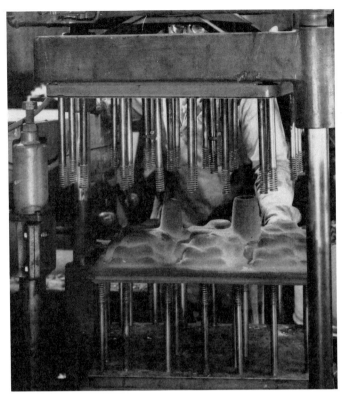

Fig. 14-10. Joining the two mold sections together.

Shell molding is well suited for mass-production. The casting produced, Fig. 14-11, has a superior finish. It also has greater accuracy than castings made by the regular sand casting technique.

CASTING IN THE METALS LAB

While several foundry processes just discussed can be used in the metals lab, SAND CASTING is most often used. It is also the most widely used of the industrial casting techniques.

The sand casting technique used in a school lab is similar to that used in industry. The major differences are casting size and the quantity of castings produced.

Sand castings are cast in MOLDS made of a mixture of sand and clay, Fig. 14-12. The sand is used in the moist stage and is called a GREEN SAND MOLD. The mold is made by packing the sand in a box called a FLASK, around a pattern of the shape to be cast. Parts of the flask separate to allow easy removal of the pattern.

A GATING SYSTEM is used to get the molten metal to the mold cavity. This consists of vertical openings, called SPRUES. These are connected to the mold cavity by grooves called GATES and RUNNERS.

Upon cooling, the pattern is removed. The shell halves are bonded together using a special adhesive, Fig. 14-10. Like regular sand molds, shell molds must be destroyed to remove the casting.

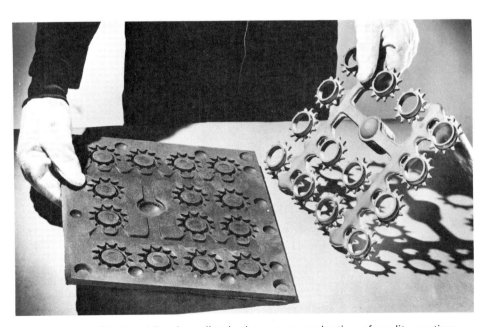

Fig. 14-11. Shell molding is well suited to mass production of quality castings.

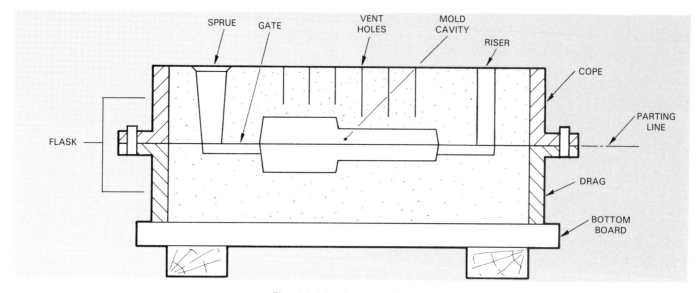

Fig. 14-12. Sand mold.

Metals shrink as they cool. Therefore, steps must be taken to supply additional metal to the parts of the casting that cool last. If this is not done, hollow parts may occur in the finished casting. These reservoirs of extra metal are called RISERS or FEEDERS.

Sand molds can be used only once. They are destroyed in removing the finished casting.

SAND MOLD CONSTRUCTION

In order to produce a sound casting in the metals lab, a certain sequence of operations should be followed. This sequence is outlined in the following sections.

PATTERNMAKING

The cavity in the sand mold is made with a PATTERN, Fig. 14-13. A SIMPLE PATTERN is made in one piece. SPLIT PATTERNS are patterns with two or more parts. They are used to make castings of more complex shape.

A pattern must have DRAFT, Fig. 14-14. Draft is a slight taper. It permits the pattern to be lifted from the sand without damaging the mold.

The pattern must be made slightly larger than the casting. This is because metal shrinks as it cools from the molten state. The amount of shrinkage will depend on the metal being cast.

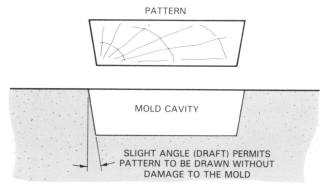

Fig. 14-13. The split pattern (top) is used to make castings of more complex shape than the simple pattern (bottom).

Fig. 14-14. A slight angle (draft) on the pattern permits it to be easily drawn from the mold.

146

Openings or hollow spaces are made in a casting with a sand CORE, Fig. 14-15. Cores are made from a special sand mix. When baked, this is hard enough to withstand casting pressures.

MOLDING SAND

Good molding sand is essential for good castings. Two types of sand are commonly used in the school foundry. NATURAL SAND is used as it is dug from the ground. SYNTHETIC SAND has an oil binder and no water is needed.

If a synthetic sand is not used, the sand must be TEMPERED. This means it is dampened enough to be workable. Water is added and serves as a binder. Mix the sand until it is uniformly moist. Test this by squeezing a handful of sand and breaking it in half. Properly tempered sand will break cleanly and retain the imprint of your fingers, Fig. 14-16. The sand will cling to your hand if it is too moist, and will crumble if too dry.

Fig. 14-16. Notice how cleanly properly tempered sand breaks.

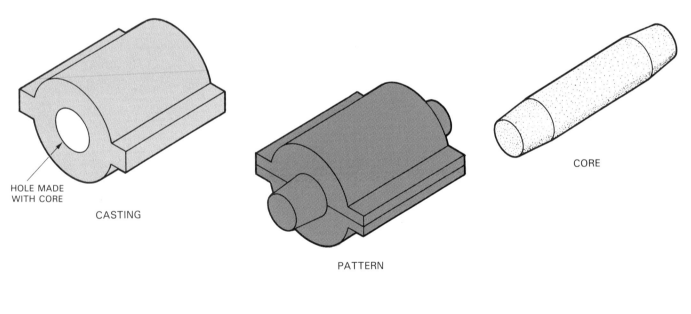

HOLE MADE
WITH CORE

CASTING

PATTERN

CORE

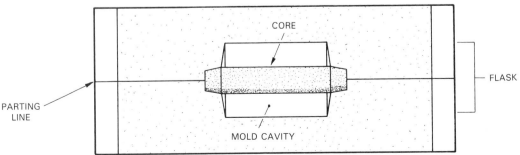

CORE

PARTING
LINE

FLASK

MOLD CAVITY

Fig. 14-15. Cores are made of a special sand and are used to produce openings in castings.

PARTING COMPOUND

PARTING COMPOUND is a waterproofing material. A light dusting will prevent moist sand from sticking to the pattern or to the mold faces.

TOOLS AND EQUIPMENT

Typical foundry tools and equipment are shown in Fig. 14-17. Their uses are explained in the next section.

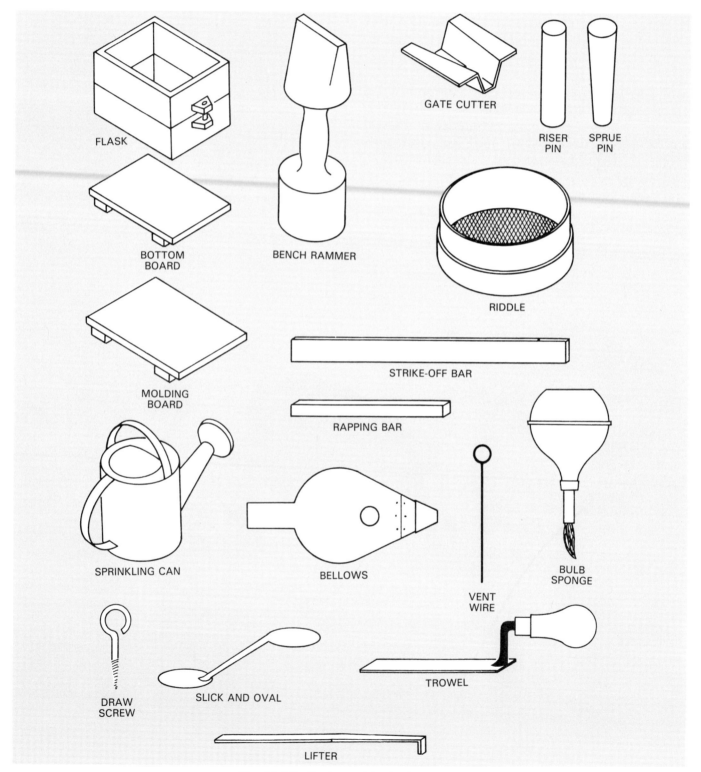

Fig. 14-17. Tools used in the foundry.

SIMPLE MOLD CONSTRUCTION AND CASTINGS

1. Temper the molding sand.
2. Clean and wax the pattern.
3. Position the drag on the molding board. Aligning pins are down. Place the pattern in position, Fig. 14-18. The flat back of the pattern is placed on the board.

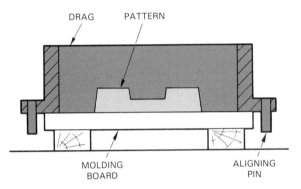

DRAG   PATTERN

MOLDING BOARD   ALIGNING PIN

Fig. 14-18. Position the drag on the molding board and position the pattern near its center.

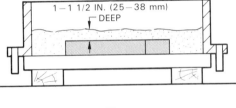

1—1 1/2 IN. (25—38 mm) DEEP

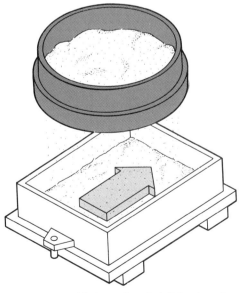

Fig. 14-19. Riddle (sift) about 1 to 1 1/2 in. deep layer of sand over the pattern.

4. Lightly dust the pattern with parting compound.
5. Fill the riddle with sand. Then sift a 1 to 1 1/2 in. (25 to 38 mm) layer of sand over the pattern, Fig. 14-19.
6. Using your fingers, pack the riddled sand around the pattern. Roughen the surface of the packed sand and fill the drag with unriddled sand.
7. Pack loose sand around the pattern and inside edges of the drag. Do this with the PEEN edge of the bench rammer, Fig. 14-20. Be careful not to hit the pattern. Ram the sand firmly enough around the pattern to give a good, sharp impression.
8. Add extra sand if necessary to fully pack the drag. Use the BUTT end of the rammer for the final packing.
9. Use a strike-off bar to remove excess sand, Fig. 14-21.

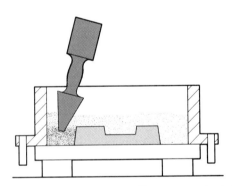

Fig. 14-20. Ram the mold using the peen end of the bench rammer. Be careful not to hit the pattern!

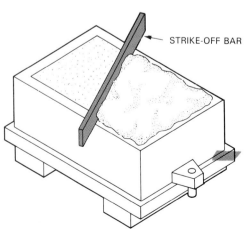

STRIKE-OFF BAR

Fig. 14-21. Remove excess sand with the strike-off bar.

10. Place the bottom board on top of the drag and roll (turn) it over.

11. Remove the molding board to expose the pattern. Examine the surface of the sand and, if necessary, smooth and level it with a trowel or slick.

12. Place the cope on the drag. Place the sprue and riser pins in the drag about 1 in. (25 mm) away from each end of the pattern, Fig. 14-22. Place the riser pin near the heaviest section of the pattern.

13. Dust parting compound over the face of the mold. This will prevent the surfaces from sticking together when the cope and drag are separated.

14. Riddle, ram, and strike off the sand in the cope, as was done before.

15. Gases are generated when the molten metal is poured into a mold. To permit these gases to escape, vent the mold with a VENT WIRE, Fig. 14-23. The vent holes should almost touch the pattern.

16. Remove the sprue and riser pins from the mold. Smooth the edges of the holes with your fingers.

17. Carefully lift the cope from the drag. Place it away from the immediate work area.

18. Use a bulb sponge to moisten the sand around the pattern. This will lessen the chance that the sand will break up when the pattern is DRAWN (removed from the sand).

19. Withdraw the pattern from the mold. Insert a draw screw into the back of the pattern. Tap the screw lightly with a rapping bar to loosen the pattern. DO NOT HIT THE BACK OF THE PATTERN!

20. Draw the pattern from the mold. Repair any defects using a slick and/or trowel, Fig. 14-24.

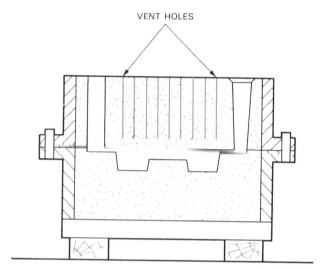

Fig. 14-23. Gases are generated when molten metal contacts moist sand. Vent holes permit the gas to escape, without damaging the mold.

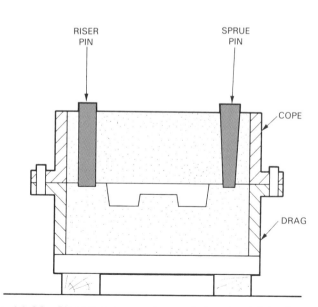

Fig. 14-22. Place the riser and sprue holes about 1 in. from the pattern. Place the riser hole near the heaviest section of the pattern.

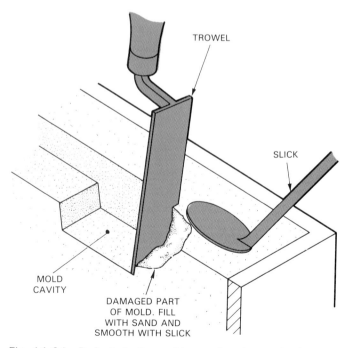

Fig. 14-24. Defects in the mold can often be repaired using a trowel and slick.

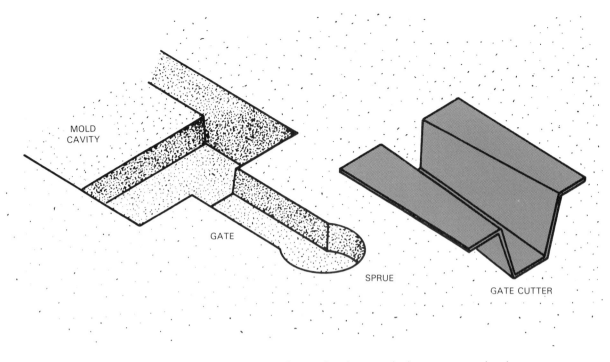

Fig. 14-25. The gate cutter is used to make the trough that connects the riser and sprue holes to the mold cavity.

21. Cut a gate from the mold cavity to the sprue hole and riser hole. Use a gate cutter, Fig. 14-25. The gate is about 1/2 in. (13 mm) wide and 1/2 in. deep. Smooth the gate surfaces with your finger or a slick.
22. Use a bellows to remove any loose sand that has fallen into the mold cavity.
23. Replace the cope on the drag.
24. Move flask to the pouring area. Allow to dry for a short time before pouring.
25. Pour metal into sprue hole carefully and rapidly. Hold the ladle or crucible close to the mold. Large molds are weighted or clamped.

This will prevent the molten metal from lifting the cope, allowing molten metal to flow out of the mold at the parting line.
26. Allow the casting to cool, then break the sand from around it.

The mold is made in much the same manner when a split pattern is used. The pattern is made in two parts. One is fitted with aligning pins, the other has holes to receive the pins. The pattern half with the holes is rammed in the drag, Fig. 14-26. The other half is placed in position after the drag has been rolled.

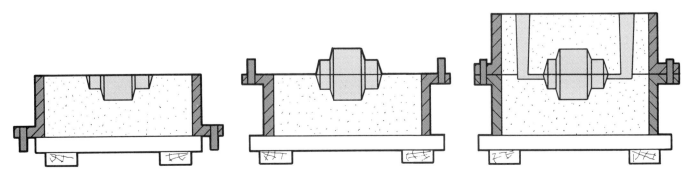

Fig. 14-26. Ramming up a split pattern. Left. Pattern half with aligning holes is rammed up first. Center. After drag is rolled over, the pattern half with the aligning pins is put in space. Right. Mold is rammed up in conventional manner.

FOUNDRY SAFETY

1. Wear protective clothing and goggles when pouring and handling molten metal.
2. UNDER NO CIRCUMSTANCES SHOULD MOIST OR WET METAL BE ADDED TO MOLTEN METAL. A VIOLENT EXPLOSION MIGHT RESULT.
3. Place hot castings in an area where they will not cause accidental burns.
4. Stand to one side of the mold as you pour. Never stand directly over it. Steam is generated when molten metal meets moist sand and this may burn you. Also, molten metal may spurt from the mold if the sand is too moist.
5. Keep the foundry area clean.
6. Do not wear oily or greasy shop clothing when working with hot metals.
7. Follow instructions carefully. DO NOT TAKE CHANCES. WHEN YOU ARE NOT SURE WHAT MUST BE DONE, ASK YOUR INSTRUCTOR.
8. Never look into the furnace when it is lighted. Stand to one side. DO NOT LIGHT THE FURNACE UNTIL YOU HAVE LEARNED THE PROPER WAY TO DO IT.

MELTING METALS

A CRUCIBLE FURNACE, Fig. 14-27, is used to melt aluminum and brass. A SOLDERING FURNACE, Fig. 14-28, is used to melt metals with lower melting temperatures. This includes lead, pewter and zinc alloys (garalloy).

A CRUCIBLE, Fig. 14-29, is used to hold aluminum and brass being melted. It is removed from the furnace with CRUCIBLE TONGS, Fig. 14-30. It is placed in a CRUCIBLE SHANK for pouring.

TURN OFF THE GAS BEFORE REMOVING THE CRUCIBLE FROM THE FURNACE.

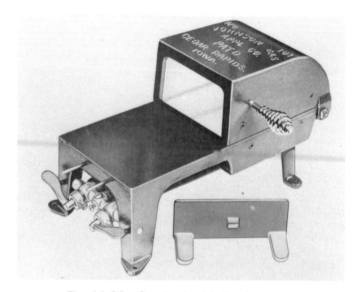

Fig. 14-28. Gas fired soldering furnace.
(Johnson Gas Appliance Co.)

Fig. 14-27. A gas fired melting furnace with safety features.
(Johnson Gas Appliance Co.)

Fig. 14-29. Crucible used to hold melted aluminum and brass.

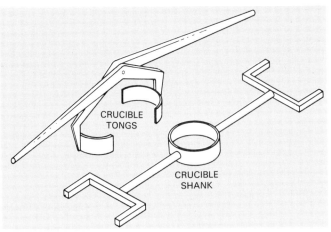

Fig. 14-30. Tongs are used to lift crucible out of furnace. The crucible is placed in the shank for pouring into the mold.

MELTING POINTS OF METAL			
Tin	232°	Garalloy	444°
Lead	327°	Aluminum	659°
Zamak	391°	Brass	956°
Zinc	420°	Copper	1084°

Fig. 14-31. Chart of melting temperatures. Temperatures are given in both degrees Fahrenheit and Celsius.

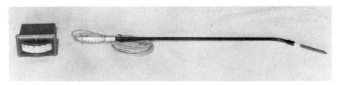

Fig. 14-32. The pyrometer probe is placed in the molten metal. The temperature is read on the direct reading gauge.

POURING METAL

Gather enough metal before lighting the furnace. Do not mix different metals. Use a crucible large enough to hold sufficient metal for the casting. Place it in the furnace.

Light the furnace. Allow the metal to come to pouring temperature, Fig. 14-31. Use a PYROMETER, Fig. 14-32, to check the temperature of the metal. If additional metal must be added to the crucible, prevent metal with moisture from being added to the molten metal. WATER AND MOLTEN METAL REACT VIOLENTLY WHEN THEY COME IN CONTACT. BE SURE TO KEEP THEM APART.

When the metal has been heated to the correct temperature, turn off the furnace. Be careful not to overheat or poor casting will result. Remove the crucible from the furnace with tongs. Place it in a crucible shank for pouring. Add FLUX and skim the SLAG or DROSS (impurities in the metal) from the surface of the metal.

Pour the molten metal rapidly. STAND TO ONE SIDE OF THE MOLD AS YOU POUR. NEVER STAND DIRECTLY OVER IT. Stop when the riser and sprue holes are full.

Allow the casting to cool, then shake out (break up) the mold.

After cutting off the sprue and riser, the casting is ready for machining and finishing.

TEST YOUR KNOWLEDGE, Unit 14

Please do not write in the text. Place your answers on a separate sheet of paper.
1. Name four casting processes that are used in industry.
2. What casting process is used most often in school labs?

MATCHING QUESTIONS: Match each of the following terms with their correct definitions.
a. Flask.
b. Cope.
c. Drag.
d. Green sand mold.
e. Mold.
f. Parting line.
g. Core.
h. Draft.
i. Bench rammer.
j. Crucible.

3. ____ Container used to hold metal that is being melted.
4. ____ Box into which sand is packed to make mold.
5. ____ Mold made with moist sand.
6. ____ Opening in sand into which molten metal is poured to produce casting.
7. ____ Bottom half of mold.
8. ____ Tool used to pack sand into flask.
9. ____ Top half of flask.
10. ____ Enables pattern to be removed from sand without damaging mold.
11. ____ Point at which flask comes apart.
12. ____ Inserts that make holes and other openings in casting.
13. List four safety precautions that must be observed when casting metals.

TECHNICAL TERMS TO LEARN

bellows
bottom board
casting
cope
core
crucible
crucible furnace
crucible shank
crucible tongs
die casting
draft
drag
dross
flask
foundry
gate
gate cutter

investment casting
lifter
lost wax casting
mold
parting compound
pattern
permanent mold
pyrometer
riddle
runner
sand casting
shell molding
slag
slick and oval
sprue
trowel

ACTIVITIES

1. Secure samples of various types of castings. Prepare a display board showing the processes followed to make each casting. Use photographs and drawings to show the steps.
2. Prepare a series of posters on safe foundry operations.
3. Demonstrate to the class the proper way to make a sand mold. Follow all safety rules.
4. Certain products require molds made of plaster. Research and prepare a paper on the plaster casting process.
5. Visit a local dentist or a dental supply shop to see how the dental profession uses investment castings. Give a short report to the class on what you observed.
6. Make arrangements to visit a foundry that uses the shell molding technique. If possible, secure a casting made by the process. Compare it with a sand mold casting. How do surface finish and dimensional accuracy compare between the two?

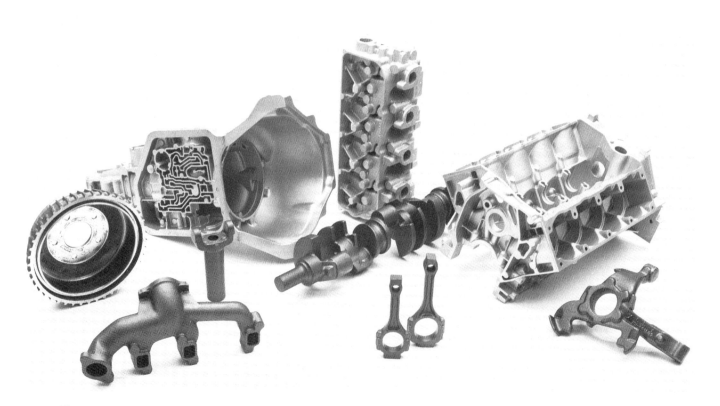

These automotive castings are made of aluminum, several types of iron, and an aluminum/grey iron composite.

Unit 15.........

Welding and Brazing

After studying this unit, you will be able to explain the three most common types of welding. In addition, you will be able to demonstrate various welding techniques in a safe manner.

WELDING is a process used to fabricate metal parts. Two or more pieces of metal are joined into a single unit. This is done by heating them to a temperature that is high enough to cause them melt and combine. A permanent joint is produced by this method.

Welding is a very important facet of modern fabricating techniques, Fig. 15-1. There are almost 100 welding and allied processes classified by the American Welding Society (AWS). Three of the most common are ARC, OXYACETYLENE, and SPOT WELDING. Welding makes it possible for most metals and their alloys to be welded to themselves, and often to each other.

Fig. 15-1. Worker puts finishing touches on a crosshead for a large press. This was made in the weldment shop of Bethlehem Steel Corporation.

155

With careful design, welded standard stock metal shapes are often simpler, lighter and, in many cases, stronger and less expensive than their cast counterparts, Fig. 15-2. Welding is often used to make combinations of castings, forgings, and stock steel shapes.

WELDING SAFETY

When welding, be sure you are shielded from the direct rays of the arc. The rays can cause serious and often permanent eye damage. Protect your eyes, face, and neck with an arc welding helmet. NEVER USE GAS WELDING GOGGLES FOR THIS PURPOSE.

Keep your sleeves down. Wear gauntlet type leather gloves to protect your arms and hands from "arc burn" and molten weld metal.

Wear a leather apron or jacket to protect your clothing from weld "spatter." WEAR LEATHER (NOT CANVAS) SHOES WHEN WELDING.

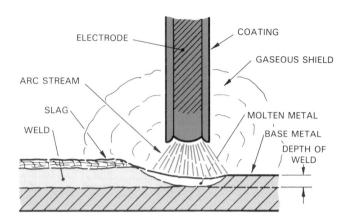

Fig. 15-3. Close-up showing electric welding procedure.

ARC WELDING

Arc welding is a joining technique that uses an electric current to generate the necessary heat for making welds. The tip of the electrode (welding rod) and a small portion of the work become molten in the intense heat, Fig. 15-3.

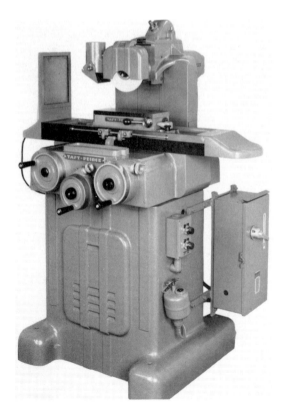

Fig. 15-2. Compare the two surface grinder models shown. Left. This grinder was made from castings.
Right. This grinder has been redesigned to make use of welded and cast components.

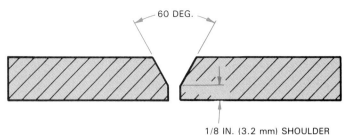

Fig. 15-5. A joint prepared for welding.

Fig. 15-4. Arc welding equipment. (Lincoln Electric)

Typical arc welding equipment is illustrated in Fig. 15-4.

PREPARING WORK FOR WELDING

Metal to be welded must be clean. It may also be necessary to shape the joint in a V. In this way, electrode metal will fuse with the parent metal better, Fig. 15-5.

Special welding symbols are used on drawings. These show the type and size of the weld to be made. Fig. 15-6 shows some of these symbols and their meaings.

STRIKING THE ARC

Adjust the machine to the correct power setting. Your instructor will help you do this. Your instructor will also help you select the correct type and size of welding rod.

Clamp the electrode into the holder, Fig. 15-7. It should be at a 90 deg. angle to the jaws.

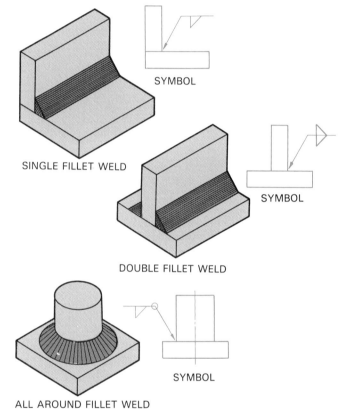

SYMBOL

SINGLE FILLET WELD

SYMBOL

DOUBLE FILLET WELD

SYMBOL

ALL AROUND FILLET WELD

Fig. 15-6. Common welding symbols.

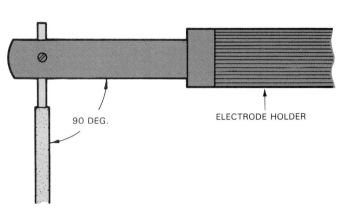

90 DEG.

ELECTRODE HOLDER

Fig. 15-7. Clamp electrode into the holder as shown.

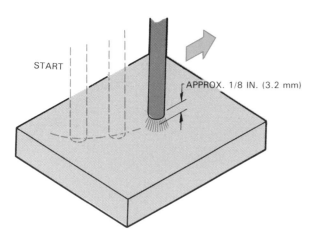

Fig. 15-8. The scratching method of striking an arc. The striking end of the electrode is dragged across the work. It might be compared to striking a match. To prevent the electrode from "freezing" to the work, withdraw the rod from the work immediately after contact has been made.

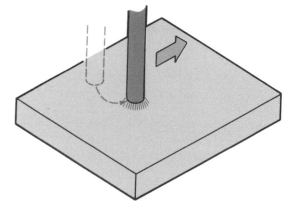

Fig. 15-9. In the tapping method of striking an arc, the electrode is brought straight down on the work. It is immediately raised on contact to provide the proper arc length.

There are two methods for striking an arc. They are the SCRATCHING method, Fig. 15-8, and the TAPPING method, Fig. 15-9.

Once the arc is established, a short arc (1/16 to 1/8 in. or 1.6 to 3.2 mm) should be held.

DEPOSITING WELD METAL

The electrode should be held at a right angle to the bead. And it should be slightly tilted in the direction of travel, Fig. 15-10.

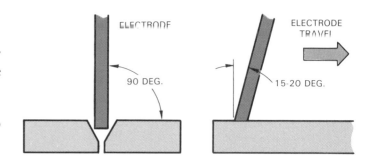

Fig. 15-10. The electrode is held at a slight angle, in the direction of travel.

Do not watch the arc. Watch the puddle of molten metal directly behind the arc and the ridge that forms as the molten metal becomes solid. Move the electrode at a uniform speed. The correct speed will be reached when the ridge formed is about 3/8 in. (9.5 mm) behind the arc. Fig. 15-11 shows weld characteristics.

Fig. 15-11. Arc weld characteristics.

ARC WELDING SAFETY

1. NEVER arc weld or watch arc welding without using a shield. Gas welding goggles or sun glasses are NOT satisfactory.
2. Wear goggles when chipping slag.
3. Wear suitable clothing for welding.
4. Do not weld where solvent or paint fumes may collect. Remove all flammable materials from the welding area.
5. Weld only in a well-ventilated area.
6. Treat any cut or burn promptly.
7. Safety goggles should be worn under your welding shield for additional safety.
8. Do not attempt to weld a container until you have determined whether flammable liquids were stored in it. Have containers steam cleaned or fill them with water before welding.
9. Use care when handling metal that has just been welded. A serious burn could result from touching a weld that has not cooled.

OXYACETYLENE WELDING

Oxyacetylene welding equipment, Fig. 15-12, includes two heavy cylinders. One is for acetylene gas, one is for oxygen. PRESSURE REGULATORS reduce high pressure in the cylinders to usable pressures. They also help maintain constant pressure at the torch. One gauge of the regulator shows cylinder pressure. The other shows pressure being delivered to the torch.

HOSES are used to transfer the acetylene and oxygen from cylinders to the torch. The oxygen hose is green and the acetylene hose is red.

The TORCH mixes the gases in the proper proportion for welding.

A WRENCH is used to fit the various connections. A SPARK LIGHTER is used to light the torch. NEVER USE MATCHES! A pair of suitable GOGGLES and heavy GLOVES are need for eye and hand protection.

FLUXES

FLUXES are needed when gas heating certain metals to be joined with solder, or by welding or brazing. The flux promotes better fusion of the metals. It also prevents harmful oxides (which cause poor weld joints) from forming.

WELDING PROCEDURE

Attach the torch tip best suited for the job (check with your instructor). Be sure it is clean, and that both valves on the torch are closed.

Open the oxygen tank valve SLOWLY until the oxygen high pressure gauge shows tank pressure. Then open the valve as far as it will go.

Turn the handscrew until the oxygen low pressure gauge shows the pressure needed for the torch tip being used. Your instructor will provide this information.

Do the same with the acetylene cylinder. However, the cylinder valve should be opened only 1 to 1 1/2 turns—do not open it any more.

Stand to one side of the regulator valves when the cylinder valves are opened.

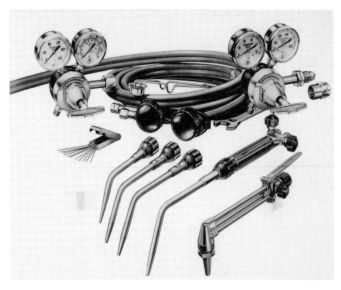

Fig. 15-12. Typical oxyacetylene welding equipment. (Marquette Mfg. Co.)

Have your instructor show you how to light and adjust the welding flame. Your instructor should also check you as you prepare the equipment for welding.

The following steps are done to close down the welding unit:

1. Shut off the acetylene valve ON THE TORCH, then on the oxygen valve.
2. Turn off each tank valve.
3. Open both valves on the torch to drain the gases from the hoses.
4. When both gauges read "zero," turn the adjusting screws on both regulators all the way out.
5. Close the torch valves. Store the torch and hoses.

MAKING A WELD

Welds can be made with or without the use of welding rod. Either type of weld is made holding the torch at a 45 deg. angle to the work, Fig. 15-13. Position the torch until the cone of the flame is about 1/8 in. (3.2 mm) from the metal. When the metal begins to melt into a puddle, move the torch along in a zigzag motion, Fig. 15-14. Do this as fast as the metal will melt and form a smooth, uniform weld. The BACKHAND GAS WELDING TECHNIQUE is shown in Fig. 15-15.

If welding rod is used, preheat it. Do this by bringing it to within 3/8 in. (9.5 mm) of the flame.

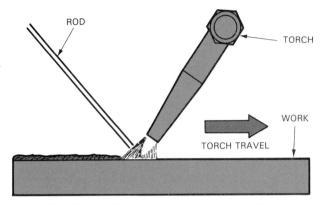

Fig. 15-13. Torch position for gas welding.

Preheating causes the rod to melt faster when it is dipped into the molten weld pool as more metal is needed.

Enough rod should be added to raise the metal in the joint into a slight crown.

A number of typical weld joints are illustrated in Fig. 15-16.

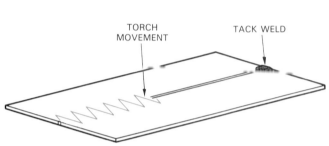

Fig. 15-14. When the metal begins to melt into a puddle, move the torch along in a zigzag motion. The tack weld at the end will prevent the pieces from spreading apart when they expand from being heated.

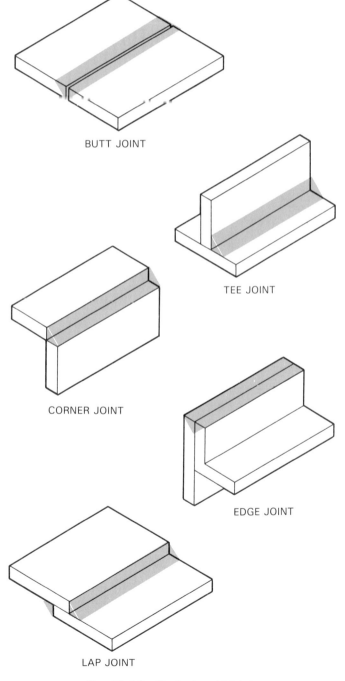

Fig. 15-16. Typical weld joints.

Fig. 15-15. Producing a smooth, strong, uniform weld using the backhand gas welding technique. The weld is made from left to right and the welding rod is between the completed weld and the torch flame. For a forehand weld, the weld is made from right to left. The flame is then between the completed weld and the welding rod.

BRAZING

There are two major differences between welding and brazing. The base metal is not melted in brazing and a nonferrous rod is used as filler metal. However, gas welding equipment is used.

The joint must be clean. Heat the pieces until they are red hot. Then heat the end of the brazing rod and dip it in flux. Hold the rod just ahead of the flame. Allow it to melt and flow into the joint. An example of a properly deposited brazed joint is shown in Fig. 15-17.

OXYACETYLENE WELDING SAFETY

1. Do not attempt to gas weld until you have received instructions on how to use the equipment.
2. Wear appropriate welding goggles.
3. Remove all flammable material from the welding area.
4. Never light the torch with matches. Use a spark lighter, Fig. 15-18.
5. Never attempt to blow dirt from your clothing with gas pressure. Your clothing may become saturated with oxygen and/or acetylene and may explode if a spark comes in contact with it.
6. For added protection, dress properly for the job. Wear welder's gloves.
7. Use care when handling work that has just been welded to avoid serious burns.
8. It is only necessary to turn off the torch if your work needs to be repositioned. However, the entire unit should be turned off when the job is completed. Carefully hang up the torch.

SPOT WELDING

A SPOT WELD is a resistance type weld in which the metals to be welded are clamped between two electrodes. An electric current is passed between the two electrodes. Resistance to the current of the metal between the electrodes heats the metal at the point of contact and fuses the pieces together, Fig. 15-19. Filler metal is not required. Spot welding can be done with a portable unit, Fig. 15-20, or a larger stationary unit, Fig. 15-21.

Fig. 15-17. An example of a properly deposited brazed joint.

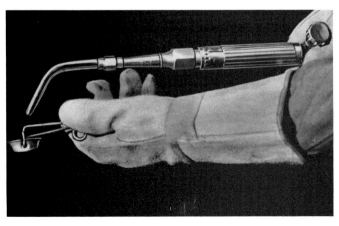

Fig. 15-18. Hold the torch away from the cylinders and pointed away from the body when lighting it. Note the gloves worn by the welder.   (Linde Co.)

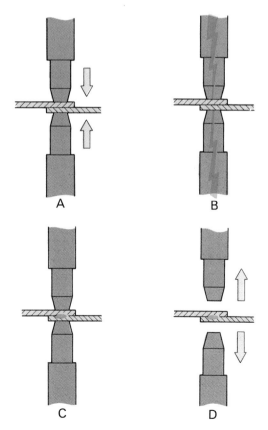

Fig. 15-19. Making a spot weld. A—Squeeze time. B—Weld time. C—Hold time. D—Off time.

Fig. 15-20. Portable spot welding unit.
(Miller Electric Mfg. Co.)

2. List the three welding techniques most commonly used.
3. There are two methods for striking an arc. Name them.
4. List five safety precautions to follow when arc welding.
5. Gases used in oxyacetylene welding are stored in:
    a. Hoses.
    b. Regulators.
    c. Cylinders.
    d. None of the above.
6. _____ prevents oxidation from forming during the welding operation.
7. There are two major differences between welding and brazing. Name them.
8. A _____ _____ is a resistance type weld.

Fig. 15-21. Manually controlled spot welding unit.
(Taylor-Winfield)

TECHNICAL TERMS TO LEARN

amperage	spot weld
arc burn	tack weld
brace	tank
butt joint	tee joint
edge joint	torch
electrode	weld
fillet weld	welding
joint	welding rod
lap joint	weld splatter
oxyacetylene	weld symbol
pressure regulator	

ACTIVITIES

1. Prepare a series of posters on arc welding safety.
2. Prepare a series of posters on oxyacetylene welding safety.
3. Secure samples of work that have been arc welded, gas welded, brazed, and spot welded.
4. Acquire drawings that show parts that must be fabricated by welding.
5. Make a chart showing the various welding symbols used on drawings.

TEST YOUR KNOWLEDGE, Unit 15

Please do not write in the text. Place your answers on a separate sheet of paper.
1. Define welding.

Unit 16 . . . .
Heat-Treating Metals

After studying this unit, you will be able to explain the reasons metal is heat-treated. You will also be able to demonstrate the annealing and case hardening heat-treating processes. You will also be able to harden and temper a steel object.

Metals must be soft in order to be machined. And they must be hard and tough enough to perform the job they were designed to do, without quickly dulling or wearing down, Fig. 16-1. These conditions are difficult to meet in the manufacture of many metal products. However, through the science of heat-treating, this is made possible. Most metals and alloys can be heat-treated.

The heat treatment of metal includes a number of processes. All of them involve CONTROLLED heating and cooling of a metal to obtain certain changes in metal properties. This might mean a change in properties such as toughness and hardness.

Fig. 16-1. Many parts on this tractor and scraper must be heat-treated to prevent them from wearing out rapidly. (Caterpillar Tractor Co.)

One heat-treating process, ANNEALING, can be used to soften some metals for easier machining. Another, CASE HARDENING, can be used to produce a very hard surface on steel. This makes the metal more resistant to wear.

Heat-treating is done by heating the metal to a predetermined temperature, Figs. 16-2, 16-3, and 16-4. Then, the metal is cooled rapidly (QUENCHING) in water, oil, or brine (salt water). Another heating (at a lower temperature) and cooling cycle may be needed to give the metal the desired degree of hardness and toughness.

HEAT-TREATING IN THE SCHOOL SHOP

There are any heat-treating processes used by industry. The following techniques can be used in the metals lab. However, before attempting any of them, the following safety precautions are recommended.

Heat-treating requires the handling of very hot metals. Wear a face shield and leather or fabric gloves. Have any burns, no matter how small, treated promptly.

ANNEALING

Some metals become hard as they are worked. They will fracture or be very difficult to work if not softened. ANNEALING reduces the hardness of metals, making them easier to machine and shape.

Annealing is done by heating the metal in a HEAT-TREATING FURNACE, Fig. 16-5. The metal is then cooled slowly in an insulating material such as ashes or vermiculite. The temperature of the furnace and the amount of time the metal is to be heated depends on the kind of metal being annealed and its size. Your instructor can help you find this information in a machinist's handbook.

Fig. 16-2. Electric heat-treating furnace.

Fig. 16-3. The thermocouple is set to the desired temperature of 1500 °F (815 °C). The furnace has reached a temperature of 800 °F (425 °C).

Fig. 16-4. The parts have reached the required temperature and are now ready for quenching. Note how the parts are placed in the furnace so they will be uniformly heated.

Fig. 16-5. A gas fired heat-treating furnace. (Johnson Gas Appliance Co.)

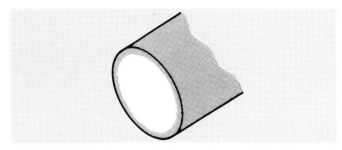

Fig. 16-6. Only a thin outer case is hardened when steel is case hardened. The center portion of the metal remains soft.

Fig. 16-7. A pyrometer is used to measure the high temperatures needed in the heat treatment of metals. (Johnson Gas Appliance Co.)

Metals like copper, silver, and nickel silver require a different annealing operation than those used with steel. These metals are heated and cooled very rapidly by quenching in water.

Some aluminum alloys are annealed by letting the heated metal cool in still air.

CASE HARDENING

CASE HARDENING adds carbon to low carbon steel so that a hard shell or case is produced, Fig. 16-6. The interior of the metal remains soft. The process is used on steel parts that need a tough, hard wearing surface, such as gears and roller bearings.

Case hardening is done by heating the steel to a bright red at 1650-1700°F (900-925°C). Use a PYROMETER, Fig. 16-7, to measure the temperature. Then roll or sprinkle case hardening compound on the heated piece until a coating of uniform thickness forms, Fig. 16-8. These powders add carbon to the surface of the steel.

Reheat according to the instructions furnished with the carburizing compound used. Then quench in clean, cold water.

Fig. 16-8. Heated piece being rolled in case hardening compound, until a coating forms. It is then reheated and plunged in the quenching fluid, according to manufacturer's instructions.

HARDENING

HARDENING is done by heating carbon or alloy steel to a certain temperature (CRITICAL TEMPERATURE), and cooling it rapidly in water, oil, or brine. The exact temperature is determined by the type of steel being hardened. This information can be found in a machinist's handbook.

Be careful when quenching the heated metal. Dip it into the liquid, Fig. 16-9. NEVER drop it in. This may cause sections of the metal to cool faster than other sections causing it to warp or crack.

Properly hardened steel will be "glass hard" and too brittle for most uses. Hardness can be tested by trying to file the metal with an old file. The file will not cut if the steel has been properly hardened.

Another heat-treating process must be performed to make this brittle steel usable. This process is called tempering.

TEMPERING

Tempering should be done immediately after hardening. The brittle steel may crack if exposed to sudden changes in temperature.

The process removes some of the hardness and reduces brittleness.

To do tempering, use the following steps.

1. Polish the piece to be tempered with abrasive cloth.
2. Reheat to the correct tempering temperature. Use a COLOR SCALE, Fig. 16-10, as a guide. Quench the steel when the proper color has been reached.
3. Temper small tools by placing them on a steel plate that has been heated red hot. Have the point of the tool extending beyond the edge of the plate, Fig. 16-11. Quench the piece when the correct color has reached the tool point.

Degrees Fahrenheit	Temper Colors	Tools
380	Very Light Yellow	Tools that require maximum hardness — lathe centers, lathe tools
420	Light Straw	Drills, taps, milling cutters
460	Dark Straw	Tools that need both hardness and toughness — punches
500	Bronze	Cold chisels, hammer faces
540	Purple	Screwdrivers, scribers
580	Dark Blue	Wrenches, chisels
620	Pale Blue	Springs, wood saws

Fig. 16-10. Tempering colors and temperatures for 0.95 percent carbon steel.

ROTATE WORK BEING QUENCHED

Fig. 16-9. General work can be quenched using a rotary motion. However, long, slender work should be plunged into the quenching fluid in an up-and-down motion. This prevents the piece from warping.

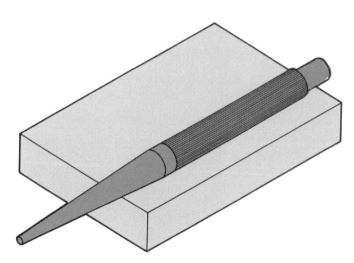

Fig. 16-11. Tempering small tools on a steel plate. It is important that the tool be in continuous motion during the tempering process, or portions of the tool will get overheated.

SAFETY

1. Wear goggles and the proper protective clothing: leather or fabric gloves and an apron (never one that is greasy or oil-soaked).
2. Heat-treating involves metal heated to very high temperatures. Handle it with the appropriate tools.
3. Never look at the flames of the furnace unless you are wearing tinted goggles.
4. Do not light the furnace until you have been instructed in its operation. If you are not sure how it should be done, ask for further instructions.
5. Be sure the area is properly ventilated and that all solvents and flammable materials have been removed.
6. Do not stand over the quenching bath when immersing heated metal.

TEST YOUR KNOWLEDGE, Unit 16

1. Heat treating involves the _____ heating and cooling of metals.
2. A heat treating process used to soften metals for easier machining.
   a. Tempering.
   b. Case hardening.
   c. Annealing.
   d. None of the above.
3. Define quenching.
4. Case hardening:
   a. Adds carbon to low carbon steel.
   b. Is used on steel parts that need a hard wearing surface
   c. Leaves the interior of the metal soft.
   d. All of the above.
5. A _____ is used to measure the temperature of the furnace.
6. List live safety precautions to follow when heat treating metals.

TECHNICAL TERMS TO LEARN

anneal
brittle
carburize
case harden
color scale
cooling
critical temperature
glass hard
harden
heat treat
pyrometer
quench
temper
temper colors
toughness

ACTIVITIES

1. Secure examples of products that have been heat-treated.
2. Demonstrate how to anneal a piece of metal.
3. Demonstrate how to case harden a piece of low carbon steel.
4. Demonstrate how to harden and temper a center punch made from carbon steel.
5. Prepare a poster on one of the safety precautions that should be observed when heat-treating metals.

Unit 17 . . . .

Machining Technology

After studying this unit, you will be able to explain the functioning of and uses for a lathe. You will be able to set up a lathe for operation and safely perform several lathe operations. In addition, you will be able to discuss the uses and operations of shapers, milling machines, bands saws, grinding machines, and planing machines. And, finally, you will be able to explain the manual and computer-assisted operations of numerical control systems.

Many kinds of machine tools are found in the MACHINE SHOP. MACHINE TOOLS are power-driven tools. They may be used to mass produce accurate, uniform parts used in such machinery as printing presses, washers, and trains, Fig. 17-1.

THE LATHE

The lathe is a versatile machine tool. Rotating work is shaped by a cutting tool that is fed against

Fig. 17-1. Many machined parts are used in the construction of this high-speed train, which tilts as it goes around curves at speeds of up to 100 miles per hour. (Siemens)

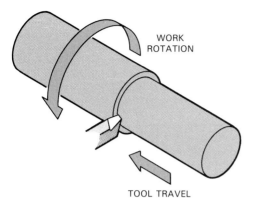

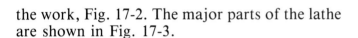

Fig. 17-2. The lathe rotates work against a cutting tool that shapes the work.

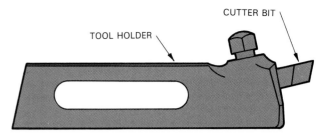

Fig. 17-4. Lathe tool holder and cutter bit.

the work, Fig. 17-2. The major parts of the lathe are shown in Fig. 17-3.

PREPARATION FOR LATHE OPERATION

Become familiar with the names and locations of the lathe parts. Learn what each does. Get permission to operate the various handwheels and levers of the lathe with the power off. The parts should move freely. There should be no binding.

Lubricate the lathe before operating it. Use the lubricants specified by the manufacturer.

Clean the lathe after each working period. Use a paint brush to remove the chips. NEVER USE YOUR HANDS. Wipe all surfaces with a soft cloth.

LATHE CUTTING TOOLS AND TOOL HOLDERS

The lathe cuts metal with a small piece of metal called a CUTTER BIT, Fig. 17-4. The cutter bit used in the school lab is usually made from a special alloy steel. This special alloy is called HIGH SPEED STEEL (HSS).

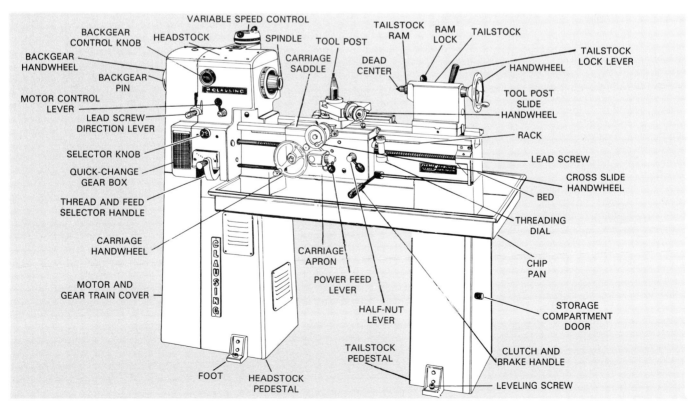

Fig. 17-3. Parts of the cutting lathe.   (Clausing)

On most lathes the cutter bit must be supported in a TOOL HOLDER. Tool holders are made in STRAIGHT, RIGHT-HAND, and LEFT-HAND shapes, Fig. 17-5. This allows for many different machining operations.

CUTTING TOOL SHAPES

Some cutting tools used for general turning are shown in Fig. 17-6. The cutter bit should have a keen, properly shaped cutting edge. The type of work and the kind of metal being cut will determine the shape to grind the cutter bit.

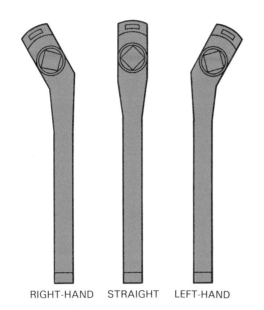

RIGHT-HAND   STRAIGHT   LEFT-HAND

Fig. 17-5. Shapes of tool holders available.

ROUGHING CUTS are used to reduce the work diameter quickly to an approximate size (about 1/32 in. oversize).

The FINISH CUT brings the work to EXACT size. The work surface is also made smooth.

The cutter bit is sharpened on a BENCH or PEDESTAL GRINDER, Fig. 17-7. The bench grinder is a grinder fitted to a bench or table. The grinding wheel mounts directly to the motor shaft. The pedestal grinder is usually larger than the bench grinder. It is equipped with a base (pedestal) that is fastened to the floor.

CAUTION: Always wear goggles when doing *any* grinding. Be sure all guards and safety shields are in place and securely fastened. Because it is not always possible to check the wheels on a grinder each time it is used, stand to one side of the machine when it is first turned on, until it reaches operating speed. This will keep you clear of flying pieces if a wheel shatters.

Before attempting to grind a cutter bit, be sure the tool rest is positioned with a space of about 1/16 in. (1.6 mm) between the tool rest and the grinding wheel, Fig. 17-8.

HOLDING WORK ON THE LATHE

Different kinds of work require different methods of holding. Two methods are the 3-jaw universal and the 4-jaw independent chucks.

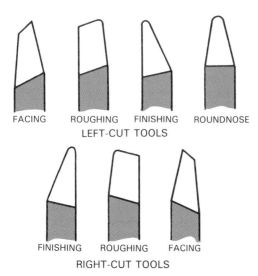

FACING   ROUGHING   FINISHING   ROUNDNOSE
LEFT-CUT TOOLS

FINISHING   ROUGHING   FACING
RIGHT-CUT TOOLS

Fig. 17-6. Common cutting tools used on the lathe.

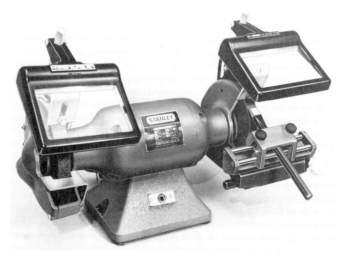

Fig. 17-7. Typical bench grinder.   (The Stanley Works)

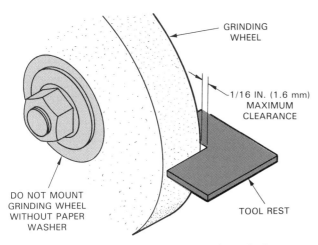

Fig. 17-8. Adjusting the tool rest for grinding.

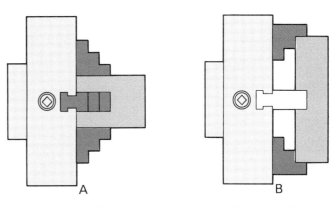

Fig. 17-10. A—Chuck jaw position for holding small diameter work. B—Chuck jaw position for holding large diameter work.

CHUCKS, Fig. 17-9, are the easiest and fastest method for mounting work for turning. They fit on the headstock spindle.

The jaws on a 3-JAW UNIVERSAL CHUCK all operate at one time. The jaws automatically center round or hexagon shaped stock.

Each jaw on a 4-JAW INDEPENDENT CHUCK operates individually. This permits irregular shaped work (square, rectangular, octagonal, etc.) to be centered.

The jaws can be reversed on the 4-jaw independent chuck to hold large diameter work, Fig. 17-10. Another set of jaws must be used with the 3-jaw universal chuck.

At first, it may appear difficult to center work on a 4-jaw chuck. Practice is all that is required.

Center the work approximately by using the concentric rings on the chuck face as a guide, Fig. 17-11. Final centering can be done using a piece

Fig. 17-9. Top. The 3-jaw universal chuck. Bottom. 4-jaw independent chuck.   (L.W. Chuck Co.)

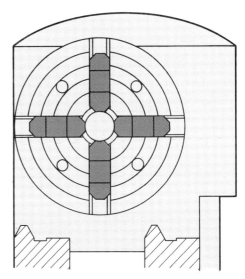

Fig. 17-11. Concentric rings on face of 4-jaw independent chuck can be used for approximate centering of work.

Fig. 17-12. Using chalk to center work in a 4-jaw chuck. The chalk mark indicates the ''high point.'' Loosen jaw opposite chalk mark, then tighten jaw on chalked side. Use small, gradual adjustments rather than large adjustments.

Fig. 17-13. The facing operation. Note that a right-hand tool holder is used.

of chalk, Fig. 17-12. Rotate the chuck slowly and bring the chalk into contact with the work. Slightly loosen the jaw(s) opposite the chalk mark. Then tighten the jaw(s) on the side where the chalk mark is located. Continue the operation until the work is centered. The cutter bit may be used instead of chalk if the work is large enough.

REMOVE THE CHUCK KEY FROM THE CHUCK BEFORE TURNING ON THE LATHE.

FACING STOCK HELD IN A CHUCK

FACING is the term used when the end or face of the stock is machined square. The tool is positioned on center and mounted as shown in Fig. 17-13. The cut can be made in either direction.

PLAIN TURNING

Plain turning, Fig. 17-14, is done when the work must be reduced in diameter. One precaution must be noted. If the work projects from the chuck more than a few inches, it should be center drilled and supported with the tailstock center, Fig. 17-15. (Also refer to Fig. 17-27.) This will prevent the work from springing away from the cutting tool while it is being machined.

Fig. 17-14. Plain turning. A left-hand tool holder is used for most operations of this type. It will permit maximum clearance between the rotating chuck and the lathe carriage.

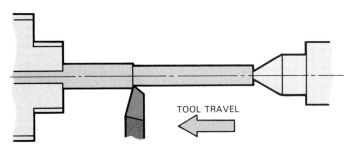

Fig. 17-15. Support long or slender work with the tailstock center. Otherwise the resulting "chatter" will cause a poor surface finish or work cut on a slight taper.

DO NOT FORGET TO LUBRICATE THE TAILSTOCK (DEAD) CENTER. Without lubrication, the tailstock center will heat up and "burn" off. Lubrication can be done with either a dab of white lead mixed with machine oil or a commercially prepared center lubricant.

The first operation in plain turning is called ROUGH TURNING. The diameter is reduced to within 1/32 in. (0.8 mm) of desired size. Use a LEFT-HAND TOOL HOLDER to hold the cutter bit. Position the tool holder as shown in Fig. 17-16.

CAUTION: Before starting the lathe, be sure that the cut can be made without danger of the rotating chuck striking the tool holder or compound, Fig. 17-17.

The tool cutting edge should be on center or slightly over center. There should not be too much overhang, Fig. 17-18. Too much overhang will cause a rough surface.

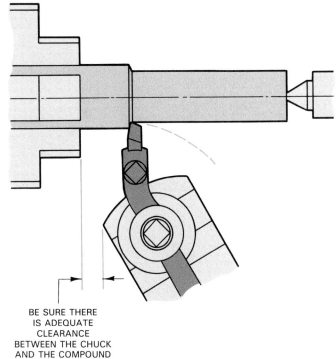

BE SURE THERE
IS ADEQUATE
CLEARANCE
BETWEEN THE CHUCK
AND THE COMPOUND

Fig. 17-17. Be sure the cut can be made without danger of the rotating chuck striking the tool holder or compound. Also, position the tool holder so it will swing clear of the work if the tool holder slips in the tool post.

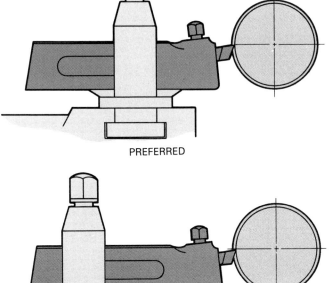

PREFERRED

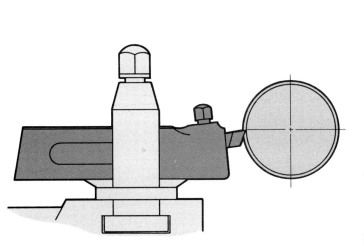

AVOID

Fig. 17-16. Tool set up for general turning.

Fig. 17-18. Top. Recommended tool set up for general turning. Bottom. Avoid excessive overhang of the tool holder.

Adjust the lathe to the proper CUTTING SPEED (revolutions per minute) and FEED. Feed is the distance the cutter travels in each revolution of the work. This will vary for different metals. See Fig. 17-19.

Make the cut from the tailstock to the headstock. Feed the cutter into the stock. Engage the power feed and make a trial cut about 1/4 in. (6.4 mm) wide. Check with a micrometer or caliper. You may have to make several roughing cuts to get the work to the desired size plus 1/32 in. (0.8 mm).

Insert a finishing tool. INCREASE the speed but DECREASE the feed. Again, make a trial cut 1/4 in. (6.4 mm) wide. DO NOT CHANGE THE CROSS FEED SETTING. Measure the diameter with a micrometer. If, for example, the work is 0.006 in. (0.152 mm) oversize, the cross feed micrometer dial is fed in 0.003 in. (0.076 mm) and another cut is taken. Check your lathe. Some of them are set differently. The cross micrometer dial must be fed in 0.006 in., if 0.006 in. of metal is to be removed. When the correct diameter is reached, finish the cut.

CUTTING TAPERS

The lathe center is cut on a TAPER. There are several ways to cut tapers on the lathe. The COMPOUND REST method of turning tapers, Fig. 17-20, is perhaps the easiest. However, the taper length is limited to the compound rest travel. The base of the compound is graduated in degrees.

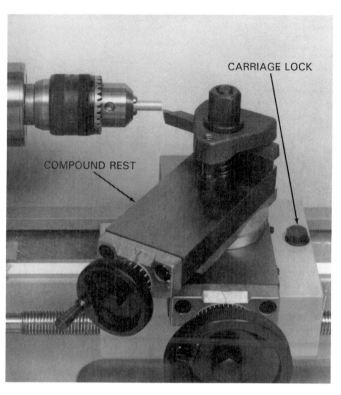

Fig. 17-20. Turning a taper using the compound rest method.

When cutting tapers, the compound rest is ALWAYS set parallel to the desired taper.

Long tapers can be cut using the TAILSTOCK SET-OVER METHOD, Fig. 17-21. To calculate the amount of set-over use the following formulas It is suggested that all fractions be converted to decimal fractions.

When taper per inch is known:

$$\text{SET-OVER} = \frac{\text{Total length of piece} \times \text{Taper per inch}}{2}$$

When taper per foot is known:

$$\text{SET-OVER} = \frac{\text{Total length of piece} \times \text{Taper per foot}}{24}$$

When the dimensions of the tapered section are known:

$$\text{SET-OVER} = \frac{\text{Total length of piece} \times (\text{Major Dia.-Minor Dia.})}{2 \times \text{Length of Taper}}$$

The set-over can be measured by using center points to determine amount of tailstock set-over, Fig. 17-22. Or it can be measured by measuring the distance between the witness marks on base of the tailstock. See Fig. 17-23.

STOCK DIA. IN IN.	MACHINE STEEL	BRASS	ALUMINUM
3/8	960	1700	2100
1/2	720	1200	1600
5/8	576	960	1280
3/4	500	800	1066
1	360	600	800
1 1/4	288	480	640
1 1/2	240	400	540
2	180	300	400

Fig. 17-19. Speeds for various metals are given in revolutions per minuts (rpm) and are only approximate. Increase or decrease as necessary for the job being machined. Feeds will vary from 0.010-0.020 in. for roughing cuts to 0.002-0.010 in. for finishing cuts.

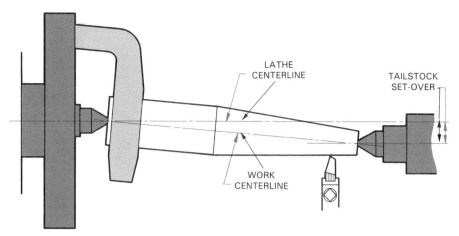

Fig. 17-21. Tailstock set-over method of turning tapers. The work must be mounted between centers.

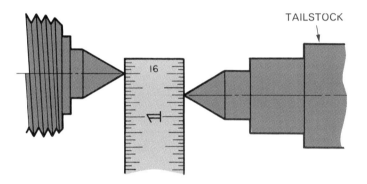

Fig. 17-22. The set-over can be measured using the center points.

When using the tailstock set-over method of turning tapers the work must be mounted between centers, Fig. 17-24.

You can also cut tapers by using the taper attachment that is built on many lathes, Fig. 17-25. The taper attachment is a guide that provides an accurate way to cut tapers.

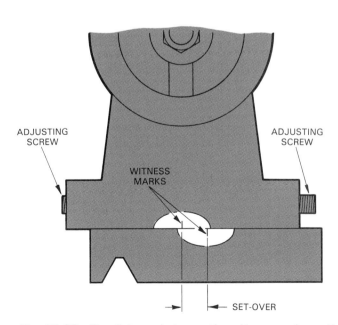

Fig. 17-23. The distance between the witness marks on the base of the tailstock can be used to measure the amount of set-over.

Fig. 17-24. Working between centers.

175

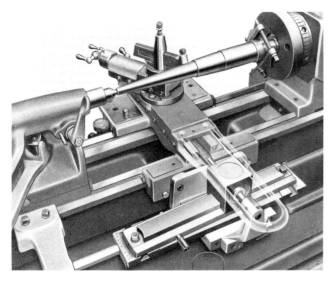

Fig. 17-25. Lathe fitted with taper attachment. When using this method to cut tapers, the work can be mounted in a chuck or between centers.   (Clausing)

Fig. 17-27. Locating stock center using a 3-jaw chuck.

TURNING BETWEEN CENTERS

Much lathe work is done with the stock mounted between centers. Refer back to Fig. 17-24. The chuck is replaced with a FACEPLATE. A LIVE CENTER and a SLEEVE are inserted in the headstock spindle. A DEAD CENTER is placed in the tailstock. The work is connected to the faceplate with a DOG.

Before stock can be turned between centers, it is necessary to drill a CENTER HOLE in each end. Center holes are drilled with a COMBINATION DRILL AND COUNTERSINK, Fig. 17-26.

There are several ways to locate the center of the stock. An easy way is to mount the work in a 3-jaw chuck. Face the stock to length and drill the center holes, Fig. 17-27. Fig. 17-28 shows a properly drilled center hole.

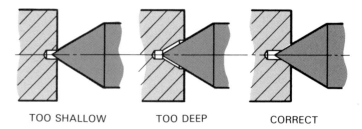

TOO SHALLOW   TOO DEEP   CORRECT

Fig. 17-28. Drilling center holes.

Center holes can also be located using the CENTER HEAD of the combination set, Fig. 17-29. The holes are drilled on a drill press.

Fig. 17-26. Combination drill and countersink (center drill).
(Greenfield Tap and Die)

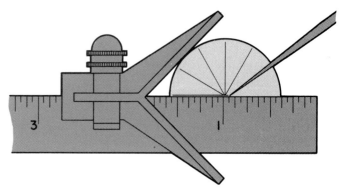

Fig. 17-29. Using the center head to locate the center of round stock.

The centers must run true for accurate work. Check center alignment by bringing them together, Fig. 17-30. A tapered piece will result if they are not aligned. Adjust the tailstock to bring them into alignment.

Clamp a dog on one end of the stock. Place a dab of lubricant (white lead and oil) in the center hole at the tailstock end. Insert the centers in the holes. Adjust the tailstock center until it is snug enough to prevent the lathe dog from "clattering." Check the adjustment from time to time. The heat generated during the machining operation causes the work to expand. The tailstock center may burn off if too much heat is generated.

The cutting operation is identical to machining work mounted in a chuck.

If the work must be reversed to machine its entire length, protect the section under the dog setscrew. This can be done by inserting a piece of soft copper or aluminum sheet, Fig. 17-31.

DRILLING

Drilling can be done on the lathe. Hold the work in a chuck and mount a Jacobs chuck in the tailstock to grip the drill, Fig. 17-32.

Start the hole by first "spotting" the work with a center drill.

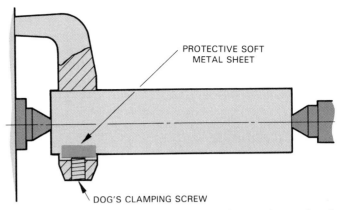

Fig. 17-31. Protect the work by placing a piece of soft aluminum or copper under the clamping screw.

Fig. 17-32. Drilling with a straight shank drill held in a Jacobs chuck.

Drills up to 1/2 in. (12.7 mm) diameter are held in a Jacobs chuck. Larger drills are mounted in the tailstock spindle. See Fig. 17-33.

Fig. 17-30. Center alignment can be checked by bringing centers together.

Fig. 17-33. Drilling on the lathe.

177

A PILOT HOLE (small hole) should be drilled first if a drill larger than 1/2 in. (12.7 mm) diameter is used, Fig. 17-34.

BORING

BORING, Fig. 17-35, is done when a hole is not a standard drill size. It is also done when a very accurate hole diameter is needed.

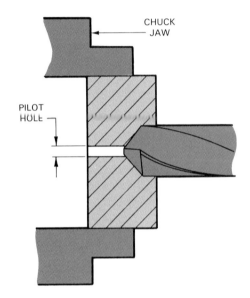

Fig. 17-34. A pilot hole permits larger drills to cut easier and faster.

A BORING TOOL HOLDER supports the BORING BAR. A cutter bit is inserted in the boring bar. The hole is first drilled slightly smaller than the desired diameter. The cutter tool is set on center with the boring bar parallel to the centerline of the hole. The cutting is done in much the same manner as is external turning.

KNURLING

KNURLING, Fig. 17-36, is the operation that presses horizontal or diamond shaped serrations on the circumference of the stock. This provides a gripping surface.

To knurl, complete the following steps.

1. Mark off the section to be knurled.
2. Put the lathe into back gear (slow speed) with a fairly rapid feed.
3. Position the knurling tool so that both knurl wheels bear evenly and squarely on the work.
4. Start the lathe and feed the knurl slowly into the work until a pattern develops. Engage the automatic feed. USE A LUBRICANT ON THE KNURL WHEELS. After the knurl has traveled the desired distance, reverse the spindle rotation. Apply additional pressure. Repeat until a good knurl has formed.

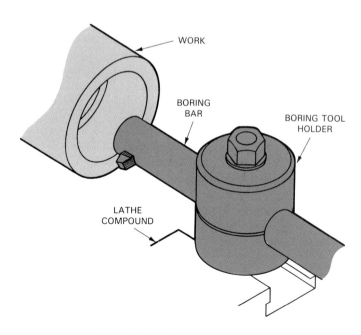

Fig. 17-35. Boring on the lathe.

Fig. 17-36. Knurling.

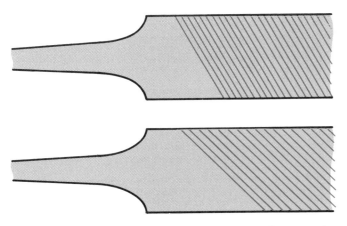

Fig. 17-37. Top. Long angle lathe file. Bottom. Compare the long angle file with this regular file.

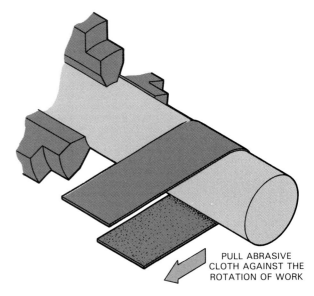

PULL ABRASIVE CLOTH AGAINST THE ROTATION OF WORK

Fig. 17-39. Polishing on the lathe. Do not forget to protect the lathe ways from the abrasive particles.

FILING AND POLISHING ON THE LATHE

If the cutter bit is properly sharpened, there should be no need to file or polish work machined on the lathe. However, due to lack of experience, you may wish to smooth and polish a machined surface.

A fine mill file or long angle lathe file should be used, Fig. 17-37. Take long even strokes across the rotating work. Hold the file as shown in Fig. 17-38. Keep the file clean and free from chips.

A filed surface can be made very smooth by using fine grades of abrasive cloth, Fig. 17-39. Apply oil to the abrasive cloth. Keep the cloth moving across the rotating work. It is recommended that you protect the lathe ways from the abrasive particles.

CUTTING THREADS ON THE LATHE

Threads can be cut on many lathes, Fig. 17-40. The cutter bit is sharpened to the shape of the desired threads. The feed and speed selector controls are adjusted to move the carriage and cutter bit across the work. This is done at a rate that will cut the desired number of threads per inch.

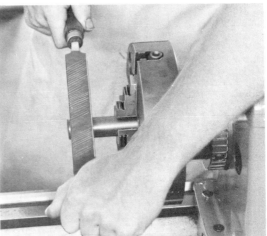

Fig. 17-38. Left. Left-hand filing method. The hands are clear of the rotating chuck. Right. Right-hand filing method. The left hand and arm must be over the revolving chuck.

Fig. 17-40. Cutting threads.

Cutting threads is a complex operation. The correct way to set up the lathe and how threads are cut is best demonstrated by your instructor.

THE SHAPER

The SHAPER, Fig. 17-41, is another machine tool often found in the metals lab. It is used primarily to machine flat surfaces, Fig. 17-42. However, a skilled machinist can use it to cut curved and irregular shapes, grooves, and keyways. The cutting tool is mounted to a ram which moves back and forth across the work.

Mount the work in the vise or clamp it directly to the worktable. The table can be moved horizontally or vertically. The head, to which the tool holder is mounted, can be pivoted for angular cutting, Fig. 17-43.

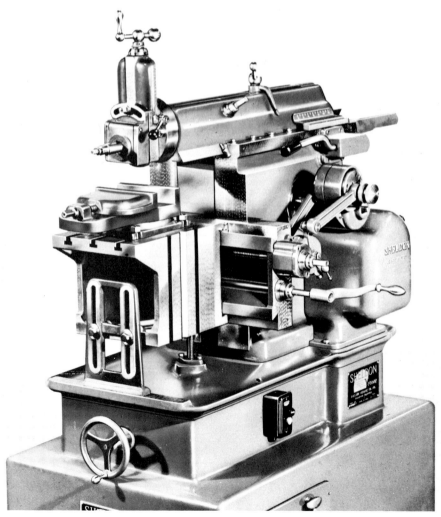

Fig. 17-41. The shaper.   (Sheldon Machine Co., Inc.)

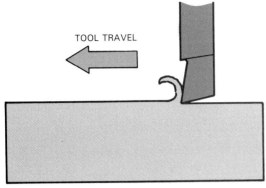

TOOL TRAVEL

WORK IS STATIONARY

Fig. 17-42. How a shaper works.

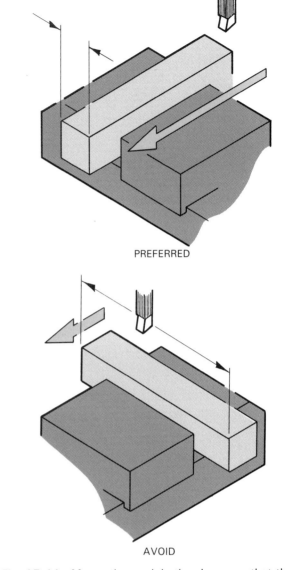

PREFERRED

AVOID

Fig. 17-44. Mount the work in the shaper so that the work will be done in the least amount of time.

Fig. 17-43. The head of the shaper can be pivoted to make angular cuts.

Position the work so that the cut can be made in the shortest possible time, Fig. 17-44. The STROKE (length of cut) is adjustable and should be positioned as shown in Fig. 17-45.

SHAPER SAFETY

KEEP YOUR FINGERS CLEAR OF THE CUTTING TOOL WHILE ADJUSTING THE STROKE.

DO NOT RUB YOUR FINGERS ACROSS THE WORK WHILE THE TOOL IS CUTTING.

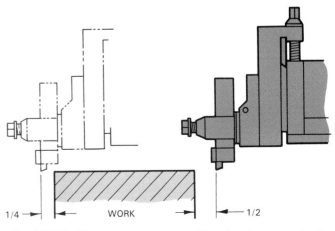

1/4   WORK   1/2

Fig. 17-45. The correct way to position the shaper stroke for cutting.

THE MILLING MACHINE

Industry uses many types of milling machines. The VERTICAL MILLING MACHINE, Fig. 17-46, and the HORIZONTAL MILLING MACHINE, Fig. 17-47, are most commonly found in the school shop.

Milling machines operate by a rotating multi-toothed cutter being fed into a moving piece of work, Fig. 17-48. The horizontal milling machine uses a cutter mounted on an arbor to smooth and shape metal, Fig. 17-49. The cutter used on a vertical milling machine is called an END MILL. It clamps in the machine spindle, Fig. 17-50.

Special attachments permit gears to be cut on the horizontal milling machine, Fig. 17-51.

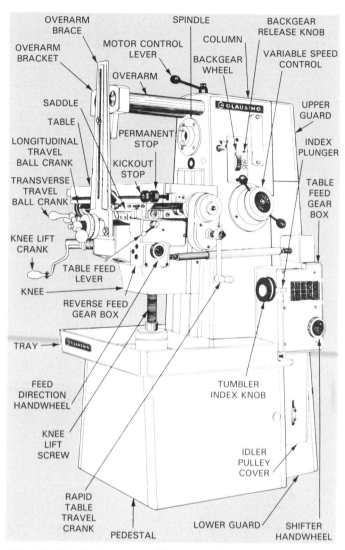

Fig. 17-47. Horizontal milling machine with the parts identified.

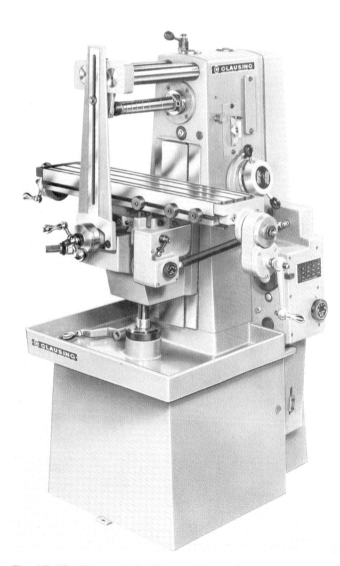

Fig. 17-46. The vertical milling machine. (Cincinnati Milacron)

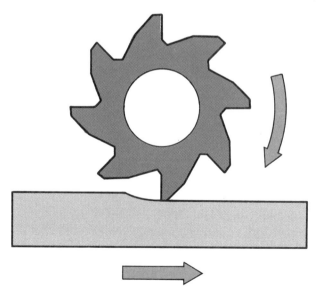

Fig. 17-48. How the milling machine works.

One kind of unique machine tool is a combination LATHE/MILLING MACHINE, Figs. 17-52 and 17-53. It is being used often in school labs. The machine tool is used for basic milling and lathe operations.

Fig. 17-49. The cutter on the horizontal milling machine is mounted on an arbor.

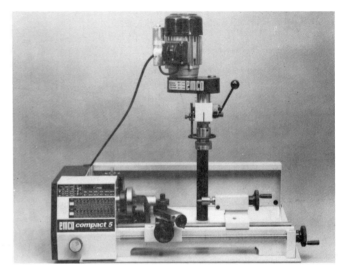

Fig. 17-52. The lathe/miller is a combination lathe and milling machine.

Fig. 17-50. An end mill is used to do the cutting in a vertical milling machine.

Fig. 17-51. Cutting gears. A dividing head is used to space the gear teeth.

Fig. 17-53. The milling machine portion of the lathe/miller.

183

Milling machines range in size from a small vertical milling machine similar to those used in the school metals lab, to the 50 hp horizontal milling machine shown in Fig. 17-54.

OTHER MACHINE TOOLS

Many other types of machine tools are used by industry. Several of the more widely used machines are discussed in the following sections.

BANDSAW

The cutting operation done on the METAL CUTTING BANDSAW, Fig. 17-55, is called BAND MACHINING. The bandsaw used one-piece saw blade to do the cutting. Cutting can be at any angle or in any direction, Fig. 17-56.

PRECISION GRINDING MACHINES

There are many types of precision grinding machines. The SURFACE GRINDER, Fig. 17-57, is frequently found in school labs. The machine uses a grinding wheel to produce a smooth, accurate surface on material regardless of its hardness. The work moves back and forth under the grinding wheel, Fig. 17-58. There are two types of surface grinders: the planer type and the rotary type.

Fig. 17-54. This 50 hp horizontal milling machine can make a cut 1/8 in. (3 mm) deep by 12 in. (305 mm) wide. (National Machine Tool Builders Assoc.)

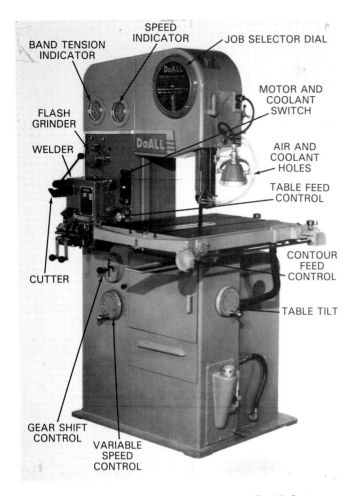

BAND TENSION INDICATOR
SPEED INDICATOR
JOB SELECTOR DIAL
FLASH GRINDER
WELDER
MOTOR AND COOLANT SWITCH
AIR AND COOLANT HOLES
TABLE FEED CONTROL
CUTTER
CONTOUR FEED CONTROL
TABLE TILT
GEAR SHIFT CONTROL
VARIABLE SPEED CONTROL

Fig. 17-55. Metal cutting bandsaw. (DoAll Co.)

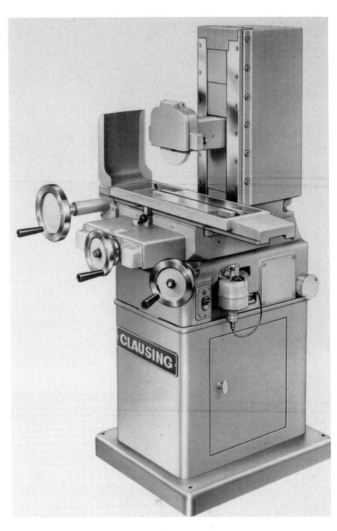

Fig. 17-57. Surface grinder.

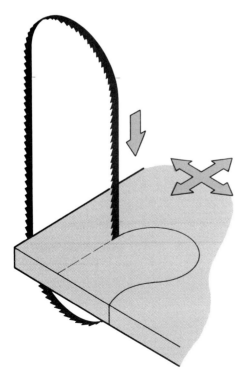

Fig. 17-56. Bandsaws machine at any angle or in any direction. The length of the cut is unlimited.

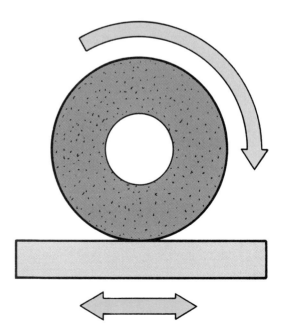

Fig. 17-58. How the surface grinder works.

PLANING MACHINES

PLANING MACHINES produce horizontal, vertical, and angular surfaces on metal much like the shaper does.

On the PLANER, Fig. 17-59, the material is mounted on the worktable. The worktable moves back and forth under the cutting tool, Fig. 17-60. The planer is used to machine large, flat surfaces.

The BROACH employs a long tool with many cutting surfaces. Each tool is slightly higher than the one before. Each increases in size to the exact size required, Fig. 17-61.

The tool is pushed or pulled across the surface to be machined, Fig. 17-62. Many flat surfaces on automobile engines are broached.

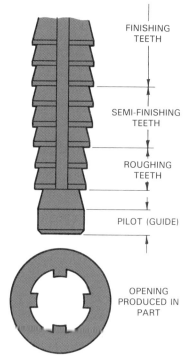

Fig. 17-61. Typical broaching tool.

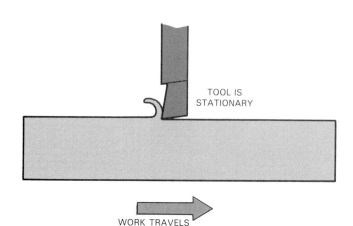

Fig. 17-59. Large planer. Note the size of the work being machined. (G.A. Gray Co.)

Fig. 17-60. How the planer works.

Fig. 17-62. Vertical broach machining the flat surface of compressor cylinder heads.
(National Machine Tool Builders Assoc.)

186

COMPUTER-ASSISTED MANUFACTURING TECHNOLOGY

The machine tools in your school metals lab are operated by hand controls. You must turn a handwheel or pull a lever to move the work against the cutting tool, Fig. 17-63. Some of the machines may also have power feed mechanisms.

Fig. 17-63. Some of the machines in your school's metals lab may be similar to those shown. They are operated by hand controls.

Fig. 17-64. This robot, or automated cell, consists of several machines with robotics material handling. Parts to be machined are delivered and finished parts are removed automatically as required. The cell becomes a fully automatic process through the application of robotics and other forms of automation. (Kearney & Trecker Corp.)

Industry employs many machine tools that perform machining operations automatically, even to the point where robots load and unload the machine, Fig. 17-64. In the system known as CAM (COMPUTER-ASSISTED MANUFACTURING or COMPUTER-AIDED MANUFACTURING), a computer "tells" the machine the required sequence of operations to be performed, the distance and direction the work is to travel, where the cutting is to be done, and the cutting tool(s) to be utilized.

NUMERICAL CONTROL or NC is the most widely used form of CAM. NC is an automated manufacturing technique. Coded numerical instructions, Fig. 17-65, direct a machine tool

PREPARATORY FUNCTIONS (G-CODES)*	
CODE	**FUNCTION**
G00	Rapid traverse (slides move only at rapid traverse speed).
G01	Linear interpolation (slides move at right angles and/or at programmed angles).
G02	Circular interpolation CW (tool follows a quarter part of circumference in a clockwise direction).
G03	Circular interpolation CCW (tool follows a quarter part of circumference in a counterclockwise direction).
G04	Dwell (timed delay of established duration. Length is expressed in X or F word).
G33	Thread cutting.
G70	Inch programming.
G71	Metric programming.
G81	Drill.
G90	Absolute coordinates.
G91	Incremental coordinates.

*G-CODES may vary on different NC machines.

MISCELLANEOUS FUNCTIONS (M-CODES)*	
CODE	**FUNCTION**
M00	Stop machine until operator restart.
M02	End of program.
M03	Start spindle—CW.
M04	Start spindle—CCW.
M05	Stop spindle.
M06	Tool change.
M07	Coolant on.
M09	Coolant off.
M30	End program and rewind tape.
M52	Advance spindle.
M53	Retract spindle.
M56	Tool inhibit.

*M-CODES may vary on different NC machines.

Fig. 17-65. Example of NC codes for preparatory and miscellaneous functions.

through a sequence of operations that produce the required part shape. Known as a PROGRAM, the coded instructions consist of ALPHANUMERIC DATA (letters, numbers, punctuation marks, and special characters). Each identifies a specific machine function.

NC coded information is sometimes punched into paper or mylar tape, Fig. 17-66, or recorded on magnetic tape, but is more often placed directly into the on-board machine tool computer, Fig. 17-67, as electronic data. Information also may be transmitted to a machine's control unit through a computer network.

The programmed information instructs small electric motors on the machine tool, called SERVOS, telling them how far and in what direction the work is to move. It also tells the cutting tool when to start cutting, how deep to cut, and when to stop cutting.

Present day NC equipment may be CNC (COMPUTER NUMERICAL CONTROL) or DNC (DIRECT NUMERICAL CONTROL). With CNC, one computer typically controls one machine tool, Fig. 17-68. DNC involves a single master computer linked to several machine tools and able to operate them simultaneously or individually.

Fig. 17-67. CNC milling/drilling machine found in many school metals labs. Note the on-board computer.
(Dyna Electronics, Inc.)

Fig. 17-68. With CNC, one computer controls one machine. The machinist can input the program directly into the computer.
(Bridgeport Machines, Inc.)

Fig. 17-66. Tape used on manually programmed NC machines and the tape code.

188

CARTESIAN COORDINATE SYSTEM

Work positioning is by the CARTESIAN COORDINATE SYSTEM, Fig. 17-69. This system is the basis of all NC programming. The X and Y axes are horizontal work movements. The Z axis is vertical work or cutting tool movement.

There are two basic NC movement systems:
- POINT-TO-POINT. There is no concern what path the tool taes when moving from Point A to Point B. See Fig. 17-70. This system is widely used for drilling, spot welding, and punching openings in sheet metal. A computer is not usually needed to prepare point-to-point programs.
- CONTOUR OR CONTINUOUS PATH. Employed to profile and contour complex two- and three-dimensional workpieces, Fig. 17-71. The cutting tool remains in continous contact with the work. Programming cannot be accomplished without a computer.

CNC technology has reached the position where a engineer can, using COMPUTER GRAPHICS, design a part and see how it will work with other parts in the assembly, Fig. 17-72. When the design has been confirmed, the computer is directed to figure out the tool paths required to make it. The tool paths are converted into a detailed sequence of commands. These commands are carried out by the proper CNC machine tool.

Fig. 17-71. Auto body dies (shaped steel blocks used to form body sections) are machined using contour or continuous path NC milling. (Buick)

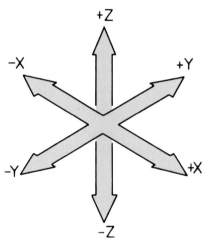

Fig. 17-69. The Cartesian Coordinate System is the basis of all NC programming.

Fig. 17-72. Computer-Aided Design (CAD) starts by defining the outline of the part being designed. After being analyzed for correct specifications, cutter paths for NC machining are defined and modified to meet production needs. Here, an engineer is starting to design an engine mount for a new type of aircraft. (Beech Aircraft Corp.)

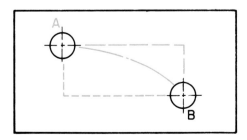

Fig. 17-70. In point-to-point NC systems, there is no concern what path is taken when the tool moves from Point A to Point B.

The technology that makes all of this possible is called CAD/CAM (COMPUTER-AIDED DESIGN/COMPUTER-AIDED MANUFACTURING).

ROBOTICS

Industrial ROBOTS, Fig. 17-73, are found in numerous applications. They can be programmed to do many types of jobs: loading and unloading machines, drilling, spot welding, Fig. 17-74, inspection, and paint spraying. They are often found performing jobs that would be tedious or hazardous for human workers. Many varieties of robots have been developed, Fig. 17-75.

MACHINING SAFETY

1. Have ALL guards in place before operating any machine.
2. When using the drill press, clamp the work to the table or mount it solidly in a vise. Otherwise, the work might spin rapidly, possibly causing injury.
3. Never reverse a machine before it comes to a full stop. This could cause the chuck on some lathes to spin off.
4. ALWAYS remove the chuck key from the lathe or drill press chuck.
5. Stop machines before making measurements and adjustments.
6. Do not operate portable electric power tools in areas where thinners and solvents are used and stored. A serious fire or explosion might result.
7. Roll up sleeves and remove dangling jewelry before starting to work.
8. ALWAYS WEAR GOGGLES.
9. Get cuts, burns, and bruises properly treated.
10. Do not wear loose clothing when operating machines. The clothing may get caught in a machine, causing injury.

Fig. 17-74. Industrial robots like these are usually found performing jobs that are tedious or hazardous for human workers. (Ford Motor Co.)

Fig. 17-73. A typical industrial-type robot. It has great freedom of movement.

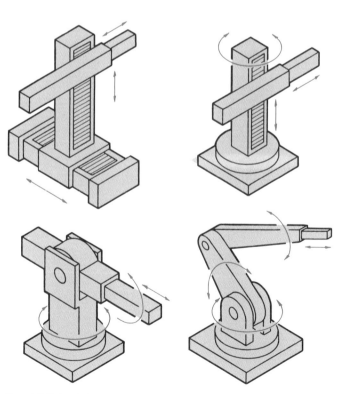

Fig. 17-75. A few variations of industrial robot design. Their movements are planned for performing specific jobs.

TEST YOUR KNOWLEDGE, Unit 17

Please do not write in the text. Place your answers on a separate sheet of paper.

1. _____ _____ are power driven tools
2. What object is used to clean a lathe?
   a. Hands.
   b. Paint brush.
   c. Screwdriver.
   d. Vacuum.
3. What is a cutter bit?
4. A _____ cut is used to quickly reduce the diameter of work.
5. What operation would you perform to reduce work in diameter?
   a. Facing.
   b. Boring.
   c. Plain turning.
   d. None of the above.
6. Cutting speed is measured in:
   a. Revolutions per minute.
   b. Revolutions per second.
   c. Revolutions per hour.
   d. None of the above.
7. Feed is the distance the _____ travels in each revolution of work.
8. List two ways to cut tapers on the lathe.
9. What machine tool is used to machine flat surfaces?
10. What cutting operation is done on the band saw?
11. In numerical control, work is positioned using the _____ _____ _____.

MATCHING QUESTIONS: Match each of the following terms with their correct definitions.
a. Boring.   d. Center head.
b. Boring tool holder.   e. Center holes.
c. Knurling.
12. ____ Operation that presses horizontal or diamond-shaped serrations on stock.
13. ____ Drilled with a combination drill and countersink.
14. ____ Done when a hole is not standard flat size.
15. ____ Used to locate center holes.
16. ____ Supports a boring bar.
17. Name two types of milling machines.
18. List five safety rules to follow in the machine shop.
19. It costs $25 to manufacture a part using conventional machine tools. The cost is reduced by 20 percent when the part is manufactured on a CNC machine tool. How much money will be saved using a CNC machine tool to produce 500 parts?

TECHNICAL TERMS TO LEARN

band saw
band machining
bench grinder
boring
broach
Cartesian coordinate system
center hole
computer-aided drafting
computer-aided manufacturing
computer graphics
Computer Numerical Control (CNC)
compound
concentric
cross feed
cutter bit
cutting speed
dead center
Distributive Numerical Control (DNC)
dog
drill
end mill
facing
head stock
high speed steel
horizontal milling machine
independent chuck
Jacobs chuck
knurl
lathe
machine tool
Numerical Control (NC)
parallel
pedestal grinder
planner
program
revolutions per minute
robot
shaper
spindle
surface grinder
tailstock
taper
threads
tool holder
turning
universal chuck
vertical milling machine

ACTIVITIES

1. Carefully clean and lubricate a lathe in your school shop. Use the lubrication chart furnished with the lathe to be certain that you do not overlook critical points.
2. After securing permission from your instructor, operate the various handwheels and levers on the lathe. THE POWER MUST BE OFF. Learn what each does. Do not force any movement.
3. Sharpen a cutter bit.
4. Prepare a check list and keep a record of the various operations you perform on the lathe. Prepare a similar chart for other machines that you operate.
5. Prepare a series of posters on the safe operation of machine tools.

Unit 18 . . . .

Entrepreneurship Activity

After completing the activity in this unit, you will be able to describe the place of the entrepreneur in the American economy. In addition, you will have gained first-hand experience in the business world. This includes experience in organizing, financing, and operating your own small manufacturing business. You will do many of the things large business does, on a smaller scale. You will obtain experience that will make you a better employee when you are ready for your first full-time job.

AN INTRODUCTION TO PRODUCTION

It has been said the average person will work in at least seven different occupations during their lifetime. It is also said that the technologies that will be involved in four of them have not yet been invented or discovered.

These new technologies will be developed and put into production by **entrepreneurs.** They are the men and women (either individually or as a group) who originate new business ventures and create jobs. They are willing to risk capital (money) and time to establish a new enterprise and make a profit if the business is a success. Entrepreneurs and the businesses they establish are thought by many to be the backbone of the American economy.

Entrepreneurs enjoy the challenge of starting a new business. However, after the venture is started and operating, many of them turn day-to-day operations over to men and women with managerial skills.

You will have the experience of being an entrepreneur if your class decides to manufacture a product by the means described in this unit.

ESTABLISHING A BUSINESS ENTERPRISE

The business activity in this unit may be changed to meet local conditions and restrictions.

The procedure to follow in a typical setup includes:

1. Deciding on a product.
2. Selecting a name for your new company.
3. Electing company officials.
4. Determining approximate amount of operating capital (money) needed to finance the business.
5. Selling shares of stock to raise operating capital.
6. Determining the manufacturing steps required, and sequence of operations.
7. Providing jigs and fixtures needed for mass production.
8. Developing sales plan; promoting product sales.
9. Dissolving the business and reimbursing stockholders.

DECIDE ON PRODUCT

At your first meeting (with your instructor serving as advisor) decide on the product to be manufactured. Select one of the tested products covered later in this unit.

SELECT COMPANY NAME

The name selected should be appropriate, businesslike, and brief.

This is a class activity in which all students are expected to participate. Therefore, each classmember should come up with a good name for the new company that is being organized.

It is suggested that each class member write one or more names on a slip of paper. The slips should be collected, proposed names discussed, and a vote taken. The vote will determine which company name is to be used.

Note: Do not include Incorporated, or Corporation after the company name. Each of these is a legal term which can be used only in cases where a state charter has been obtained.

COMPANY OFFICIALS

If your company is to be a success, it must be run in an efficient, businesslike manner. This means you will need capable company officials and capable workers. It is suggested that you elect:

1. General Manager.
2. Office Manager.
3. Purchasing Agent.
4. Sales Manager.
5. Safety Director.

Duties of the company officials are described in the following paragraphs. Each office should be discussed before holding an election.

DUTIES OF GENERAL MANAGER

Your General Manager will be expected to:

1. Exercise general supervision over entire activity.
2. Train workers, assign workers to jobs.
3. Check on, and be responsible for, product quality and manufacturing efficiency.
4. Approve bills to be paid by Office Manager. Approve purchase orders before making purchases.
5. Prepare and submit reports as required by your Advisor (instructor).

6. Cooperate with your Advisor and other Company officials.

DUTIES OF OFFICE MANAGER

The Office Manager should:

1. Maintain attendance records. Check absentees for valid excuses.
2. Keep company's financial records (8 1/2 x 11 loose leaf notebook suggested).
3. Keep a record of all money received on RECEIPTS page of record book, Fig. 18-1.
4. All cash receipts should be deposited in a local bank and a checking account established.
5. Pay all bills (invoices previously approved by your General Manager) by writing checks. Make a complete record in your checkbook. Show dates and amount of money deposited in checking account, and checks written. Show the balance. This is the amount in bank, after each check is written. See Fig. 18-2. Be sure

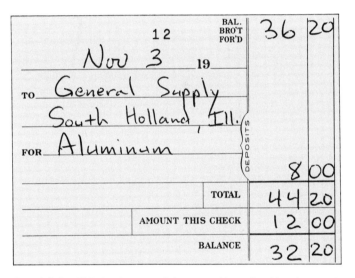

Fig. 18-2. This business activity record is a checkbook record of bills paid.

A-1 PRODUCTS, 123 W. Taft, South Holland, Ill. 60473

RECEIPTS

Date	Item	Quantity	Sold To	Sold By	Amount

Fig. 18-1. Business activity records for cash receipts.

your figures are correct. This is the only record your company has of the cash on hand.

6. Keep stock sales and ownership records.
7. Cooperate with your Advisor and other company officials.

DUTIES OF PURCHASING AGENT

The Purchasing Agent should:

1. Check with Advisor to obtain materials and supplies needed to manufacture product selected.
2. Arrange to have stock certificates, purchase orders, and other business forms printed.
3. Have purchase orders approved by General Manager before issuing order.
4. Obtain materials required from school stock or purchase from outside source.
5. Cooperate with Advisor and other company officials.

DUTIES OF SALES MANAGER

The Sales Manager should:

1. Help decide how product is to be packaged, and provide instructions on product use, to include on the package. This is done after a product sample is available.
2. Plan sales program; decide on price to charge

for product, where and how product is to be sold. Note: All students participating in this activity will be expected to sell the company's products (also stock).
3. Cooperate with Advisor and other company officials.

DUTIES OF SAFETY DIRECTOR

The Safety Director should:

1. Enforce safety rules.
2. Stop all horseplay and call attention to undesirable conduct.
3. Be alert to hazards.
4. Take steps to eliminate possible accident causing problems.
5. See to it that equipment and tools are in good operating condition.
6. Make sure machine guards are in place and students are using eye protection and protective clothing as specified by the Advisor.
7. Immediately report all injuries, even minor ones, to the Advisor.
8. Cooperate with Advisor and other company officials.

All company officials should be provided with identification badges, Fig. 18-3.

RAISING CAPITAL

Operating your new business requires money (capital). This capital will be used to pay bills until cash is available from the sale of your product. Many corporations raise money by selling stock to the public. It is sugggested you do the same.

Getting stock certificates printed and sold, and keeping the necessary records, is the duty of the Office Manager. See Fig. 18-4.

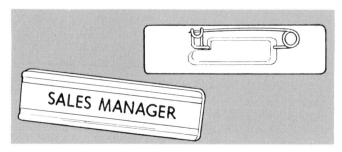

Fig. 18-3. Identification badge for company official.

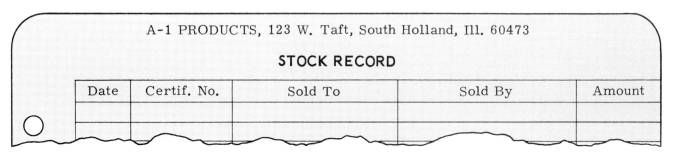

A-1 PRODUCTS, 123 W. Taft, South Holland, Ill. 60473				
STOCK RECORD				
Date	Certif. No.	Sold To	Sold By	Amount

Fig. 18-4. Stock ownership record.

STOCK CERTIFICATE

A–1 PRODUCTS
South Holland, Ill.

One Share

Par Value 50¢

Certificate Number ____________

Redeemable Within
One Year After Issue

Date Issued ____________

This Certifies That (please print)

First Name ____ Initial ____ Last Name ____

Street Address ____ City ____ State ____ Zip ____

Is the Owner of One Share, Par Value 50¢, of the stock of A–1 Products.

Stockholder's Signature ____________ for A–1 Products ____________

Stockholder by signature, okays operation of Company by Student Officials elected by Student Stockholders.

Fig. 18-5. Sample stock certificate form.

An example might help to illustrate this task. Let us say you need $40.00. This may be raised by selling 80 shares of stock at 50 cents each. See Fig. 18-5 for a suggested stock certificate form.

Stock certificates might be run off on a duplicating machine on two different colors of stock. Make 100 copies of each color. Yellow and white are suggested. Number the certificates 1 to 100.

Each student should purchase a share of stock at 50 cents. Sell stock on your own time. It is a good idea to make your first sale to yourself.

Use a ball point pen and carbon paper to fill out the stock certificate form. Put the white copy on top. On the share you sell to yourself sign where the stockholder's signature is required. Also sign as a representative of your company. Keep the white copy. Turn in the yellow copy (carbon) and the 50 cents to your Office Manager. It is his or her job to keep an accurate record of stock sales. The Office Manager must also see to it that the cash turned in is deposited in the bank. See Fig. 18-6.

It is suggested you limit stock sales to one share per customer. The stock should be divided so each

DEPOSITED WITH
SOUTH HOLLAND TRUST & SAVINGS BANK
SOUTH HOLLAND, ILLINOIS

NAME A-1 PRODUCTS

ADDRESS SOUTH HOLLAND, ILL.

DATE 11-1 19____

ACCOUNT NUMBER
487

	DOLLARS	CENTS
CURRENCY	7	00
COIN	3	40
CHECKS		
TOTAL	10	40
LESS CASH DEDUCTION		
TOTAL DEPOSIT	10	40

LIST ADDITIONAL CHECKS ON REVERSE SIDE

CHECKS DEPOSITED CANNOT BE DRAWN AGAINST UNTIL THEY HAVE BEEN COLLECTED BY THE BANK

Fig. 18-6. All cash received from product sales is deposited in the bank and bills are paid by check.

student has roughly the same number of shares to sell. When contacting those persons who might purchase stock, (local businessworkers, parents, neighbors, friends) be businesslike. Briefly describe your company and its operations. Be enthusiastic. Give your prospect the idea that he or she is buying a share of a "going business," and is NOT throwing money away. Tell him or her you cannot ensure results in advance, but that your company expects to make profits. Also assure your prospect that when the business is closed, you will redeem the stock at full value (50 cents per share) and pay a small dividend.

After a share of stock has been sold, fill out the stock certificate as just described. Please print. Ask your purchaser to read the certificate to make sure everything is understood and is agreeable. Then ask purchaser to sign. Hand the top (white) copy to your purchaser.

SETTING A PRICE AND SELLING A PRODUCT

In setting a selling price for your product, determine the total cost of making each item. Then add about 25% to this to cover the cost of material wasted, and to pay a dividend to stockholders when the business is closed.

Each participant in the project is expected to help sell the company's product.

If the product selected for manufacture is small, such as the two items described in this unit, make the products in advance. Then you can provide "on the spot" delivery.

Keep an current record of all sales. This includes quantity sold, name of customer, and amount col-

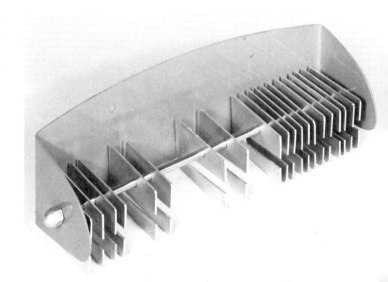

Fig. 18-8. Tie rack suitable for mass production.

lected. Turn these records and any money collected over to your Office Manager for handling.

At the end of the mass production project, the company you formed should be liquidated (closed). Money in the bank (after all bills are paid) should be divided in an equal manner among stockholders.

Include with each of the checks a memo informing each stockholder that the business is being closed. Fig. 18-7 shows a sample memo.

MASS PRODUCTION IN THE METALS LAB

Two mass production projects with proven student interest are the tie rack and the contemporary lamp.

(today's date)

TO: A-1 stockholders

FROM: A-1 company officials

SUBJECT: A-1 Products liquidation

A-1 Products, the business experience activity you helped finance by buying a share of stock, is being liquidated.

The check, in the amount of *(insert dollar amount of check)* is enclosed. This is intended to redeem the stock you purchased. The stock certificate you have does not need to be returned to us.

Thank you very much for your support of our project.

Fig. 18-7. Sample memo to send to stockholders telling of A-1 Products liquidation.

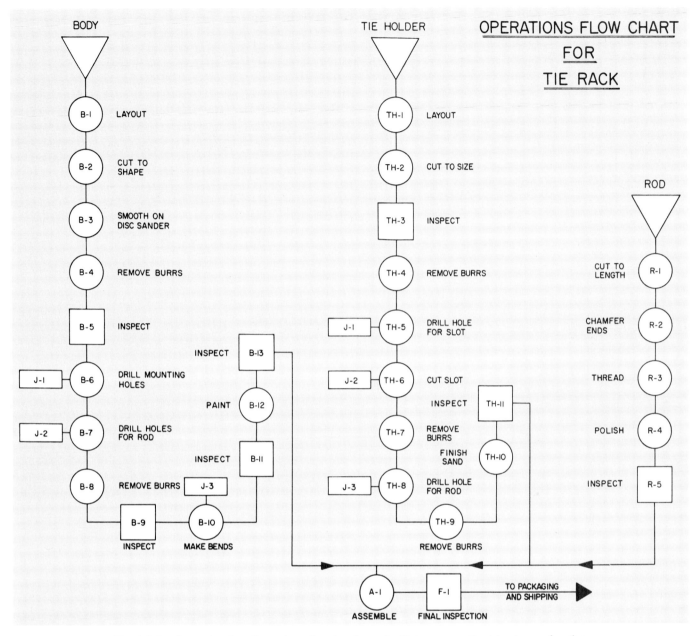

Fig. 18-9. A production flow chart for the tie rack. Only one method is shown for the manufacture of the tie holder.

IMPORTANT: No production project should be attempted until product samples are made. This will assure that the project can be made with the equipment available.

MASS-PRODUCING A TIE RACK

The TIE RACK, Fig. 18-8, provides unique production problems. But it is simple enough to be produced in a short time.

The PRODUCTION FLOW CHART, Fig. 18-9, shows a suggested sequence to follow in production. It includes such steps as manufacturing, inspecting, assembling, and finishing operations. The facilities and equipment located in your shop may require some changes.

Tie rack plans are shown in Fig. 18-10. A tie rack of the size indicated will hold about 20 ties. A smaller rack may be made up by using shorter body pieces.

BODY

The body (main part) of the tie rack is made from .080 in. (2.3 mm) half-hard aluminum sheet. Make a pattern on .030 aluminum and use it to

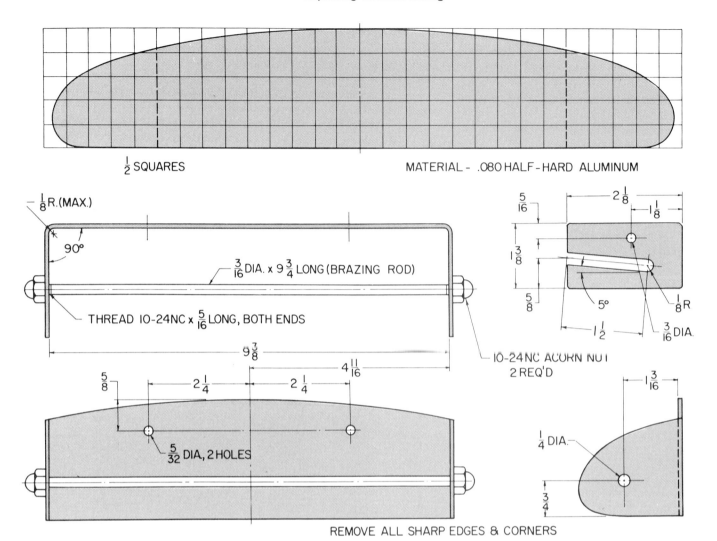

$\frac{1}{2}$ SQUARES

MATERIAL - .080 HALF-HARD ALUMINUM

$\frac{1}{8}$ R.(MAX.)

90°

$\frac{3}{16}$ DIA. x 9 $\frac{3}{4}$ LONG (BRAZING ROD)

THREAD 10-24NC x $\frac{5}{16}$ LONG, BOTH ENDS

9 $\frac{3}{8}$

$\frac{5}{16}$

2 $\frac{1}{8}$

1 $\frac{1}{8}$

1 $\frac{3}{8}$

$\frac{5}{8}$

5°

$\frac{1}{8}$ R

1 $\frac{1}{2}$

$\frac{3}{16}$ DIA.

10-24NC ACORN NUT
2 REQ'D

$\frac{5}{8}$

2 $\frac{1}{4}$

2 $\frac{1}{4}$

4 $\frac{11}{16}$

$\frac{5}{32}$ DIA, 2 HOLES

1 $\frac{3}{16}$

$\frac{1}{4}$ DIA.

$\frac{3}{4}$

REMOVE ALL SHARP EDGES & CORNERS

Fig. 18-10. Tie rack plans.

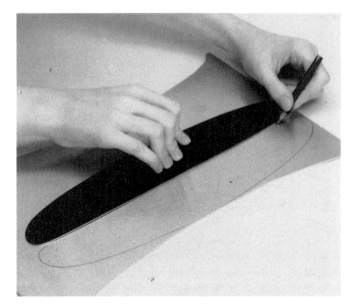

Fig. 18-11. Make a metal template and use it to transfer the outline to the aluminum sheet.

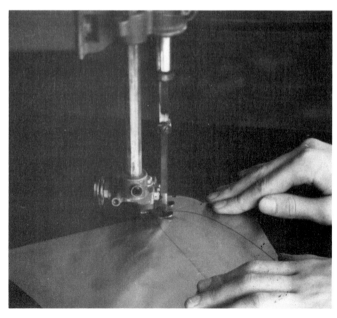

Fig. 18-12. Cutting outlined shape on a jig saw.

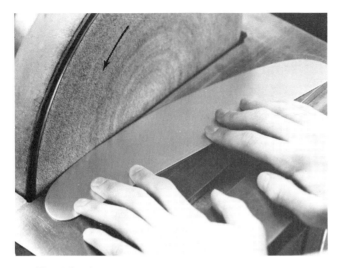

Fig. 18-13. Using disk sander to smooth edges.

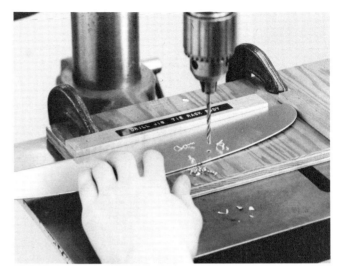

Fig. 18-15. Jig shown in Fig. 18-14 may also be used to position work for drilling the mounting holes.

trace the body outline on the metal, Fig. 18-11. Use a soft lead pencil or fine-point marker. Cut the metal to shape on a jigsaw, Fig. 18-12. Use a fine-toothed (24T-32T) blade or a bandsaw, if available.

Rough edges of the metal are smoothed on a disk sander, Fig. 18-13. Use a fine (3/0-4/0) abrasive disc. Or, rough edges can be smoothed by hand. Be very careful. Make certain all burrs are removed.

The 1/4 in. (6.35 mm) holes for the 3/16 in. (1.01 mm) rod are drilled using a simple jig to hold

the part in position, Fig. 18-14. The same jig can be used to position the work for drilling the mounting holes, Fig. 18-15. Remove all burrs.

The 90 deg. bends are formed using a shop-made bending jig. Fig. 18-16 shows a bend being

Fig. 18-14. Jig used to position metal for drilling holes that will hold rod.

Fig. 18-16. Making bends with a shop-made bending jig.

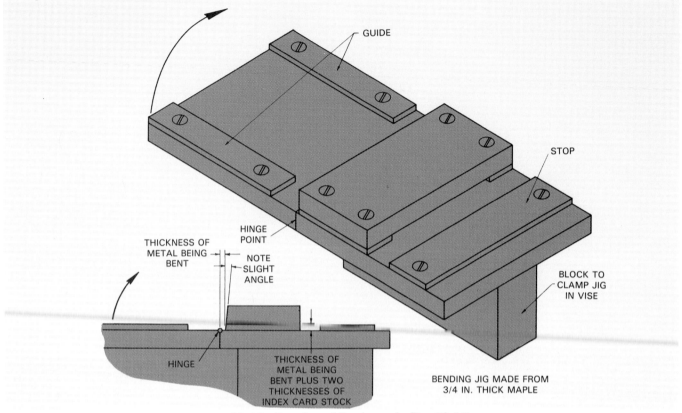

THICKNESS OF METAL BEING BENT

NOTE SLIGHT ANGLE

HINGE POINT

GUIDE

STOP

BLOCK TO CLAMP JIG IN VISE

HINGE

THICKNESS OF METAL BEING BENT PLUS TWO THICKNESSES OF INDEX CARD STOCK

BENDING JIG MADE FROM 3/4 IN. THICK MAPLE

Fig. 18-17. Drawing of jig shown in Fig. 18-16.

made with the jig. Fig. 18-17 shows a working drawing of a shop-made jig. There are two guides on the bending jig. Therefore, it can be used to make both of the required bends.

After carefully inspecting the tie rack body, it is ready to be cleaned and painted, Fig. 18-18. Spray paints are easier to clean-up afterwards than are conventional paints. Store the completed bodies until needed for final assembly.

TIE HOLDERS

There are several ways the holders (for individual ties) can be made, Fig. 18-19. They may

Fig. 18-18. Painting tie rack body with spray paint.

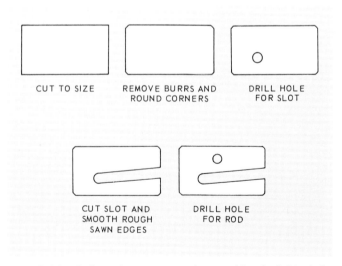

CUT TO SIZE

REMOVE BURRS AND ROUND CORNERS

DRILL HOLE FOR SLOT

CUT SLOT AND SMOOTH ROUGH SAWN EDGES

DRILL HOLE FOR ROD

Fig. 18-19. Follow these steps when making individual tie holders.

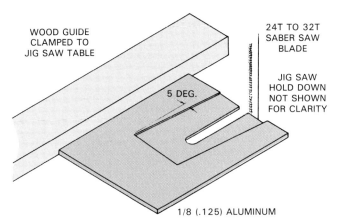

WOOD GUIDE
CLAMPED TO
JIG SAW TABLE

24T TO 32T
SABER SAW
BLADE

5 DEG.

JIG SAW
HOLD DOWN
NOT SHOWN
FOR CLARITY

1/8 (.125) ALUMINUM

Fig. 18-20. Fixture and setup for cutting slots in individual tie holders.

be cut to individual size on squaring shears, on a jigsaw or bandsaw, Fig. 18-20. Or, the slots may be cut quickly using a small milling machine. After removing burrs, round corners to remove the sharp edges. Then, carefully sand until smooth.

Inspect each part. Has each part been properly cleaned and smoothed?

When the slot in the holder is cut on a jigsaw or bandsaw, drill a hole at the end of the slot. Use a drill jig to position the part to drill the hole. It is not necessary to lay out each holder separately, if the fixture shown in Fig. 18-20 is used.

It is also possible to manufacture the holders in strip form. Using squaring shears, cut a strip of aluminum sheet as wide as the tie holder is long. The length of the strip will be set by the size of the squaring shears. The strip can also be cut on a jigsaw or bandsaw.

Lay out tie holders on the strip. Allow material for the cut, if a saw is to be used to cut the strip into individual tie holders.

The holes at the base of the slots are drilled first. Drill a hole in the first tie holder on the strip. Then place the hole over the aligning dowel on the drill jig, Fig. 18-21. After CAREFULLY aligning the jig, drill a hole in the second holder. Do not forget to clamp the jig firmly to the drill press. Drill the second hole. Remaining holes are positioned for drilling by moving the strip over so the last drilled hole is fitted over the aligning pin. Drill the required holes and remove the burrs. This may be done by using a countersink mounted in the drill press.

The slots in the tie holder are cut using the fixture shown in Fig. 18-22. A guide must be clamped to the jigsaw table. Make first cut in all holders,

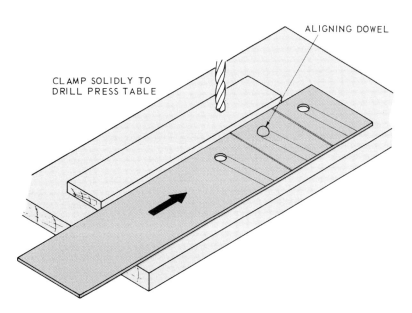

ALIGNING DOWEL

CLAMP SOLIDLY TO
DRILL PRESS TABLE

Fig. 18-21. Drill jig used to drill hole at bottom of slot, when tie holders are made in strip form.

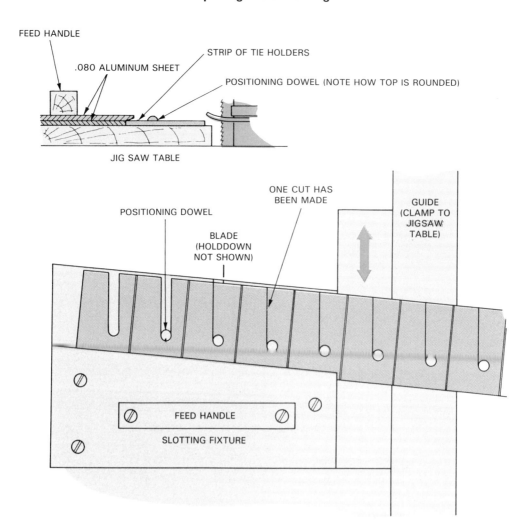

Fig. 18-22. Fixture used to position strip of tie holders so slots can be cut.

then adjust position of guide for second cut. The fixture can be mounted on the miter gauge if the slots are to be cut on a bandsaw.

The same fixture can be used if a jigsaw or bandsaw is used to cut the individual holders from the strip.

Remove all burrs and rough edges with a file.

The hole that will mount the tie holder on the rod can now be drilled. Use the jig shown in Fig. 18-23 to position the piece. In drilling it is important that the parts be fitted into the jig as shown.

After burrs are removed, sand, clean, and inspect the holder. Store until needed for assembly.

Fig. 18-23. This jig positions holder for drilling mounting hole. It is important that the part be fitted in the jig as shown.

ROD

The rod is made from 3/16 in. dia. (4.7 mm) brazing rod. However, 3/16 in. dia. cold finished steel rod may be substituted.

Cut the material to length. Using a grinder, round each end slightly. This will make threading easier.

Thread both ends. Remove any burrs, polish, and inspect.

FINAL ASSEMBLY

Parts ready for assembly are shown in Fig. 15-24. The assembly line can be operated as outlined.

1. Attach one acornnut to rod.
2. Slide rod through one end of body.
3. Fit holders to rod.
4. Slide rod thorugh other end of body.
5. Attach second acorn nut to rod.
6. Make a final inspection.

MASS-PRODUCING A TABLE LAMP

Mass-producing the lamp, shown in Fig. 18-25, involves a number of metalworking procedures. For construction details on the lamp, see Fig. 18-26, on pages 204 and 205.

Fig. 18-25. Mass-produced table lamp.

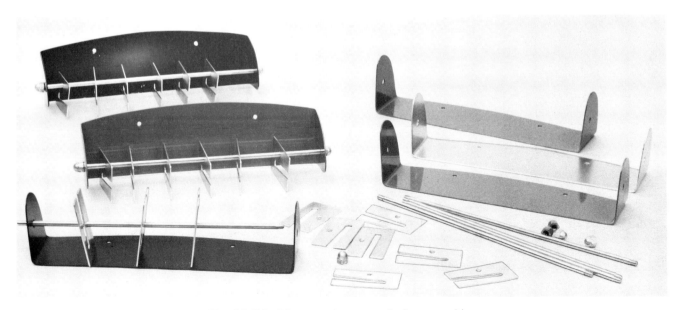

Fig. 18-24. These parts are ready for assembly.

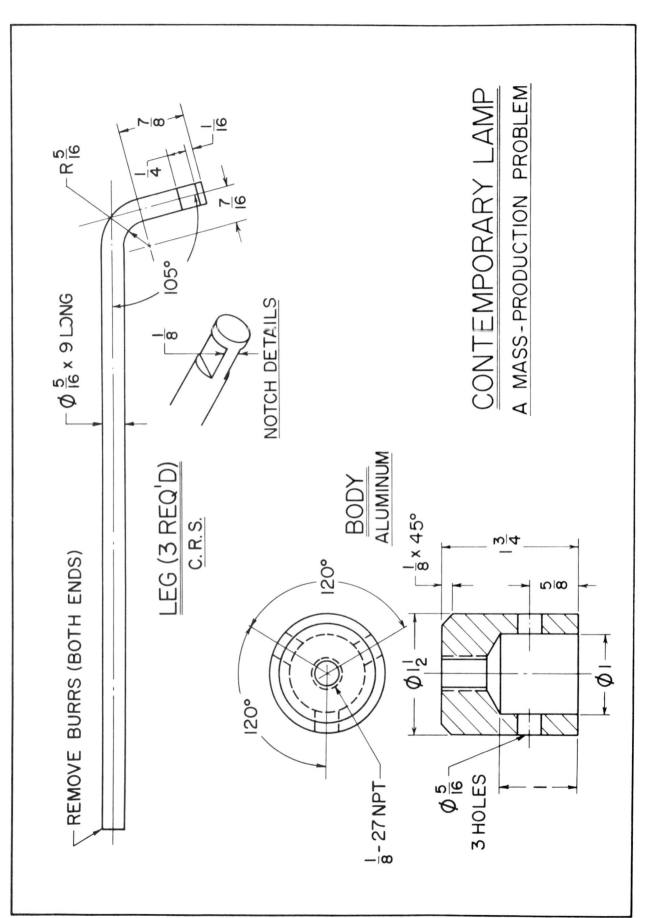

REMOVE BURRS (BOTH ENDS)

Ø 5/16 × 9 LONG

R 5/16

105°

7/8

1/4

1/16

7/16

LEG (3 REQ'D)
C.R.S.

1/8

NOTCH DETAILS

BODY
ALUMINUM

120°

120°

1/8 - 27 NPT

Ø 5/16
3 HOLES

Ø 1 1/2

Ø 1

1/8 × 45°

1 3/4

5/8

CONTEMPORARY LAMP
A MASS-PRODUCTION PROBLEM

Fig. 18-26. Plans for the lamp shown in Fig. 18-25.

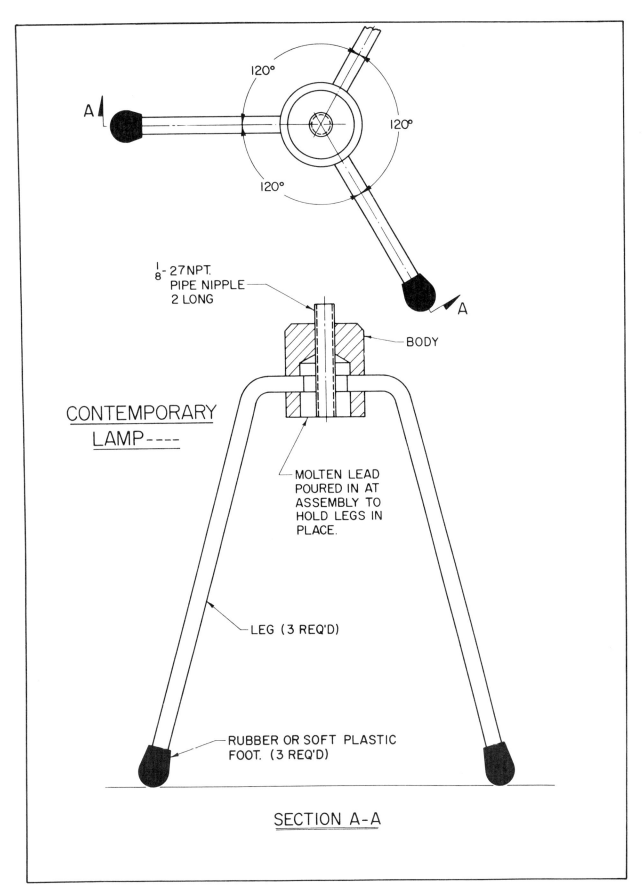

120°

120°

120°

$\frac{1}{8}$-27 N.P.T.
PIPE NIPPLE
2 LONG

A

A

BODY

CONTEMPORARY
LAMP----

MOLTEN LEAD
POURED IN AT
ASSEMBLY TO
HOLD LEGS IN
PLACE.

LEG (3 REQ'D)

RUBBER OR SOFT PLASTIC
FOOT. (3 REQ'D)

SECTION A-A

Fig. 18-26. Plans for lamp shown in Fig. 18-25. (continued)

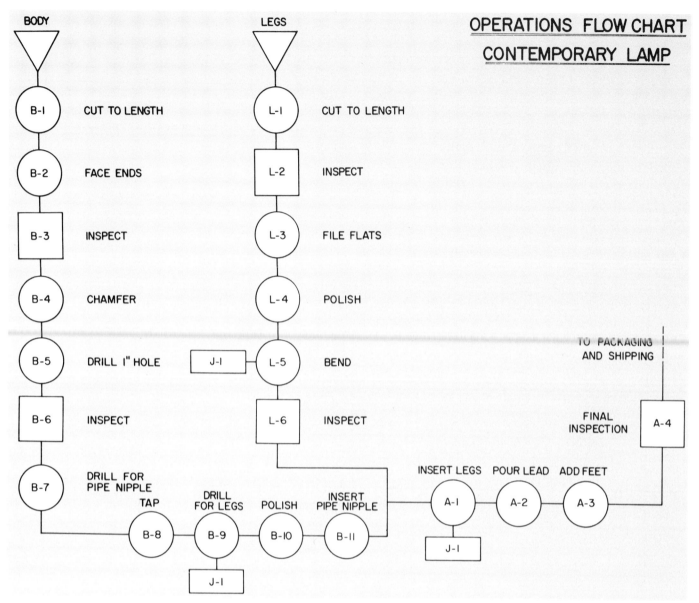

Fig. 18-27. Flow chart shows manufacturing sequences of various parts.

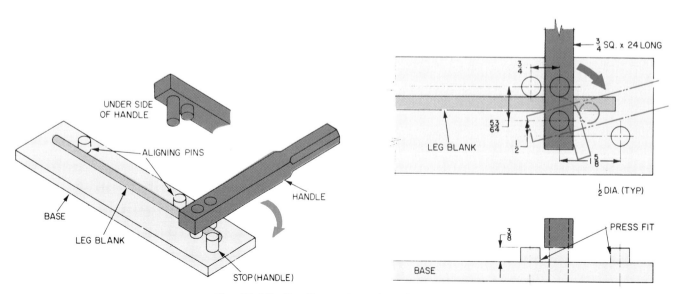

Fig. 18-28. Bending tool used to shape legs.

An OPERATIONS FLOW CHART is given in Fig. 18-27. At each step, students assigned the task of preparing production equipment should ask if there is any way to improve production or if there is any way to improve the product. Any approved changes should be noted and incorporated into the plan.

A bending tool used to form the legs is shown in Fig. 18-28. A drill jig used to locate the holes for the legs is shown in Fig. 18-29.

Figs. 18-30 and 18-31 show gauges designed to make the length of the legs and the angle at which the legs are bent the same.

To attach the legs to the body, molten metal is used. It is poured into the body cavity of the base. This is done after positioning the pipe nipple and legs, Fig. 18-32. Special training for handling of molten metals is a "must."

Another solution is to pack plastic steel around the positioned legs. The rubber or plastic feet, lamp fixtures, wire, and plug must be purchased commercially. Choose a shade of appropriate size and shape as the final step.

PRODUCTION PROBLEM IDEAS

You have seen how two student-designed production problems have been accomplished. The following projects are offered as ideas. Your class may use them or research and develop a project of your own design. In either case, you will have the opportunity to solve a production problem in your school metals lab.

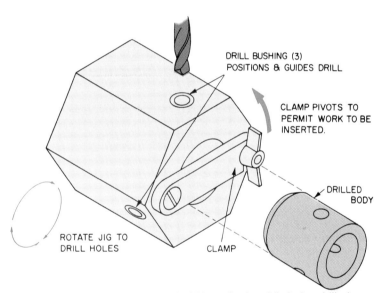

Fig. 18-29. Drill jig used to hold lamp body while being drilled.

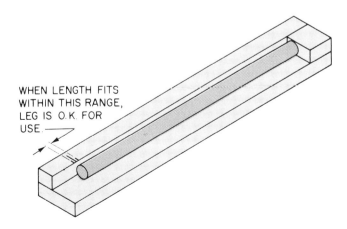

Fig. 18-30. Gauge used to check length of legs.

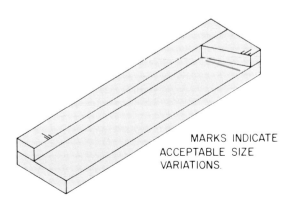

Fig. 18-31. Gauge used to check angle of bend in leg.

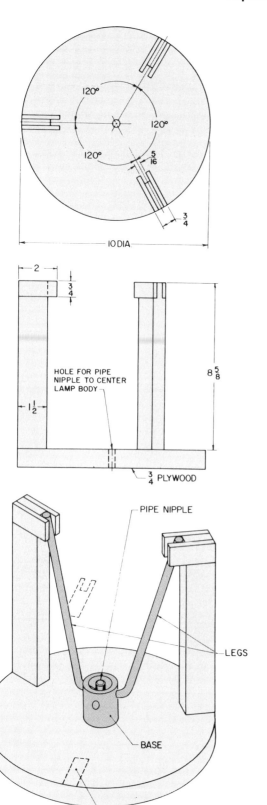

Fig. 18-32. Fixture holds legs while molten lead is poured.

PRODUCTION PROBLEM IDEA I: TRIVET

A trivet is a device used to prevent hot dishes, pans, etc., from damaging the surface of a table or a countertop. The trivet is fabricated from nine pieces of metal. The tooling needed is shown in Fig. 18-33.

PRODUCTION PROBLEM IDEA II: GARDEN TROWEL

The garden trowel is inexpensive to produce. Although it has only two pieces, a number of operations are required to produce them.

When manufacturing the trowel, all of the information needed is shown in Fig. 18-34 (top), except that the length of the 1/8 in. x 1/2 in. hot rolled steel handle is not furnished. Can you calculate the length of the metal?

The trowel can be painted flat black or a bright color.

PRODUCTION PROBLEM IDEA III: LETTER HOLDER

The letter holder, Fig. 18-34 (bottom), offers many design variations. The accent strip can be initials or any simple geometric form. Assemble by soldering.

After the letter holder has been assembled and cleaned and polished, it should be given a thin coat of clear lacquer to prevent the brass from tarnishing.

SAFETY NOTE: WEAR APPROPRIATE SAFETY EQUIPMENT AND HAVE AMPLE VENTILATION WHEN SPRAYING LACQUER OR PAINT.

REVIEW OF ACTIVITY

1. What problems were encountered in mass-producing your project? How could they have been avoided?
2. How do you think that the project could have been improved?
3. What was the most interesting part of the activity? Why was it interesting?
4. What was the most challenging part of the activity? Why was it challenging?

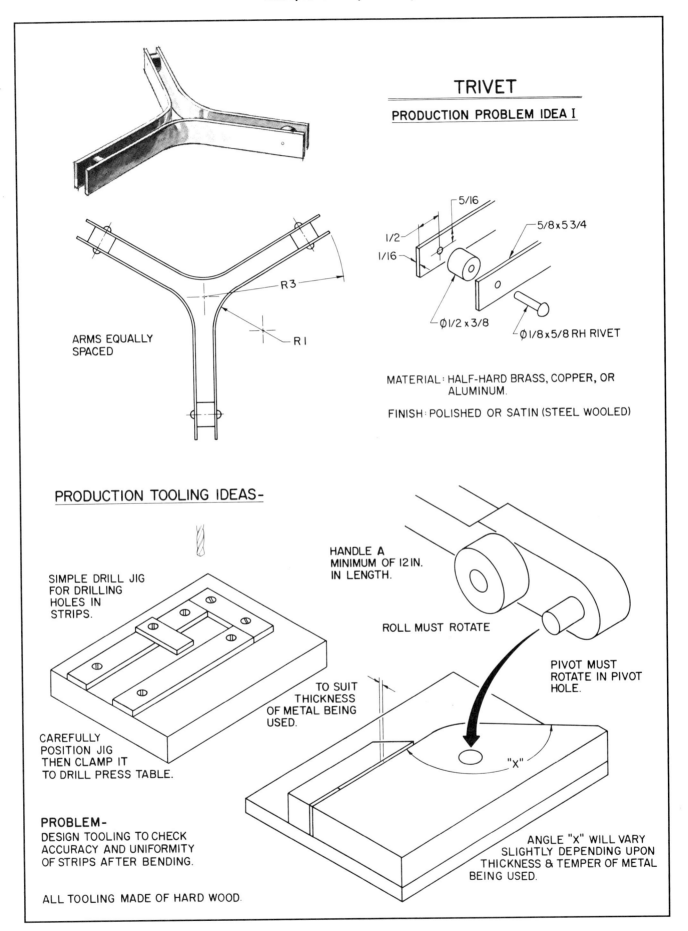

TRIVET

PRODUCTION PROBLEM IDEA I

5/16
1/2
1/16
5/8 x 5 3/4
Ø 1/2 x 3/8
Ø 1/8 x 5/8 RH RIVET

ARMS EQUALLY
SPACED

R 3
R 1

MATERIAL: HALF-HARD BRASS, COPPER, OR
ALUMINUM.

FINISH: POLISHED OR SATIN (STEEL WOOLED)

PRODUCTION TOOLING IDEAS—

SIMPLE DRILL JIG
FOR DRILLING
HOLES IN
STRIPS.

CAREFULLY
POSITION JIG
THEN CLAMP IT
TO DRILL PRESS TABLE.

PROBLEM—
DESIGN TOOLING TO CHECK
ACCURACY AND UNIFORMITY
OF STRIPS AFTER BENDING.

ALL TOOLING MADE OF HARD WOOD.

HANDLE A
MINIMUM OF 12 IN.
IN LENGTH.

ROLL MUST ROTATE

PIVOT MUST
ROTATE IN PIVOT
HOLE.

TO SUIT
THICKNESS
OF METAL BEING
USED.

"X"

ANGLE "X" WILL VARY
SLIGHTLY DEPENDING UPON
THICKNESS & TEMPER OF METAL
BEING USED.

Fig. 18-33. Trivet project.

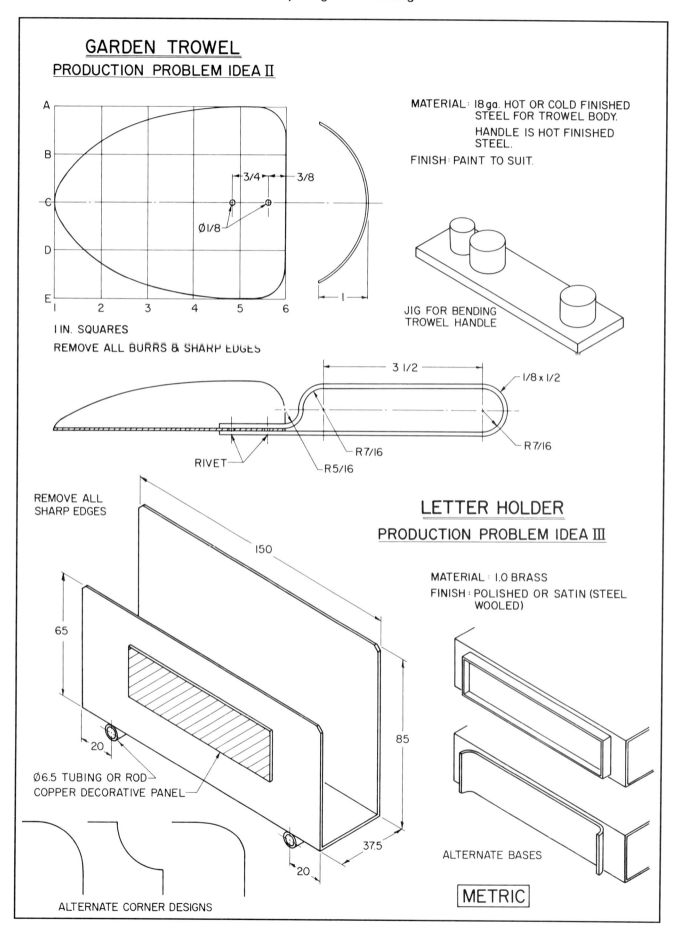

GARDEN TROWEL
PRODUCTION PROBLEM IDEA II

MATERIAL: 18 ga. HOT OR COLD FINISHED STEEL FOR TROWEL BODY.

HANDLE IS HOT FINISHED STEEL.

FINISH: PAINT TO SUIT.

3/4 3/8

Ø1/8

1 IN. SQUARES

REMOVE ALL BURRS & SHARP EDGES

JIG FOR BENDING TROWEL HANDLE

3 1/2

1/8 x 1/2

RIVET

R 7/16

R 5/16

R 7/16

REMOVE ALL SHARP EDGES

LETTER HOLDER
PRODUCTION PROBLEM IDEA III

MATERIAL: 1.0 BRASS

FINISH: POLISHED OR SATIN (STEEL WOOLED)

150

65

85

20

37.5

20

Ø6.5 TUBING OR ROD

COPPER DECORATIVE PANEL

ALTERNATE BASES

ALTERNATE CORNER DESIGNS

METRIC

Fig. 18-34. Garden trowel and letter holder projects.

TEST YOUR KNOWLEDGE, Unit 18

Please do not write in the text. Place your answers on a separate sheet of paper.

1. A company name should be appropriate, businesslike, and _____.
2. Which of the following does NOT need to be elected when electing company officials?
   a. Art director.
   b. General manager.
   c. Office manager.
   d. Safety director.
3. Which company official is expected to conduct general supervision over the entire activity?
4. Who is expected to maintain attendance records?
5. Many companies raise money by selling _____.
6. What is the formula for determining product selling price?

TECHNICAL TERMS TO LEARN

business activity
employee
entrepreneur
financing
flow chart
General Manager
liquidate
loss
manufacturing
mass production
Office Manager
product
profit
prospect
Purchasing Agent
receipts
records
Safety Director
sales
Sales Manager
stock
stockholder
supervision

ACTIVITIES

1. Visit a factory that mass-produces a product. Then, visit a shop that produces objects on a limited basis.
2. Discuss the financing of a small business with a banker. Report to your class.
3. Discuss the steps followed to advertise a product with an advertising professional. How would you advertise the tie rack described in this unit?

Unit 19 . . . .

Projects

Designing and constructing metalworking projects will teach you to think and to plan.

Your projects should be items you are interested in making. The projects, when completed, should compare favorably, in quality, with items available commercially.

NAPKIN RINGS

Material: Aluminum.

Finish: Polished or satin finish.
Remove burrs, sharp edges.

The designs shown are but a few of the many geometric forms that can be used for this project. Use your imagination and design your own.

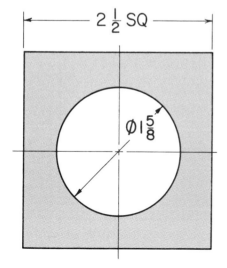

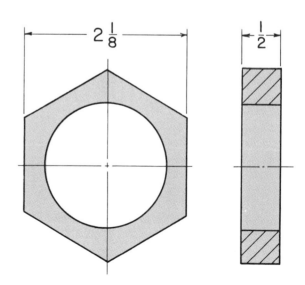

SCREWDRIVER

1. Material: Handle—Aluminum.
   Shank—Drill Rod.

2. Forge blade to shape.

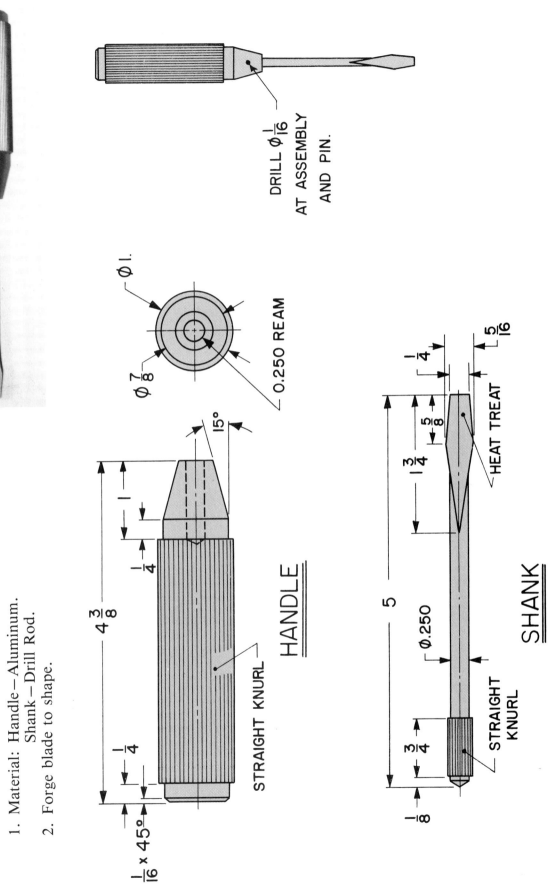

DRILL $\phi\frac{1}{16}$
AT ASSEMBLY
AND PIN.

ϕ 1.

$\phi\frac{7}{8}$

0.250 REAM

15°

1

$\frac{1}{4}$

$4\frac{3}{8}$

$\frac{1}{4}$

$\frac{1}{16}$ × 45°

STRAIGHT KNURL

HANDLE

$\frac{1}{4}$

$\frac{5}{16}$

$\frac{5}{8}$

$1\frac{3}{4}$

HEAT TREAT

5

ϕ.250

$\frac{3}{4}$

STRAIGHT
KNURL

$\frac{1}{8}$

SHANK

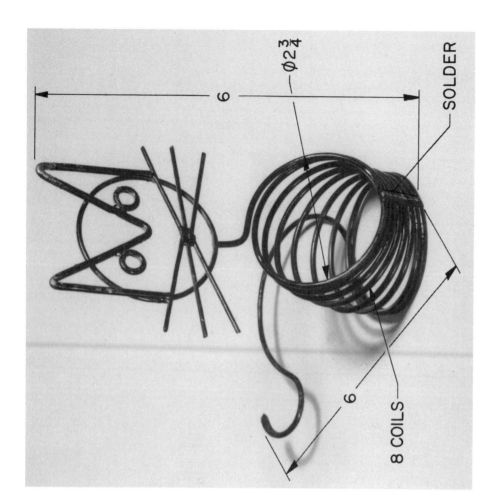

6

Ø$2\frac{3}{4}$

SOLDER

8 COILS

6

1. Use 1/8 in. (3.2 mm) diameter wire to form the figure. This may be copper wire, brazing rod, or steel coat hangers.
2. Solder all joints.
3. Finish by painting flat black.

WIRY CAT

$\frac{1}{2}$ SQUARES

FACE DETAILS

SMALL PLANTER

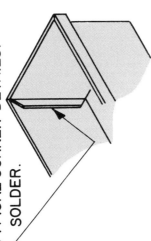

TYPICAL CORNER DETAILS. SOLDER.

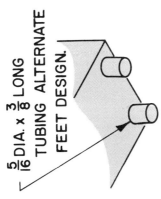

$\frac{5}{16}$ DIA. x $\frac{3}{8}$ LONG TUBING ALTERNATE FEET DESIGN.

1. Material: 18 ga. copper or brass.
2. Finish: Planish. Buff all exterior surfaces. Apply satin finish to interior surfaces. Protect polished surfaces with clear lacquer spray.

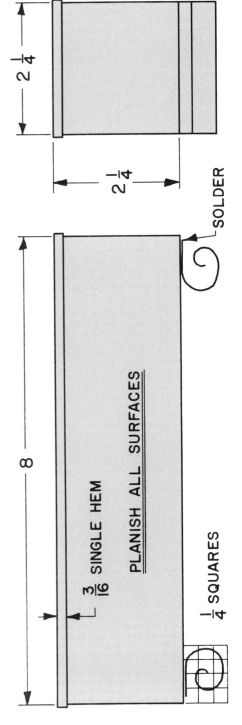

$2\frac{1}{4}$

$2\frac{1}{4}$

SOLDER

8

$\frac{3}{16}$ SINGLE HEM

PLANISH ALL SURFACES

$\frac{1}{4}$ SQUARES

215

COLD CHISEL

1. Material: 7/16 hexagonal or octagonal tool steel.
2. Heat and forge to shape.
3. File smooth and grind chamfer on chisel head.
4. Heat treat and sharpen.

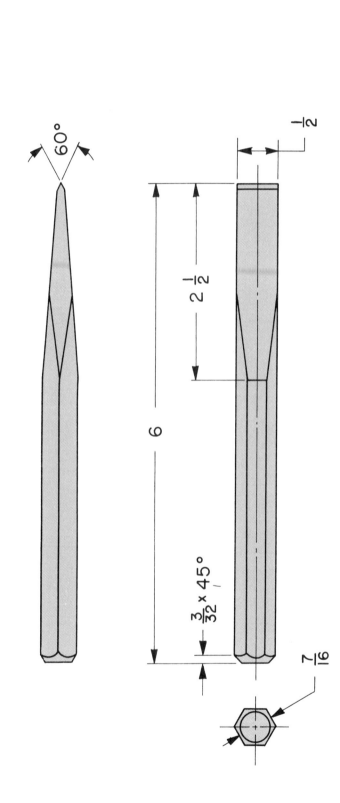

60°

6

2 1/2

1/2

3/32 x 45°

7/16

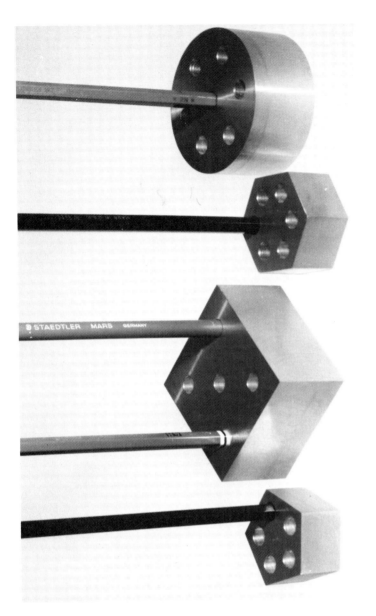

PENCIL HOLDERS

1. Material: Aluminum.
2. Finish: Polished or as machined.
3. Attach felt to bottom.
4. Remove all burrs and sharp edges.

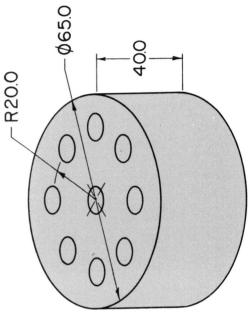

R20.0

ø65.0

40.0

6-8 HOLES EQUALLY SPACED

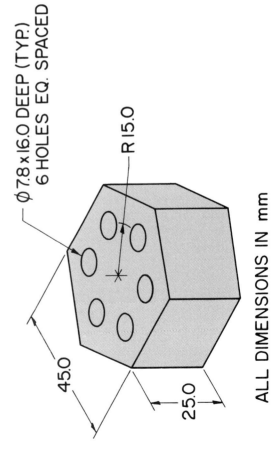

ø7.8 x 16.0 DEEP (TYP.)
6 HOLES EQ. SPACED

R 15.0

45.0

25.0

ALL DIMENSIONS IN mm

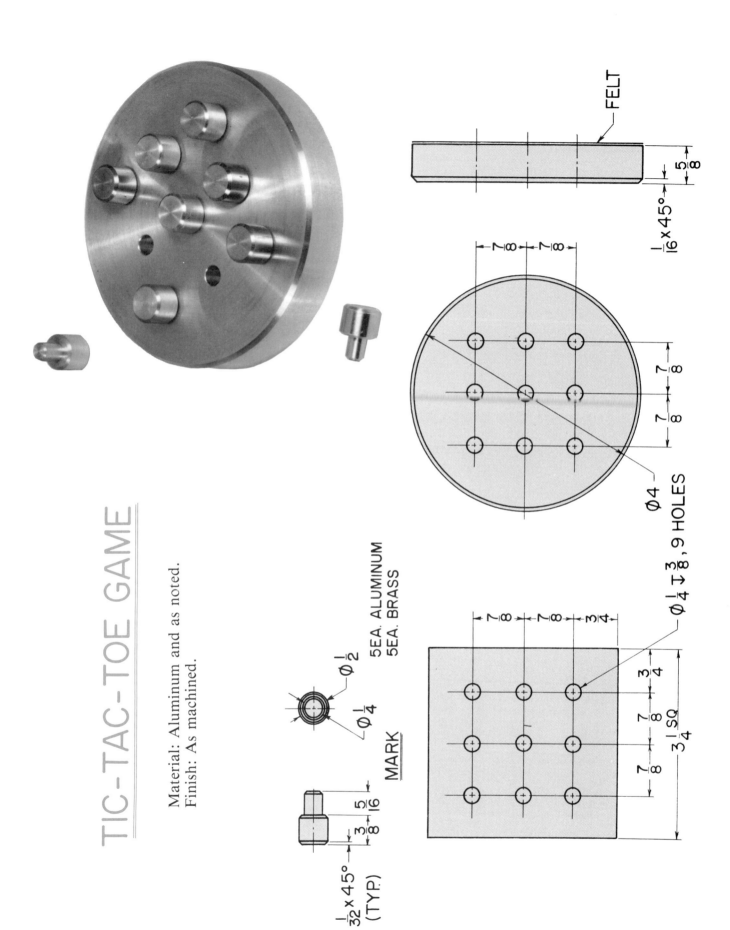

TIC-TAC-TOE GAME

Material: Aluminum and as noted.
Finish: As machined.

FELT

$\frac{5}{8}$

$\frac{1}{16} \times 45°$

$\frac{7}{8}$ $\frac{7}{8}$

$\frac{7}{8}$

$\frac{7}{8}$

$\varnothing 4$

$\varnothing \frac{1}{4} \bar{\downarrow} \frac{3}{8}$, 9 HOLES

$\frac{7}{8}$ $\frac{7}{8}$ $\frac{3}{4}$

$\frac{3}{4}$

$\frac{7}{8}$

$3\frac{1}{4}$ SQ

$\frac{7}{8}$

$3\frac{1}{4}$

$\varnothing \frac{1}{2}$

$\varnothing \frac{1}{4}$

5 EA. ALUMINUM
5 EA. BRASS

MARK

$\frac{5}{16}$

$\frac{3}{8}$

$\frac{1}{32} \times 45°$
(TYP.)

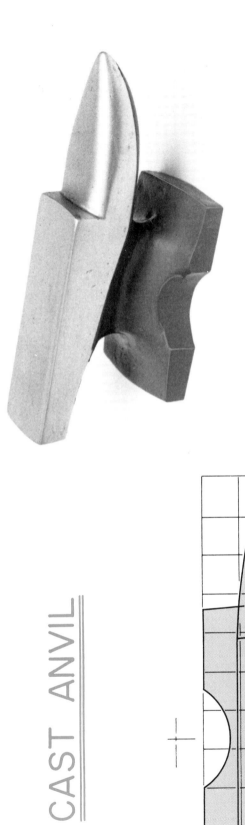

CAST ANVIL

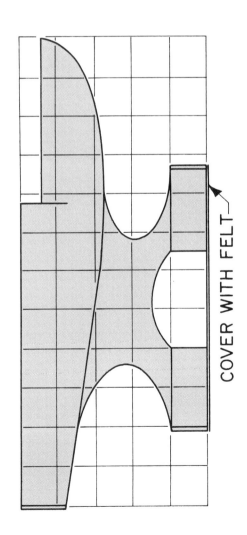

½ SQUARES

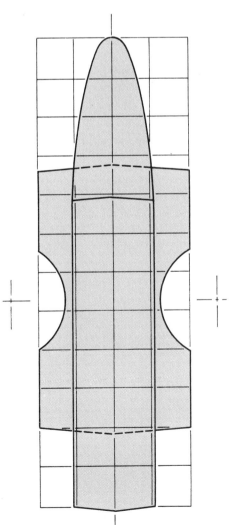

COVER WITH FELT

219

PATIO TABLE

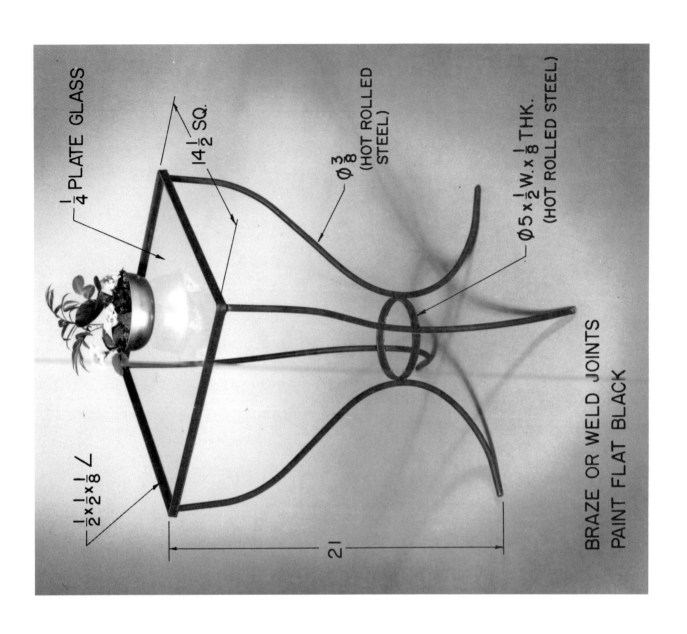

¼ PLATE GLASS

14½ SQ.

Ø⅜ (HOT ROLLED STEEL)

Ø5 x ½ W. x ⅛ THK. (HOT ROLLED STEEL)

½ x ½ x ⅛

21

BRAZE OR WELD JOINTS
PAINT FLAT BLACK

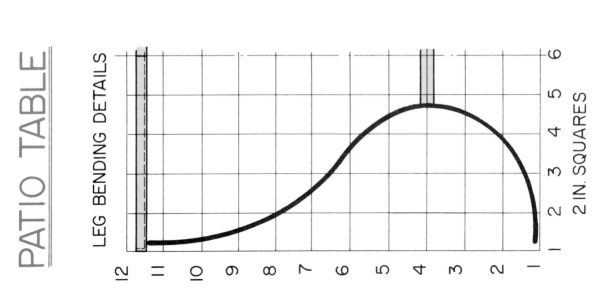

LEG BENDING DETAILS

2 IN. SQUARES

MAIL BOX DESIGN PROBLEM

Design and develop patterns, then manufacture a mail box that will meet postal regulations. Get ideas and basic dimensions from mail order catalogs and home planning magazines. Use 26 ga. sheet metal in either a plain or embossed pattern. It may be made from copper, brass, or aluminum. Larger mail boxes can be made from galvanized sheet steel. Join seams by spot welding or soldering.

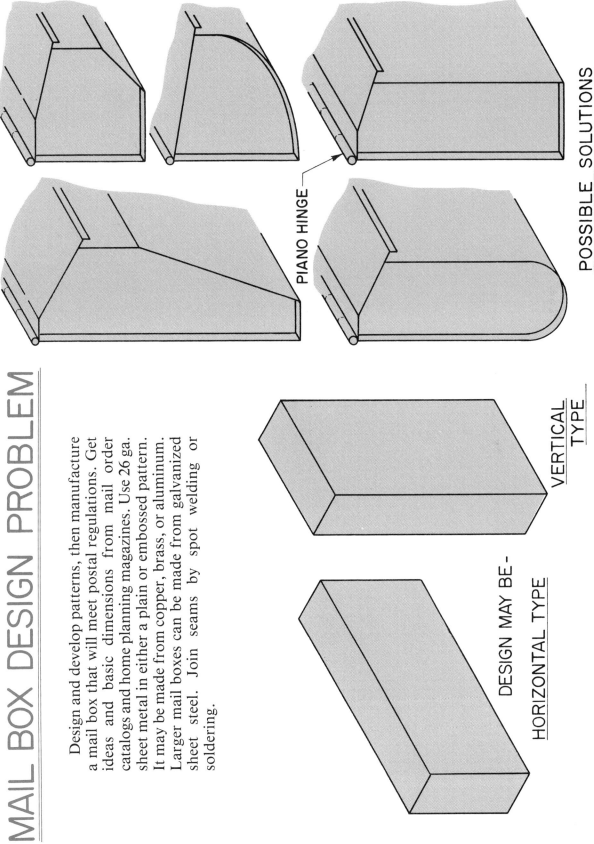

POSSIBLE SOLUTIONS

PIANO HINGE

VERTICAL TYPE

HORIZONTAL TYPE

DESIGN MAY BE -

MACHINED PAPER WEIGHT

Material: Aluminum, brass, or cold finished steel.
Finish: As machined or polished.

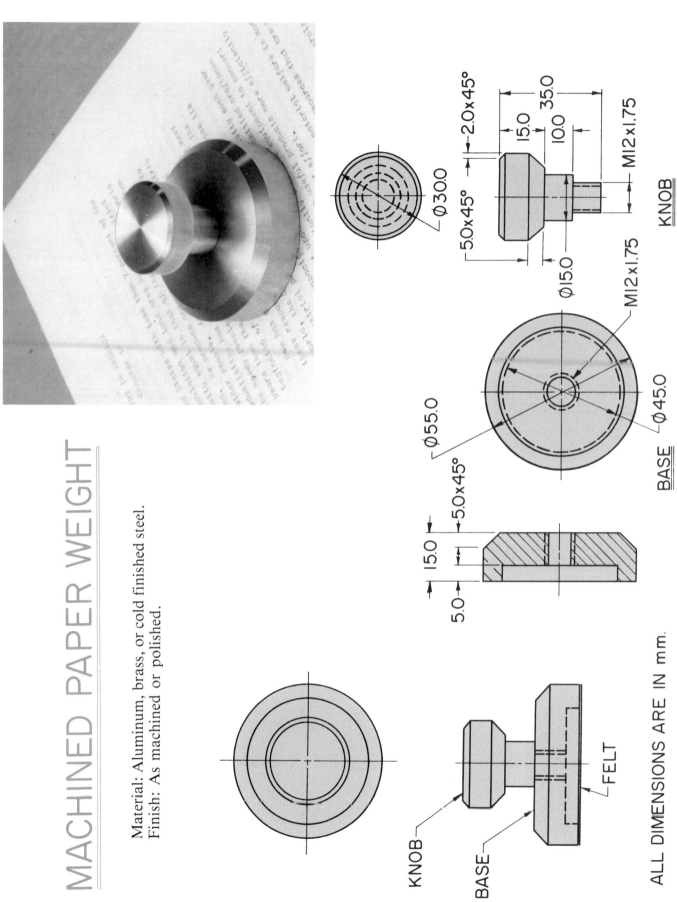

Ø30.0

2.0x45°
35.0
15.0
10.0
5.0x45°
Ø15.0
M12x1.75

KNOB

Ø55.0
M12x1.75
Ø45.0
5.0x45°
15.0
5.0

BASE

KNOB
BASE
FELT

ALL DIMENSIONS ARE IN mm.

222

HANDYMAN'S SPECIAL

1. Cold finished steel may be used. However, precision ground tool and die steel is preferred.
2. Saw and file or machine the head to shape. It is recommended that the handle slot be milled.
3. Shape the handle to the size shown. Drill holes for the handle. Fit the handle to the head and drill mounting holes.
4. Heat treat the hammer head, screwdriver, and bottle opener end of the handle. Harden and temper if tool and die steel is used. Case harden if cold finished steel is used.
5. Polish.
6. Mount the wooden handles.

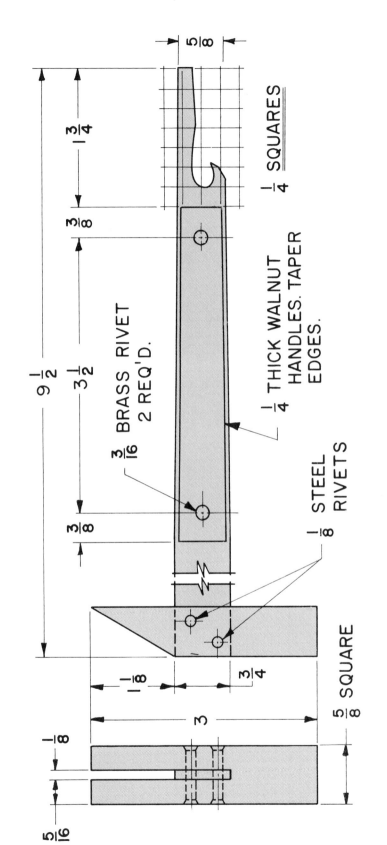

1. Material: 0.025 aluminum. The roof should be made of 0.025 embossed aluminum.
2. Use round head rivets and sheet metal screws for assembly.
3. Paint the outside surfaces light green. The roof may be left natural.
4. Design a suitable mount.
5. Remove all sharp edges and burrs.

DESIGN PROBLEM

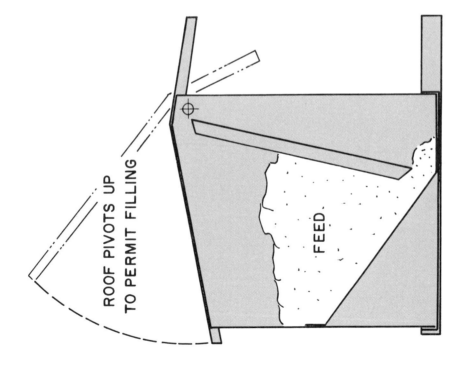

ROOF PIVOTS UP TO PERMIT FILLING

FEED.

TYPICAL CROSS-SECTION OF BIRD FEEDER SHOWN

TRIVET

Trivets are used to prevent hot pans and pots from scorching or damaging tabletops.
1. Material: Brass or hot finished steel. Walnut handle.
2. Finish: Brass — Polished. Steel — Painted flat black.
3. Remove all sharp edges.
4. Smooth all brazed joints.

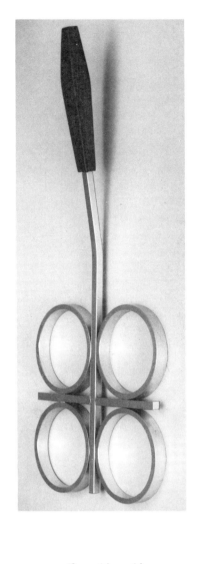

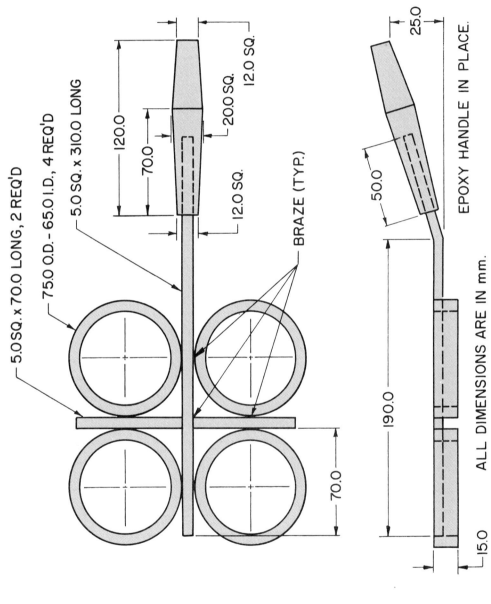

5.0 SQ. x 70.0 LONG, 2 REQ'D

75.0 O.D. - 65.0 I.D., 4 REQ'D

5.0 SQ. x 310.0 LONG

120.0

12.0 SQ.

20.0 SQ.

70.0

12.0 SQ.

BRAZE (TYP.)

70.0

25.0

50.0

190.0

15.0

EPOXY HANDLE IN PLACE.

ALL DIMENSIONS ARE IN mm.

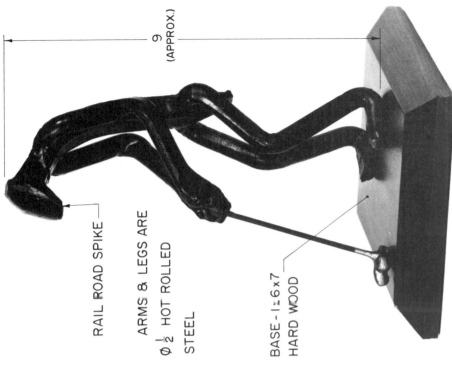

9 (APPROX.)

RAIL ROAD SPIKE

ARMS & LEGS ARE
$\varnothing \frac{1}{2}$ HOT ROLLED
STEEL

BASE - 1:6x7
HARD WOOD

DESIGN PROBLEM

Material: As noted on photo.
Finish: Paint metal figure flat black.

This is a project that can be used as a gift for a friend who is a golf enthusiast.

Using a little "think power" you can come up with a variation of the spike man that can be used to depict another sport or occupation.

Be careful to remove all burrs and rough edges before applying the finish.

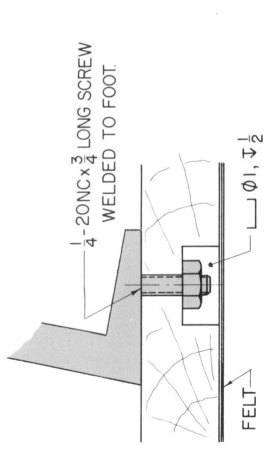

$\frac{1}{4}$ - 20NC x $\frac{3}{4}$ LONG SCREW
WELDED TO FOOT.

$\varnothing 1, \mp \frac{1}{2}$

FELT

CENTER PUNCH

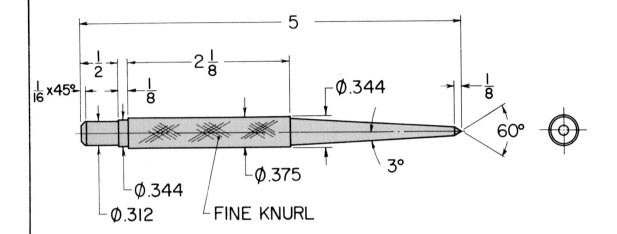

MACHINING SEQUENCE:

1. CUT A PIECE OF DRILL ROD $5\frac{1}{2}$ LONG.
   A. FACE BOTH ENDS.
   B. CENTER DRILL ONE END.

2. MACHINE CENTER DRILLED END AS FOLLOWS:

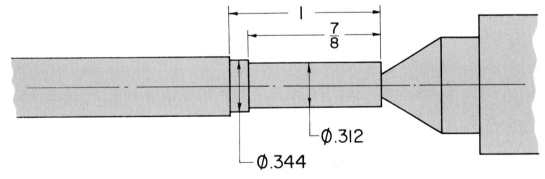

3. KNURL.

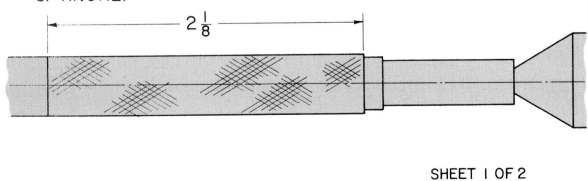

4. REVERSE WORK IN CHUCK.

5. MACHINE TO DIAMETER.

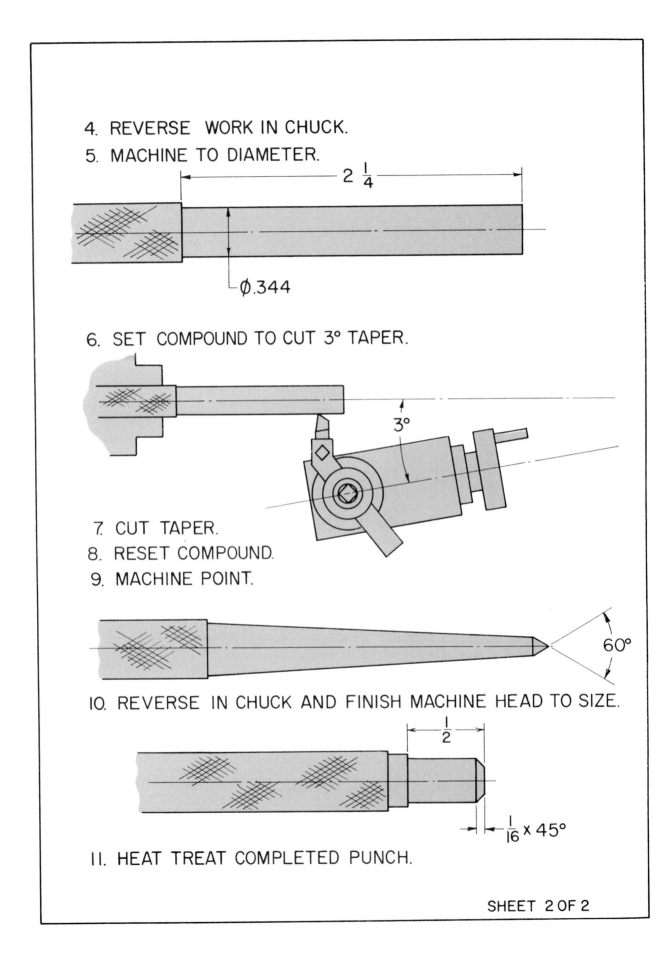

2 $\frac{1}{4}$

Ø.344

6. SET COMPOUND TO CUT 3° TAPER.

3°

7. CUT TAPER.

8. RESET COMPOUND.

9. MACHINE POINT.

60°

10. REVERSE IN CHUCK AND FINISH MACHINE HEAD TO SIZE.

$\frac{1}{2}$

$\frac{1}{16}$ × 45°

11. HEAT TREAT COMPLETED PUNCH.

SHEET 2 OF 2

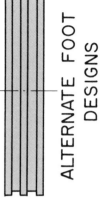

RAISED BOWL

1. Material: 14 ga. copper, brass, pewter, or aluminum.
2. Finish: Planish all surfaces and buff all exterior surfaces. Apply a satin finish to the interior of the bowl.
3. Solder base to bowl body.

$\phi 2\frac{1}{2}$

ALTERNATE FOOT DESIGNS

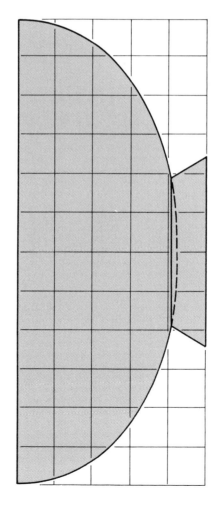

1 IN. OR $\frac{1}{2}$ IN. SQUARES

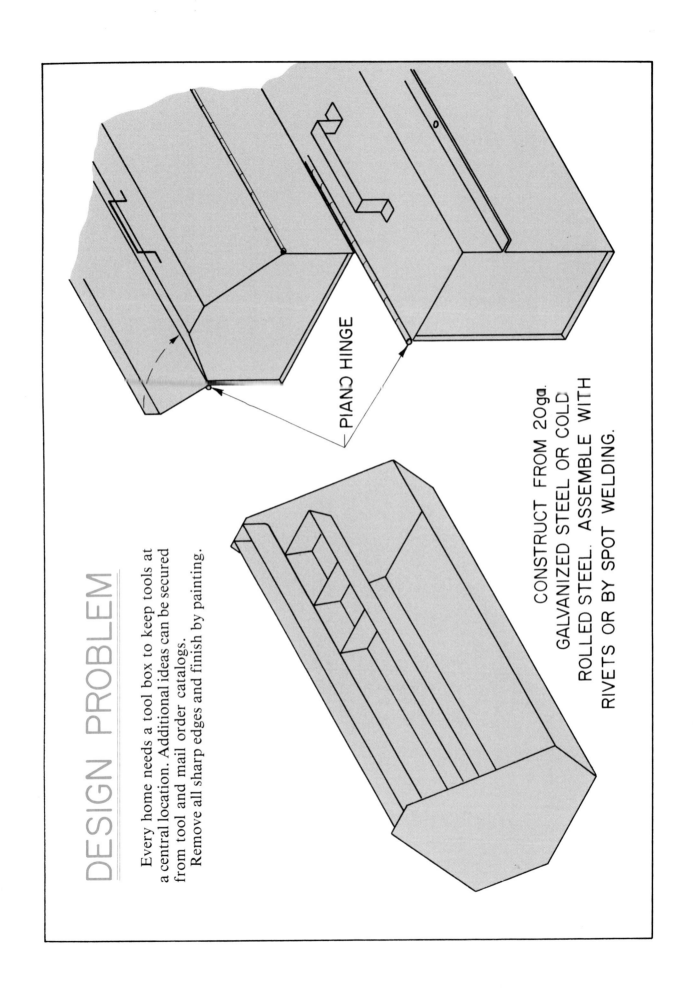

DESIGN PROBLEM

Every home needs a tool box to keep tools at a central location. Additional ideas can be secured from tool and mail order catalogs.

Remove all sharp edges and finish by painting.

PIANO HINGE

CONSTRUCT FROM 20ga. GALVANIZED STEEL OR COLD ROLLED STEEL. ASSEMBLE WITH RIVETS OR BY SPOT WELDING.

CANDLE HOLDER

Material: Cast aluminum.
Finish: Polished or satin finish.

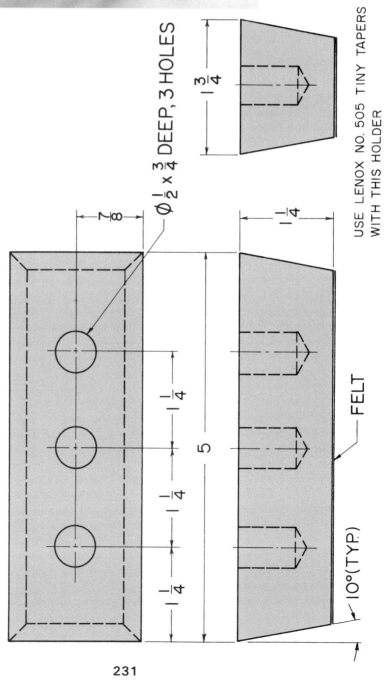

$\emptyset \frac{1}{2} \times \frac{3}{4}$ DEEP, 3 HOLES

$1\frac{3}{4}$

USE LENOX NO. 505 TINY TAPERS
WITH THIS HOLDER

$\frac{7}{8}$

$1\frac{1}{4}$

$1\frac{1}{4}$

$1\frac{1}{4}$

$1\frac{1}{4}$

5

$1\frac{1}{4}$

FELT

10°(TYP.)

231

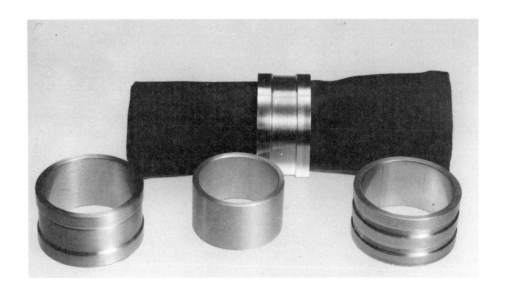

NAPKIN RINGS

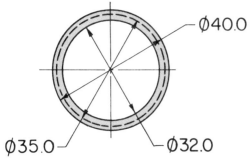

⌀40.0

⌀35.0

⌀32.0

1. Material: Aluminum or brass.
2. Finish: As machined, polished, or satin finish. Brass may be silver plated.
3. Remove all sharp edges and burrs.

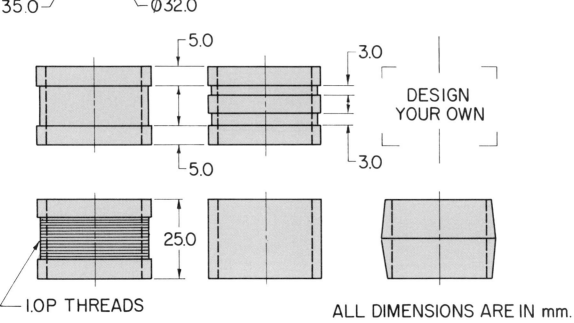

5.0

5.0

3.0

3.0

DESIGN YOUR OWN

25.0

1.0P THREADS

ALL DIMENSIONS ARE IN mm.

CHOW TIME CHIME

Material: Hot finished mild steel.
Finish: Paint flat black.

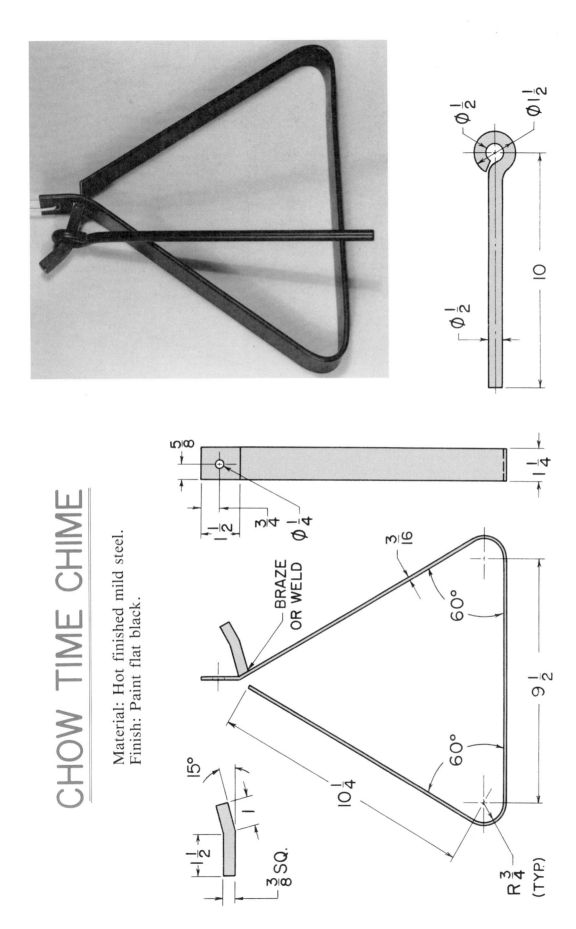

METAL STRIP SCULPTURE

This is a project for your imagination. The project illustrated is presented only as a suggestion.

Metal sculptures may be made of brass, copper, or tin plate. Assemble with solder.

Finish by polishing, painting, or electroplating. Remove all burrs and sharp edges and wash away all flux used in soldering.

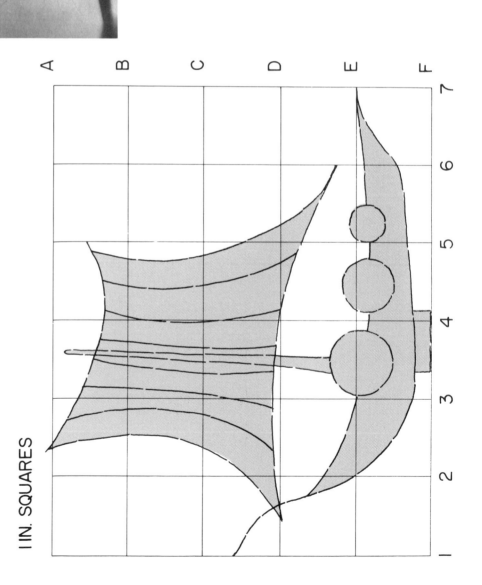

1 IN. SQUARES

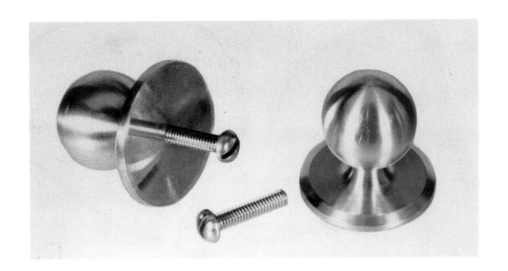

DRAWER PULL

Material: Aluminum.

Finish: Buff to a high polish or use fine abrasive paper for a satin finish.

This project provides a real challenge for the student who likes to operate the metal lathe. It is recommended that the student practice on hardwood before using the more expensive aluminum.

A full size template will make the job easier.

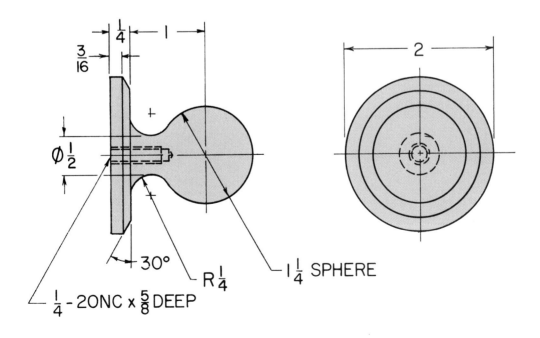

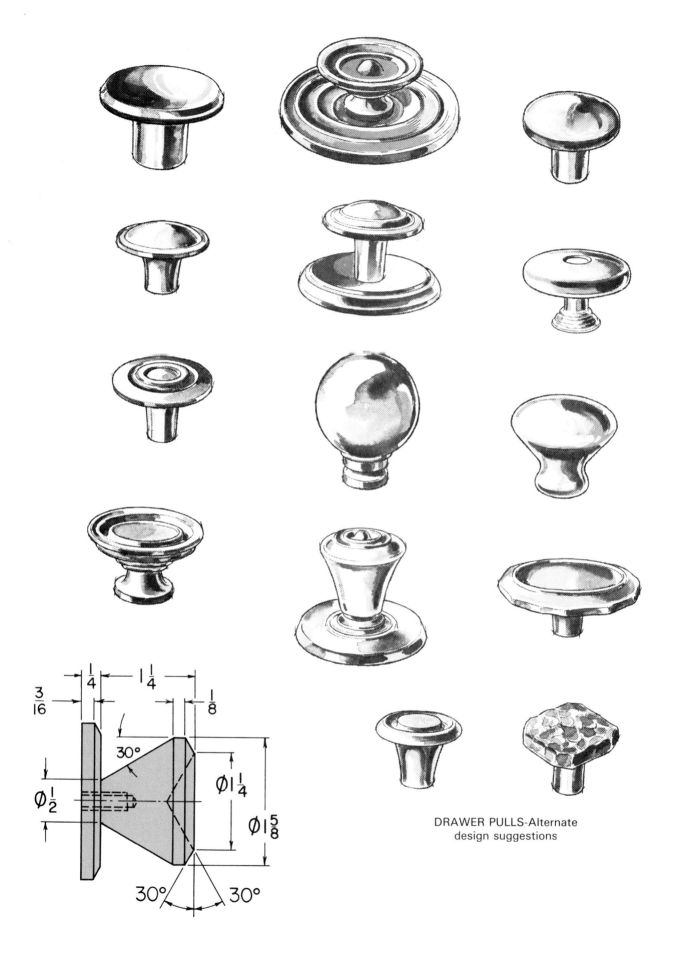

$\frac{3}{16}$

$\frac{1}{4}$

$1\frac{1}{4}$

$\frac{1}{8}$

30°

$\emptyset\frac{1}{2}$

$\emptyset 1\frac{1}{4}$

$\emptyset 1\frac{5}{8}$

30°

30°

DRAWER PULLS-Alternate
design suggestions

236

DESIGN PROBLEM

Material: Horseshoe nails and scrap metal.
Finish: Spray paint silver or gold.

These novel figures make fine gifts. Think of the many types of work and play figures you can design — ball players, golfers, swimmers, musicians, etc.

The horseshoe nails are held together by brazing, soldering, or with epoxy adhesives. Be sure the work is clean before joining the parts and painting them.

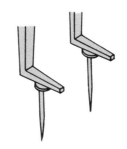

Braze or solder small nails
to feet.

$5\frac{1}{2}$

$\frac{1}{2}$ x 2 x 2 HARD WOOD

MODERN GAVEL

Material: Aluminum.
Finish: As machined.

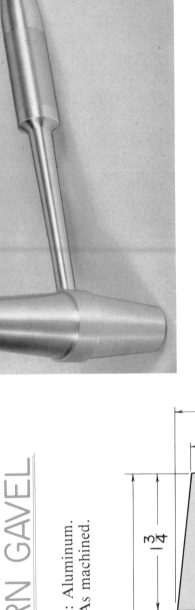

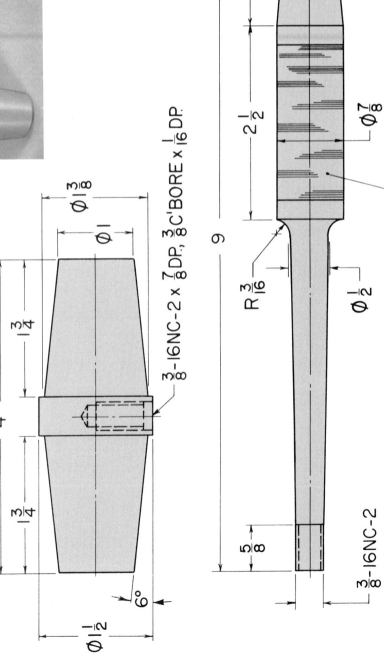

$\frac{3}{8}$-16NC-2 x $\frac{7}{8}$DP, $\frac{3}{8}$C'BORE x $\frac{1}{16}$DP.

$\phi 1\frac{3}{8}$

$\phi 1$

$1\frac{3}{4}$

$1\frac{3}{4}$

4

6°

$\phi 1\frac{1}{2}$

$\phi \frac{1}{2}$

2

$2\frac{1}{2}$

$\phi \frac{7}{8}$

40 THDS PER INCH

9

R$\frac{3}{16}$

$\phi \frac{1}{2}$

$\frac{5}{8}$

$\frac{3}{8}$-16NC-2

WIRE WALL PLAQUE

1. Use 1/8 in. diameter wire to form the figures. It may be copper wire, brazing rod, or steel coat hangers.
2. Solder all joints.
3. Finish by painting flat black.

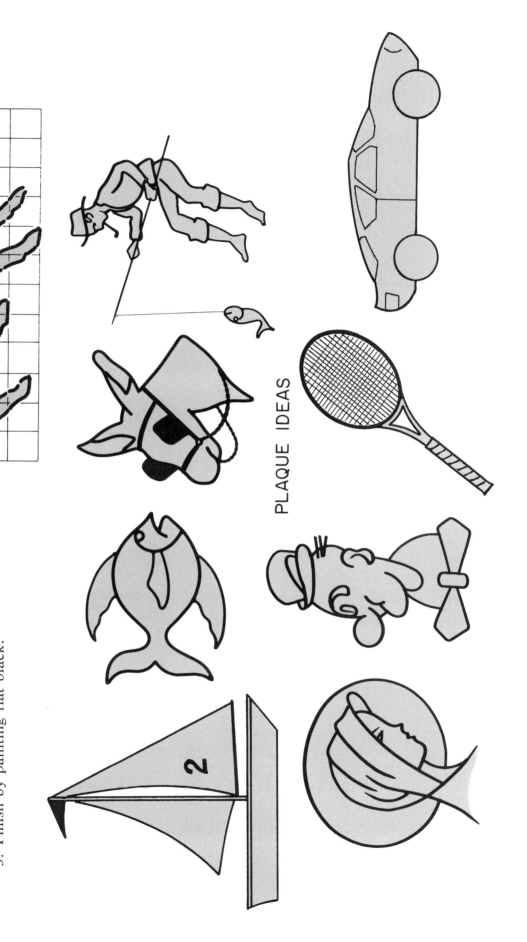

I SQUARES

PLAQUE IDEAS

BOOK ENDS

The book ends shown were made from 4 x 4 wide flange structural steel. Your book ends can be made from one of the many different shapes and sizes of structural steel and aluminum extrusions available.

Finish by removing all sharp edges and painting with colors of your choice.

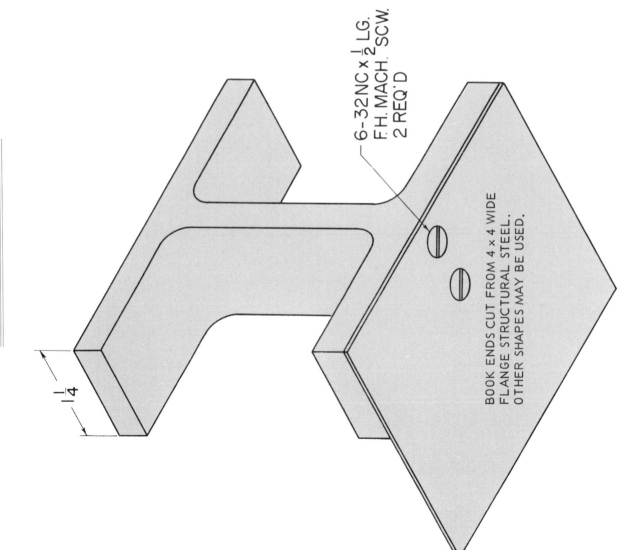

$1\frac{1}{4}$

6-32NC x $\frac{1}{2}$ LG.
F.H. MACH. SCW.
2 REQ'D

BOOK ENDS CUT FROM 4 x 4 WIDE FLANGE STRUCTURAL STEEL. OTHER SHAPES MAY BE USED.

BRACELET

Material: 16 or 18 gauge brass, aluminum, sterling silver, or nickel silver.
Finish: Buff to a high polish.

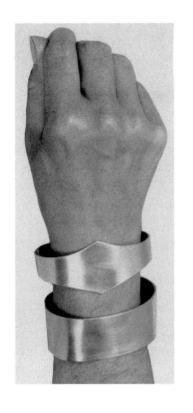

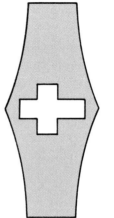

ALTERNATE DESIGNS

$\frac{3}{4}$ SQUARES

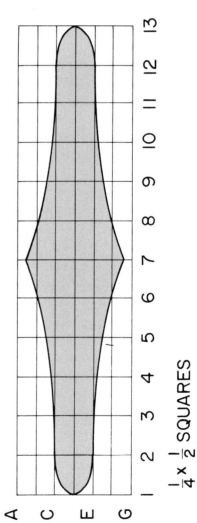

$\frac{1}{4} \times \frac{1}{2}$ SQUARES

PUNCH SET

1. Material: 3/8 dia. drill rod.
2. Heat treat after machining.
3. A pin punch set can be made by making one each of these sizes: 1/16, 1/8, 3/16, and 1/4.

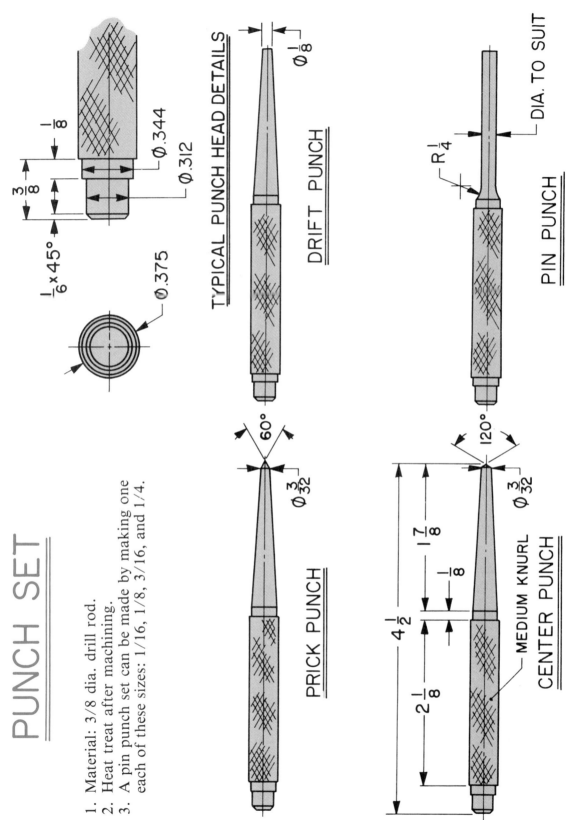

TYPICAL PUNCH HEAD DETAILS

PRICK PUNCH

DRIFT PUNCH

CENTER PUNCH

PIN PUNCH

CAST PLAQUE

1. Material: Aluminum or brass.
2. Plaques may be designed to serve as awards by mounting the casting on backing boards.

SUPPORT MAY BE ADDED TO PLAQUE TO MAKE NAMEPLATE.

15°

$\frac{3}{8}$

2

1

$1-\frac{1}{4}$ TEMPERED HARDBOARD

GLUE FRAMING TO HARDBOARD

LETTERS USED ARE COMMERCIALLY AVAILABLE. ATTACH THEM WITH MODEL AIRPLANE CEMENT.

DETAILS

LENGTH TO SUIT NAME

SEE DETAILS FOR MORE INFORMATION

NA

$2\frac{1}{2}$

LENGTH TO SUIT NAME

HAM

$\frac{3}{8}$

4

8°–10° DRAFT

BOBCATS

DESIGN PROBLEM

Design a magazine rack using the project shown as a starting point.

This is a Spanish motif which fits in with most room settings and furniture styles.

The dimensions given are approximate but will help you design a rack of suitable size.

Weld or braze all joints. Remove burrs and rough edges before painting.

Small pieces of felt cemented on the bottoms of the feet will prevent rust spots.

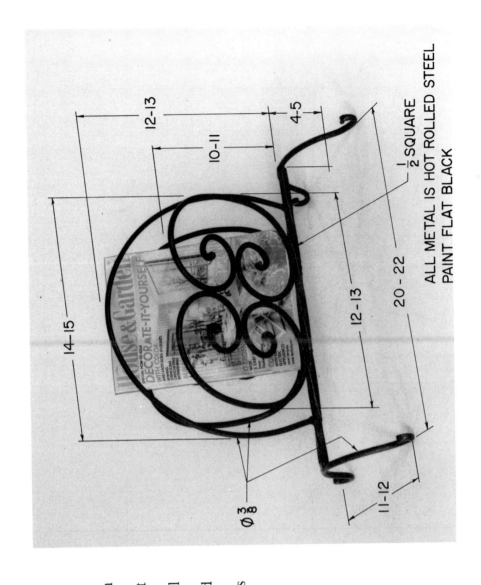

14-15

12-13

10-11

4-5

12-13

20-22

11-12

Ø 3/8

$\frac{1}{2}$ SQUARE

ALL METAL IS HOT ROLLED STEEL
PAINT FLAT BLACK

METAL SCULPTURE

1. Material: Figure – Aluminum or brass. Base – Walnut or cherry.
2. The project can be used as a trophy if an appropriate figure is selected. Ideas are available everywhere: a cougar, impala, road runner, fire bird, etc.
3. Use epoxy in figure and base.

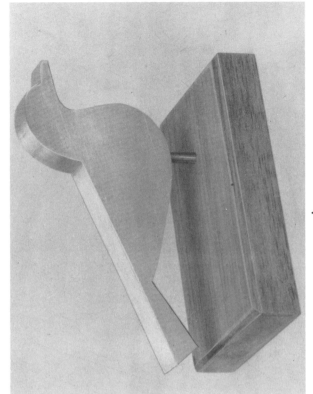

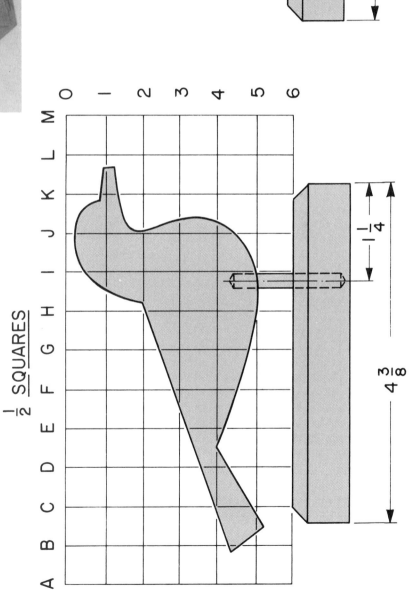

$\phi \frac{3}{16}$

$\frac{1}{2}$

$2\frac{1}{2}$

$1\frac{1}{4}$

$4\frac{3}{8}$

$\frac{1}{2}$ SQUARES

BOTTLE OPENER

Material: 1/8 - 3/16 hard brass or mild steel.
Finish: Polish.

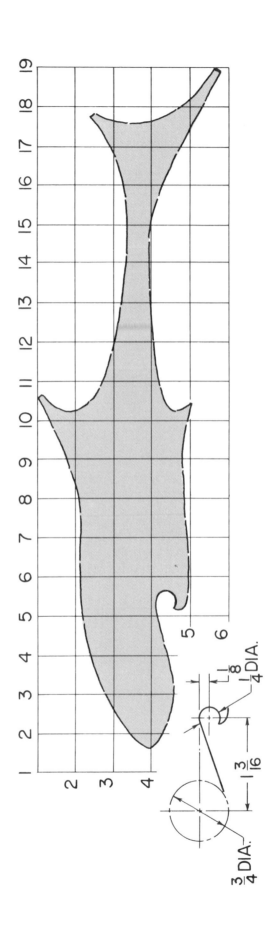

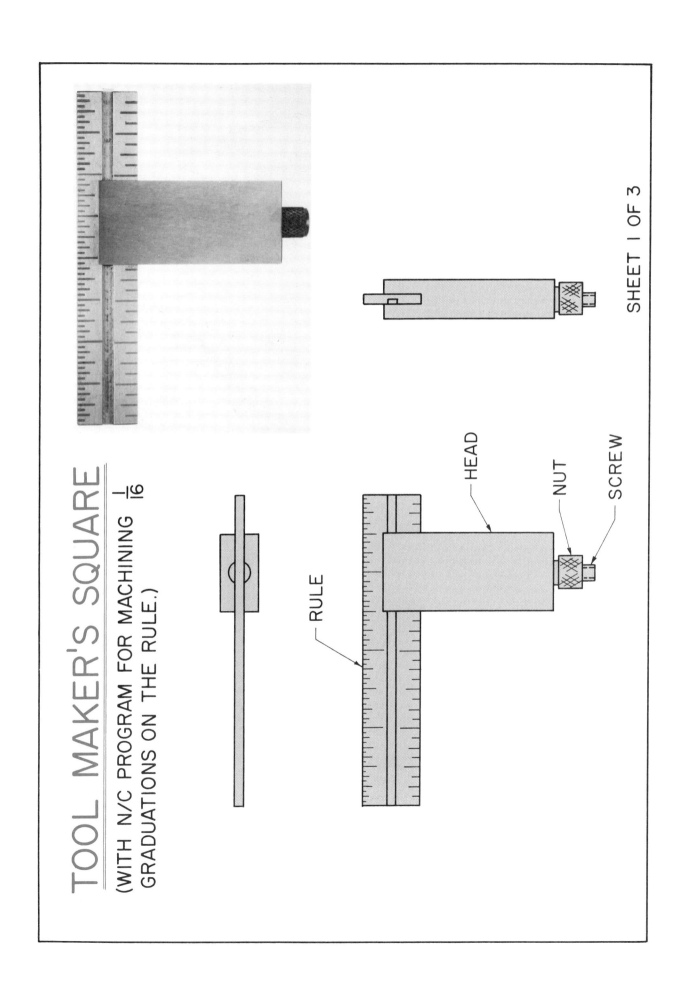

TOOL MAKER'S SQUARE

(WITH N/C PROGRAM FOR MACHINING $\frac{1}{16}$ GRADUATIONS ON THE RULE.)

RULE

HEAD

NUT

SCREW

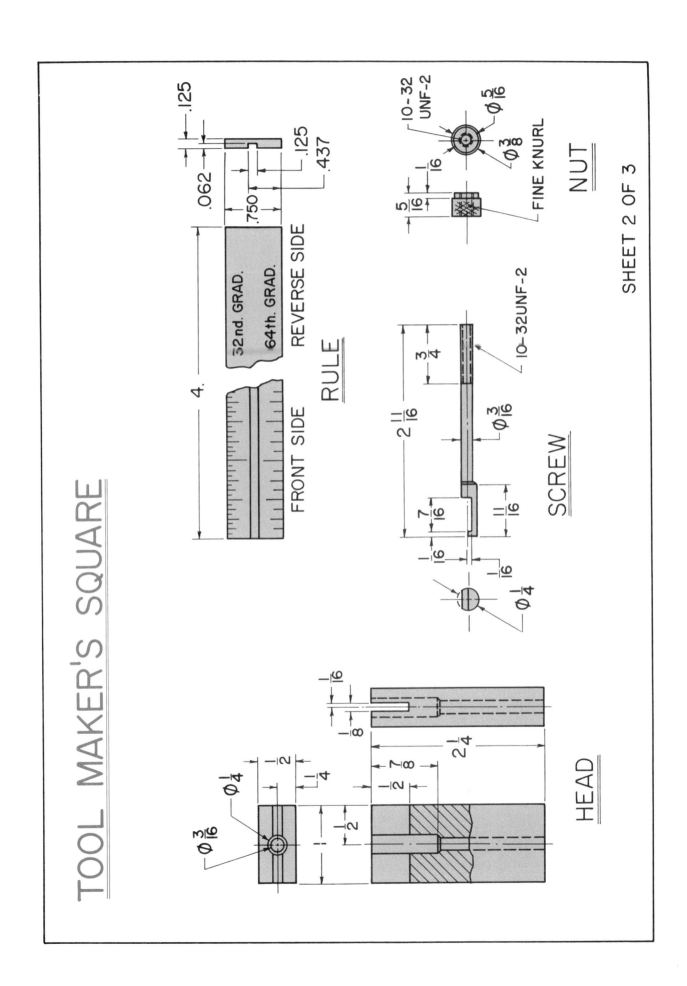

TOOL MAKER'S SQUARE

RULE

FRONT SIDE

REVERSE SIDE

32nd. GRAD.

64th. GRAD.

4.

.750

.062

.125

.437

.125

SCREW

10-32UNF-2

$\frac{3}{4}$

$2\frac{11}{16}$

$\phi\frac{3}{16}$

$\frac{7}{16}$

$\frac{11}{16}$

$\frac{1}{16}$

$\frac{1}{16}$

$\phi\frac{1}{4}$

NUT

10-32 UNF-2

$\phi\frac{5}{16}$

$\phi\frac{3}{8}$

$\frac{1}{16}$

$\frac{5}{16}$

FINE KNURL

HEAD

$\phi\frac{3}{16}$

$\phi\frac{1}{4}$

$\frac{1}{2}$

$\frac{1}{4}$

$\frac{7}{8}$

$\frac{1}{2}$

$2\frac{1}{4}$

$\frac{1}{2}$

1

$\frac{1}{16}$

$\frac{1}{8}$

248

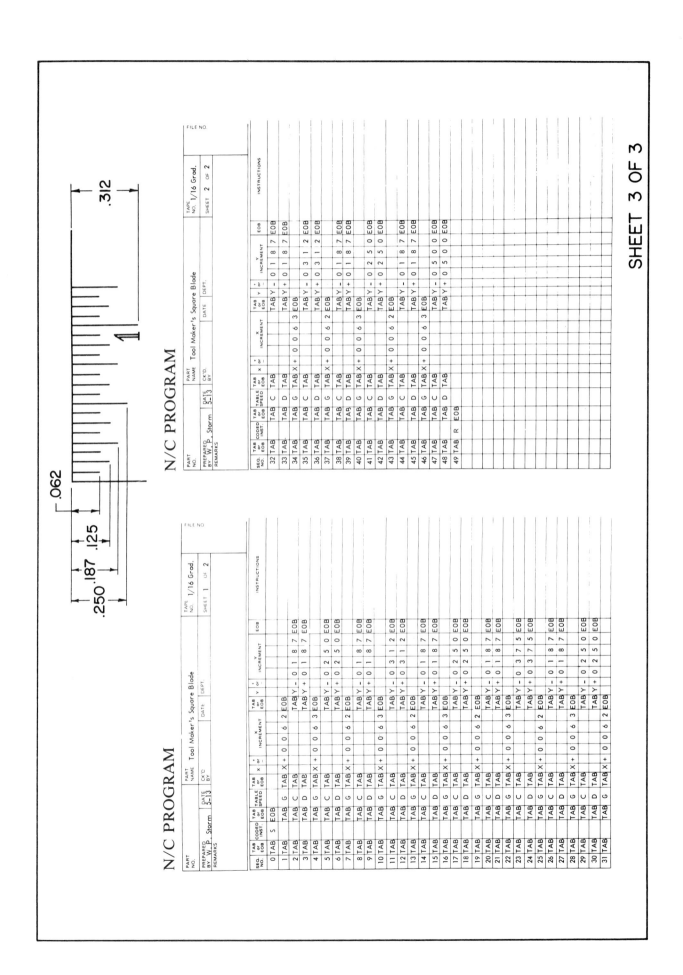

CONTEMPORARY CANDLE HOLDER

1. Material: Aluminum or brass.
2. Finish: As machined.
3. Attach felt to base.

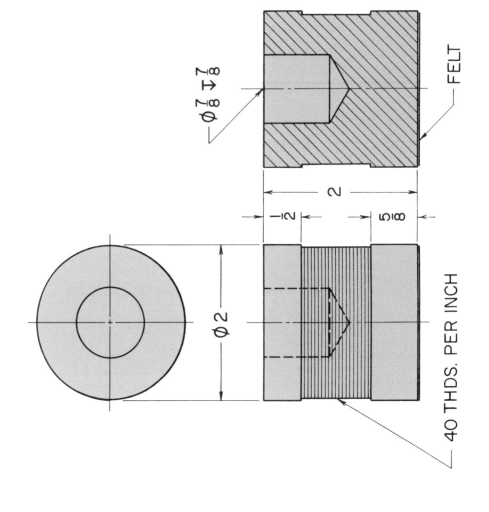

$\phi \frac{7}{8} \, \overline{\underline{\nabla}} \, \frac{7}{8}$

FELT

$\phi 2$

2

$\frac{1}{2}$

$5\frac{1}{8}$

40 THDS. PER INCH

SCOTTY TABLE LAMP

Material: 3/8 aluminum, or a pattern can be made and the figure cast as shown in photograph. The base may be made from mahogany, walnut, or cherry.

Finish: Paint flat black or use a fine abrasive and apply a satin finish.

Design Problem: Provide a way to hold the light socket and shade. It may be made from 3/8 dia. brass tubing.

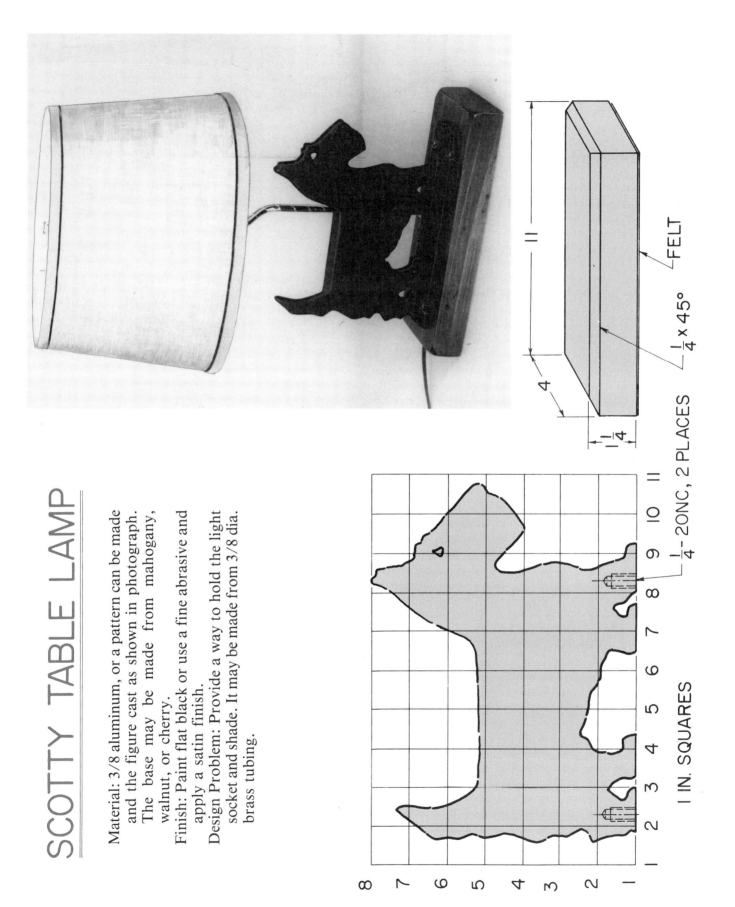

FELT

$\frac{1}{4}$ x 45°

11

4

$1\frac{1}{4}$

$\frac{1}{4}$ - 20NC, 2 PLACES

1 IN. SQUARES

Glossary

A

ABRASIVE: A material that cuts a material softer than itself.

ACUTE ANGLE: An angle of less than 90 deg.

ALIGN: Adjusting to given points.

ALLOWANCE: The limits permitted for satisfactory performance of machined parts.

ALLOY: A mixture of two or more metals fused or melted together to form a new metal.

ALUMINUM OXIDE: A manufactured abrasive. It has largely replaced emery as an abrasive when large quantities of metal must be removed.

ANNEALING: The process of heating metal to a given temperature and allowing it to cool slowly to induce softness. The exact temperature and the period of time the temperature is held depends on the metal.

ANODIZING: A surface finish for aluminum that protects it against corrosion. The process also permits the surface to be dyed a variety of colors.

ANVIL: A block of iron or steel upon which metal is forged.

ASSEMBLY: A unit fitted together from manufactured parts.

ASSEMBLY DRAWING: A drawing that shows the machinist how to assemble an object. The component parts in the drawing are usually key-numbered.

AUTOMATION: An industrial technique that substitutes mechanical labor and mechanical control for human labor and human control.

AXIS: A centerline that passes through an object about which it could rotate. Also used as a point of reference.

B

BERYLLIUM: A metal that weighs about one fourth as much as steel, yet is almost as strong. It is an "exotic metal," used in rockets and aircraft where weight is critical, and in nuclear reactors.

BEVEL: An angle that is not at right angles to another line or surface.

BLOWHOLE: A hole produced in a casting when gases are trapped during the pouring operation.

BRASS: An alloy of copper and zinc. It is bright yellow in color.

BRAZING: A process for joining metals by the fusion of nonferrous alloys that have melting temperatures above 800°F (425°C) but lower than the metals joined.

BRINELL: A term used to designate the hardness of a piece of metal.

BRITTLENESSS: Characteristics that cause a material to break easily.

BRONZE: An alloy of copper and tin. It is reddish gold in color.

BUFFING: The technique of bringing out the luster of metal. Polishing.

BURR: The sharp edge remaining on the metal after cutting or machining.

BUSHING: A bearing or a guide for a cutting tool in a fixture.

C

CARBON STEEL: Steel in which the physical and mechanical properties depend primarily on the carbon content of the metal.

CASE HARDENING: A process of surface hardening iron base metals so the surface layer or "case" of the metal is made harder than the interior or core.

CASTING: An object made by pouring molten metal into a mold.

CHAMFER: To bevel a sharp external edge.

CHASING THREADS: Cutting threads on a lathe.

CHATTER: Vibrations caused by the cutting tool springing away from the work. This produces small ridges on the machine surface.

CHIP: To cut with a chisel.

CHUCK: A device on a machine tool which holds work or cutting tools.

CLEARANCE: The distance by which one part clears another part.

CLOCKWISE: From left to right in a circular motion; the direction clock hands move.

COINING: A metalworking technique that impresses images/characters on a die and punch onto a plain metal surface.

COLOR CODING: A method used to identify steel. Each type of commonly used steel is identified by a different color.

COLOR TEMPER: Using the color range steel passes through when heated to determine the proper degree of hardness.

CONCAVE SURFACE: A curved depression in the surface of an object.

CONCENTRIC: Having a common center.

CONTOUR: The outline of an object or figure; particularly a curved or irregular outline.

CONVENTIONAL: Not original. Customary or traditional.

CONVEX SURFACE: Rounded surface raised on an object.

COOLANT: A fluid or gas used to cool the cutting edge of a tool to prevent it from burning up during the machining operation.

COPPER: A reddish brown base metal.

CORE: A body of sand or other material that is formed to the desired shape and placed in a mold to produce a cavity or opening in a casting.

COUNTERBORE: Enlarging a hole to a given depth and diameter.

COUNTERCLOCKWISE: From right to left in a circular motion. The opposite direction clock hands move.

COUNTERSINK: Chamfering a hole to receive a flat-head screw.

CUTTING FLUID: A liquid used to cool and lubricate a cutting tool and to remove chips.

D

DEAD CENTER: A stationary or non-rotating center.

DIE: A tool used to cut external threads. Also, a tool used to impart a desired shape to a piece of metal.

DIE CASTING: A method of casting metal under pressure by injecting it into the metal dies of a die casting machine.

DIVIDING HEAD: An attachment for machine tools that is used to accurately space holes, slots,

gear teeth, and flutes on round metal stock.

DRAFT: The clearance on a pattern that allows easy withdrawal of the pattern from the mold.

DRIFT: A tapered piece of flat steel used to separate tapered shank tools (like drills) from sleeves, sockets, and machine spindles.

DRILLING: Cutting round holes using a cutting tool with a sharpened point.

DRILL ROD: A carbon steel rod accurately and smoothly ground to size. Available in a large range of sizes.

DROP FORGING: Shaping metal by heating and hammering into impressions in dies.

E

ECCENTRIC: Not on a common center. A device that converts rotary motion into a reciprocating (back and forth) motion.

ECM: Abbreviation for the metal removal process, Electro Chemical Machining.

EDM: Abbreviation for the metal removal process, Electrical Discharge Machining.

EMERY: A natural (not manufactured) abrasive for grinding and polishing.

EMERY CLOTH: Cloth with emery abrasive cemented to its surface. Used to clean and polish metal.

ENTREPRENEUR: Person who originates a new business venture and creates jobs. Entrepreneurs take risks to achieve success.

EXTRUDE: To force metal through a die to produce a desired shape.

F

FACE: To make a flat surface by machining.

FACEPLATE: A circular plate that fits on to the headstock spindle and drives or carries work to be machined.

FERROUS: Denotes a family of metals in which iron is the major ingredient.

FILLET: The curved surface that connects two intersecting surfaces that form an angle.

FIXTURE: A device used to hold metal while it is being machined.

FLASK: A wooden or metal form consisting of a cope (the top portion) and a drag (the bottom portion). It is used to hold the sand that forms the mold in metal casting.

FLUTE: A groove machined in a cutting tool to help in the removal of chips. Permits coolant to reach the cutting point of the tool.

FLUX: Chemicals used in soldering, brazing, and welding to prevent oxidation and promote better fusion of the metals.

FORGE: To form metal with heat and/or pressure.

G

GALVANIZE: To coat steel with zinc.

GATE: The point where molten metal enters the mold cavity.

GAUGE: A tool used for checking the size of metal parts.

GEARS: Toothed wheels that are employed to transmit rotary motion from one shaft to another shaft without slippage.

GREEN SAND: Foundry sand moistened with water.

H

HARDENING: The process whereby certain iron-base alloys are heated and quenched (cooled) to produce a hardness superior to that of the untreated metal.

HEAT TREATMENT: The careful application of a combination of heating and cooling cycles to a metal or an alloy in the solid state to bring about certain desirable conditions such as hardness and toughness.

HERF: Abbreviation for the metal forming process, High Energy Rate Forming.

I

I.D.: Abbreviation for inside diameter.

INDEPENDENT CHUCK: A chuck in which each jaw can be moved independently of the other jaws.

INSPECTION: The measuring and checking of finished parts to determine whether they have been made according to specifications.

INTERCHANGEABLE: Refers to a part that has been made to specific dimensions and tolerances and is capable of being fitted in a mechanism in place of a similarly made part.

J

JIG: A device that holds work in position, and positions and guides the cutting tool.

K

KEY: A small piece of metal fitted in a shaft and hub to prevent a gear or pulley from rotating on a shaft.

KEYWAY: The slot or recess cut in a shaft that holds the key.

KNURLING: Operation that presses grooves into the surface of cylindrical work while it rotates in the lathe.

L

LAPPING: Technique of producing a smooth, accurate surface to a bearing or other mating part by using fine abrasives.

LATHE DOG: A device for clamping work so that is can be machined between centers.

LAY OUT: To locate and scribe points for machining and forming operations.

LIVE CENTER: A rotating center.

M

MACHINABILITY: The characteristic of a material that describes the ease or difficulty of machining it.

MACHINIST: A person who is skilled in the use of machine tools and is capable of making complex machine setups.

MAJOR DIAMETER: The largest diameter of a thread.

MANDREL: A cylindrical piece of steel used to support work for machining operations.

MILL: To remove metal with a rotating cutter on a milling machine.

MILLING MACHINE: A machine that removes metal by means of a rotary cutter.

MINOR DIAMETER: The smallest diameter of a screw thread. Also known as the "root diameter."

N

NC: Abbreviation for the National Coarse series of screw threads.

NF: Abbreviation for the National Fine series of screw threads.

NONFERROUS: Metals containing no iron.

O

O.D.: Abbreviation for outside diameter.

OFF CENTER: Eccentric, not accurate.

P

PEENING: Using the peen (rounded) end of a hammer to decorate the surface of metal.

PEWTER: An alloy of tin (91 percent), copper (1 1/2 percent), and antimony (7 1/2 percent). Modern pewter does not contain lead.

PICKLING: Chemical treatment to remove scale from metal.

PIN PUNCH: A tool made of carbon steel with a long cylindrical end that is used to remove pins and rivets. It can also be employed to punch holes in sheet metal.

PITCH: The distance from a point on one thread to a similar point on the next thread.

PLANISH: To finish or smooth the surface of sheet metal by hammering it lightly with a hammer having a mirror smooth face.

POLISH: To produce a smooth or glossy surface by friction.

PYROMETER: A device for measuring high temperatures. Temperatures are determined by measuring the electric current generated in a thermocouple (two dissimilar metals welded together) as it heats up.

Q

QUENCHING: Rapid cooling by contact with fluids or gases.

R

REAMER: A cutting tool used to finish a drilled hole to exact size.

RELIEF: An undercut or offset surface which provides clearance.

RISER: A reservoir of molten metal provided to compensate for the contraction of cast metals as they solidify.

ROCKWELL HARDNESS: A method of measuring the hardness of a piece of material using a Rockwell hardness testing machine.

ROOT DIAMETER: The smallest or "minor diameter" of a screw thread.

RUNNER: Channel through which molten metal flows from the sprue to the casting and risers.

S

SAE: Abbreviation for the Society of Automotive Engineers.

SAFE EDGE: Edge of a file which has no teeth cut in it.

SANDBLAST: To clean surfaces of castings by using sand blown at high pressure.

SCALE: Oxidation caused on metal surfaces by heating them.

SCRIBE: To draw a line with a scriber or other sharp pointed tool.

SCROLL: A curved section widely used for decorative purposes.

SETUP: The term used to describe the positioning of the work, cutting tools, and machine attachments on a machine tool.

SHEAR: To cut steel metal between two blades.

SHIMS: Pieces of sheet metal, available in various thicknesses, used between mating parts to provide proper clearances.

SILICON CARBIDE: The hardest and sharpest of the manufactured abrasives.

SLUG: Small piece of metal used as spacing material.

SOLDERING: A method of joining metals by means of a nonferrous filler metal, without fusion of the base metals. Normally carried out at temperatures lower than 800°F (425°C).

SPOTFACE: To machine a round spot on a rough surface, usually around a drilled hole. To provide seat for screw or bolt head.

SPRUE HOLE: The opening in a mold into which the molten metal is poured.

STANDARD: An accepted base for a uniform system of measurement and quality.

STRAIGHTEDGE: A precision tool used to check the accuracy of flat surfaces.

SURFACE PLATE: A plate of cast iron, cast steel, or granite that has one or more surfaces finished to a smooth, flat surface. It is used as a base for layout measurements and inspection.

T

TAP: Tool used to cut internal threads.

TAP DRILL: The drill used to make a hole prior to tapping.

TAPPING: The operation that produces internal threads with a tap. It may be done by hand or machine. Tapping also refers to the operation of removing molten metal from a furnace.

TEMPLATE: A pattern or guide.

THREAD: The act of cutting a screw thread.

TIN: A soft, shiny metal. It is nontoxic and when used as plating provides excellent protection against corrosion.

TOLERANCE: The permissible deviation from a basic dimension.

TOOL CRIB: A room or area in a machine shop where tools and supplies are stored and dispensed as needed.

TOOLROOM: The area or department where tools, jigs, fixtures, and the like are manufactured.

TRAIN: A series of meshed gears.

TRUE: On center.

TURN: To machine on a lathe.

U

UNIVERSAL CHUCK: A chuck on which all jaws move simultaneously at a uniform rate to automatically center round or hexagonal stock.

V

VENTS: Narrow openings in molds that permit gases generated during pouring to escape.

W

WHEEL DRESSER: A device utilized to true the face of a grinding wheel.

WORKING DRAWING: A drawing that gives the machinist information on how to make and assemble a mechanism.

WROUGHT IRON: Iron with most of the carbon removed. It is tough, easy to bend and weld.

X

X-RAY: An inspection technique used to find flaws in manufactured parts. The part is not damaged by the inspection process.

ACKNOWLEDGMENTS

While it would be a most pleasant task, it would be impossible for one person to develop the material included in this text by visiting the various industries represented and observing, studying, and taking the photos first-hand.

My sincere thanks to those who helped in the gathering of the necessary material, information, and photographs. Their cooperation was most appreciated.

John R. Walker

Special thanks to Mr. Gerry Greenway and the Swift Saw and Tool Supply Company in Hazel Crest, Illinois for loan of the tools for the cover design and Dr. William L. Schotta of Millersville University, Millersville, Pennsylvania for photographs used throughout the book.

Tables

FRACTIONAL INCHES
INTO DECIMALS AND MILLIMETERS

INCH	DECIMAL INCH	MILLIMETER	INCH	DECIMAL INCH	MILLIMETER
1/64	0.0156	0.3967	33/64	0.5162	13.0968
1/32	0.0312	0.7937	17/32	0.5312	13.4937
3/64	0.0468	1.1906	35/64	0.5468	13.8906
1/16	0.0625	1.5875	9/16	0.5625	14.2875
5/64	0.0781	1.9843	37/64	0.5781	14.6843
3/32	0.0937	2.3812	19/32	0.5937	15.0812
7/64	0.1093	2.7781	39/64	0.6093	15.4781
1/8	0.125	3.175	5/8	0.625	15.875
9/64	0.1406	3.5718	41/64	0.6406	16.2718
5/32	0.1562	3.9687	21/32	0.6562	16.6687
11/64	0.1718	4.3656	43/64	0.6718	17.0656
3/16	0.1875	4.7625	11/16	0.6875	17.4625
13/64	0.2031	5.1593	45/64	0.7031	17.8593
7/32	0.2187	5.5562	23/32	0.7187	18.2562
15/64	0.2343	5.9531	47/64	0.7343	18.6531
1/4	0.25	6.5	3/4	0.75	19.05
17/64	0.2656	6.7468	49/64	0.7656	19.4468
9/32	0.2812	7.1437	25/32	0.7812	19.8437
19/64	0.2968	7.5406	51/64	0.7968	20.2406
5/16	0.3125	7.9375	13/16	0.8125	20.6375
21/64	0.3281	8.3343	53/64	0.8281	21.0343
11/32	0.3437	8.7312	27/32	0.8437	21.4312
23/64	0.3593	9.1281	55/64	0.8593	21.8281
3/8	0.375	9.525	7/8	0.875	22.225
25/64	0.3906	9.9218	57/64	0.8906	22.6218
13/32	0.4062	10.3187	29/32	0.9062	23.0187
27/64	0.4218	10.7156	59/64	0.9218	23.4156
7/16	0.4375	11.1125	15/16	0.9375	23.8125
29/64	0.4531	11.5093	61/64	0.9531	24.2093
15/32	0.4687	11.9062	31/32	0.9687	24.6062
31/64	0.4843	12.3031	63/64	0.9843	25.0031
1/2	0.50	12.7	1	1.0000	25.4

MEASUREMENT SYSTEMS

ENGLISH SYSTEM	METRIC SYSTEM
MEASURES OF TIME 60 sec. = 1 min. 60 min. = 1 hr. 24 hr. = 1 day 365 dy. = 1 common yr. 366 dy. = 1 leap yr. **DRY MEASURES** 2 pt. = 1 qt. 8 qt. = 1 pk. 4 pk. = 1 bu. 2150.42 cu. in. = 1 bu. **MEASURES OF LENGTH** 12 in. = 1 ft. 3 ft. = 1 yd. 5 1/2 yd. = 1 rod 320 rods = 1 mile 5,280 ft. = 1 mile 1,760 yd. = 1 mile 6,080 ft. = 1 knot **LIQUID MEASURES** 16 fluid oz. = 1 pt. 2 pt. = 1 qt. 32 fl. oz. = 1 qt. 4 qt. = 1 gal. 31 1/2 gal. = 1 bbl. 231 cu. in. = 1 gal. 7 1/2 gal. = 1 cu. ft. **MEASURES OF AREA** 144 sq. in. = 1 sq. ft. 9 sq. ft. = 1 sq. yd. 30 1/4 sq. yd. = 1 sq. rod 160 sq. rods = 1 acre 640 acres = 1 sq. mile **MEASURES OF WEIGHT** (Avoirdupois) 7,000 grains (gr.) = 1 lb. 16 oz. = 1 lb. 100 lb. = 1 cwt. 2,000 lb. = 1 short ton 2,240 lb. = 1 long ton **MEASURES OF VOLUME** 1,728 cu. in. = 1 cu. ft. 27 cu. ft. = 1 cu. yd. 128 cu. ft. = 1 cord	The basic unit of the metric system is the meter (m). The meter is exactly 39.37 in. long. This is 3.37 in. longer than the English yard. Units that are multiples or fractional parts of the meter are designated as such by prefixes to the word "meter". For example: 1 millimeter (mm.) = 0.001 meter or 1/1000 meter 1 centimeter (cm.) = 0.01 meter or 1/100 meter 1 decimeter (dm.) = 0.1 meter or 1/10 meter 1 meter (m.) 1 decameter (dkm.) = 10 meters 1 hectometer (hm.) = 100 meters 1 kilometer (km.) = 1000 meters These prefixes may be applied to any unit of length, weight, volume, etc. The meter is adopted as the basic unit of length, the gram for mass, and the liter for volume. In the metric system, area is measured in square kilometers (sq. km. or km.^{2}), square centimeters (sq. cm. or cm.^{2}), etc. Volume is commonly measured in cubic centimeters, etc. One liter (l) is equal to 1,000 cubic centimeters. The metric measurements in most common use are shown in the following tables: **MEASURES OF LENGTH** 10 millimeters = 1 centimeter 10 centimeters = 1 decimeter 10 decimeters = 1 meter 1000 meters = 1 kilometer **MEASURES OF WEIGHT** 100 milligrams = 1 gram 1000 grams = 1 kilogram 1000 kilograms = 1 metric ton **MEASURES OF VOLUME** 1000 cubic centimeters = 1 liter 100 liters = 1 hectoliter

CONVERSION TABLES

TO REDUCE	MULTIPLY BY	TO REDUCE	MULTIPLY BY
LENGTH			
miles to km.	1.61	km. to miles	0.62
miles to m.	1609.35	m. to miles	0.00062
yd. to m.	0.9144	m. to yd.	1.0936
in. to cm.	2.54	cm. to in.	0.3937
in. to mm.	25.4	mm. to in.	0.03937
VOLUME			
cu. in. to cc. or ml.	16.387	cc. to cu. in.	0.061
cu. in. to l.	0.0164	l to cu. in.	61.024
gal. to l.	3.785	l to gal.	0.264
WEIGHT			
lb. to kg.	0.4536	kg. to lb.	2.2
oz. to gm.	28.35	gm. to oz.	0.0353
gr. to gm.	0.0648	gm. to gr.	15.432

DECIMAL EQUIVALENTS NUMBER SIZE DRILLS

NO.	SIZE OF DRILL IN INCHES	NO.	SIZE OF DRILL IN INCHES	NO.	SIZE OF DRILL IN INCHES	NO.	SIZE OF DRILL IN INCHES
1	.2280	21	.1590	41	.0960	61	.0390
2	.2210	22	.1570	42	.0935	62	.0380
3	.2130	23	.1540	43	.0890	63	.0370
4	.2090	24	.1520	44	.0860	64	.0360
5	.2055	25	.1495	45	.0820	65	.0350
6	.2040	26	.1470	46	.0810	66	.0330
7	.2010	27	.1440	47	.0785	67	.0320
8	.1990	28	.1405	48	.0760	68	.0310
9	.1960	29	.1360	49	.0730	69	.0292
10	.1935	30	.1285	50	.0700	70	.0280
11	.1910	31	.1200	51	.0670	71	.0260
12	.1890	32	.1160	52	.0635	72	.0250
13	.1850	33	.1130	53	.0595	73	.0240
14	.1820	34	.1110	54	.0550	74	.0225
15	.1800	35	.1100	55	.0520	75	.0210
16	.1770	36	.1065	56	.0465	76	.0200
17	.1730	37	.1040	57	.0430	77	.0180
18	.1695	38	.1015	58	.0420	78	.0160
19	.1660	39	.0995	59	.0410	79	.0145
20	.1610	40	.0980	60	.0400	80	.0135

NATIONAL COARSE AND NATIONAL FINE THREADS AND TAP DRILLS

SIZE	THREADS PER INCH	MAJOR DIA.	MINOR DIA.	PITCH DIA.	TAP DRILL 75 PERCENT THREAD	DECIMAL EQUIVALENT	CLEARANCE DRILL	DECIMAL EQUIVALENT
2	56	.0860	.0628	.0744	50	.0700	42	.0935
	64	.0860	.0657	.0759	50	.0700	42	.0935
3	48	.099	.0719	.0855	47	.0785	36	.1065
	56	.099	.0758	.0874	45	.0820	36	.1065
4	40	.112	.0795	.0958	43	.0890	31	.1200
	48	.112	.0849	.0985	42	.0935	31	.1200
6	32	.138	.0974	.1177	36	.1065	26	.1470
	40	.138	.1055	.1218	33	.1130	26	.1470
8	32	.164	.1234	.1437	29	.1360	17	.1730
	36	.164	.1279	.1460	29	.1360	17	.1730
10	24	.190	.1359	.1629	25	.1495	8	.1990
	32	.190	.1494	.1697	21	.1590	8	.1990
12	24	.216	.1619	.1889	16	.1770	1	.2280
	28	.216	.1696	.1928	14	.1820	2	.2210
1/4	20	.250	.1850	.2175	7	.2010	G	.2610
	28	.250	.2036	.2268	3	.2130	G	.2610
5/16	18	.3125	.2403	.2764	F	.2570	21/64	.3281
	24	.3125	.2584	.2854	I	.2720	21/64	.3281
3/8	16	.3750	.2938	.3344	5/16	.3125	25/64	.3906
	24	.3750	.3209	.3479	Q	.3320	25/64	.3906
7/16	14	.4375	.3447	.3911	U	.3680	15/32	.4687
	20	.4375	.3725	.4050	25/64	.3906	29/64	.4531
1/2	13	.5000	.4001	.4500	27/64	.4219	17/32	.5312
	20	.5000	.4350	.4675	29/64	.4531	33/64	.5156
9/16	12	.5625	.4542	.5084	31/64	.4844	19/32	.5937
	18	.5625	.4903	.5264	33/64	.5156	37/64	.5781
5/8	11	.6250	.5069	.5660	17/32	.5312	21/32	.6562
	18	.6250	.5528	.5889	37/64	.5781	41/64	.6406
3/4	10	.7500	.6201	.6850	21/32	.6562	25/32	.7812
	16	.7500	.6688	.7094	11/16	.6875	49/64	.7656
7/8	9	.8750	.7307	.8028	49/64	.7656	29/32	.9062
	14	.8750	.7822	.8286	13/16	.8125	57/64	.8906
1	8	1.0000	.8376	.9188	7/8	.8750	1-1/32	1.0312
	14	1.0000	.9072	.9536	15/16	.9375	1-1/64	1.0156
1-1/8	7	1.1250	.9394	1.0322	63/64	.9844	1-5/32	1.1562
	12	1.1250	1.0167	1.0709	1-3/64	1.0469	1-5/32	1.1562
1-1/4	7	1.2500	1.0644	1.1572	1-7/64	1.1094	1-9/32	1.2812
	12	1.2500	1.1417	1.1959	1-11/64	1.1719	1-9/32	1.2812
1-1/2	6	1.5000	1.2835	1.3917	1-11/32	1.3437	1-17/32	1.5312
	12	1.5000	1.3917	1.4459	1-27/64	1.4219	1-17/32	1.5312

LETTER SIZE DRILLS

A	0.234	J	0.277	S	0.348
B	0.238	K	0.281	T	0.358
C	0.242	L	0.290	U	0.368
D	0.246	M	0.295	V	0.377
E	0.250	N	0.302	W	0.386
F	0.257	O	0.316	X	0.397
G	0.261	P	0.323	Y	0.404
H	0.266	Q	0.332	Z	0.413
I	0.272	R	0.339		

SCREW THREAD ELEMENTS FOR UNIFIED AND NATIONAL
FORM OF THREAD

THREADS PER INCH (n)	PITCH (p) $p = \frac{1}{n}$	SINGLE HEIGHT SUBTRACT FROM BASIC MAJOR DIAMETER TO GET BASIC PITCH DIAMETER	DOUBLE HEIGHT SUBTRACT FROM BASIC MAJOR DIAMETER TO GET BASIC MINOR DIAMETER	83 1/3 PERCENT DOUBLE HEIGHT SUBTRACT FROM BASIC MAJOR DIAMETER TO GET MINOR DIAMETER OF RING GAGE	BASIC WIDTH OF CREST AND ROOT FLAT $\frac{p}{8}$	CONSTANT FOR BEST SIZE WIRE ALSO SINGLE HEIGHT OF 60 DEG. V–THREAD	DIAMETER OF BEST SIZE WIRE
3	.333333	.216506	.43301	.36084	.0417	.28868	.19245
3 1/4	.307692	.199852	.39970	.33309	.0385	.26647	.17765
3 1/2	.285714	.185577	.37115	.30929	.0357	.24744	.16496
4	.250000	.162379	.32476	.27063	.0312	.21651	.14434
4 1/2	.222222	.144337	.28867	.24056	.0278	.19245	.12830
5	.200000	.129903	.25981	.21650	.0250	.17321	.11547
5 1/2	.181818	.118093	.23619	.19682	.0227	.15746	.10497
6	.166666	.108253	.21651	.18042	.0208	.14434	.09623
7	.142857	.092788	.18558	.15465	.0179	.12372	.08248
8	.125000	.081189	.16238	.13531	.0156	.10825	.07217
9	.111111	.072168	.14434	.12028	.0139	.09623	.06415
10	.100000	.064952	.12990	.10825	.0125	08660	.05774
11	.090909	.059046	.11809	.09841	.0114	.07873	.05249
11 1/2	.086956	.056480	.11296	.09413	.0109	.07531	.05020
12	.083333	.054127	.10826	.09021	.0104	.07217	.04811
13	.076923	.049963	.09993	.08327	.0096	.06662	.04441
14	.071428	.046394	.09279	.07732	.0089	.06186	.04124
16	.062500	.040595	.08119	.06766	.0078	.05413	.03608
18	.055555	.036086	.07217	.06014	.0069	.04811	.03208
20	.050000	.032475	.06495	.05412	.0062	.04330	.02887
22	.045454	.029523	.05905	.04920	.0057	.03936	.02624
24	.041666	.027063	.05413	.04510	.0052	.03608	.02406
27	.037037	.024056	.04811	.04009	.0046	.03208	.02138
28	.035714	.023197	.04639	.03866	.0045	.03093	.02062
30	.033333	.021651	.04330	.03608	.0042	.02887	.01925
32	.031250	.020297	.04059	.03383	.0039	.02706	.01804
36	.027777	.018042	.03608	.03007	.0035	.02406	.01604
40	.025000	.016237	.03247	.02706	.0031	.02165	.01443
44	.022727	.014761	.02952	.02460	.0028	.01968	.01312
48	.020833	.013531	.02706	.02255	.0026	.01804	.01203
50	.020000	.012990	.02598	.02165	.0025	.01732	.01155
56	.017857	.011598	.02320	.01933	.0022	.01546	.01031
60	.016666	.010825	.02165	.01804	.0021	.01443	.00962
64	.015625	.010148	.02030	.01691	.0020	.01353	.00902
72	.013888	.009021	.01804	.01503	.0017	.01203	.00802
80	.012500	.008118	.01624	.01353	.0016	.01083	.00722
90	.011111	.007217	.01443	.01202	.0014	.00962	.00642
96	.010417	.006766	.01353	.01127	.0013	.00902	.00601
100	.010000	.006495	.01299	.01082	.0012	.00866	.00577
120	.008333	.005413	.01083	.00902	.0010	.00722	.00481

Using the Best Size Wires, the measurement over three wires minus the Constant for Best Size Wire equals the Pitch Diameter.

MACHINE SCREW AND CAP SCREW HEADS

FILLISTER HEAD

SIZE	A	B	C	D
#8	.260	.141	.042	.060
#10	.302	.164	.048	.072
1/4	3/8	.205	.064	.087
5/16	7/16	.242	.077	.102
3/8	9/16	.300	.086	.125
1/2	3/4	.394	.102	.168
5/8	7/8	.500	.128	.215
3/4	1	.590	.144	.258
1	1 5/16	.774	.182	.352

FLAT HEAD

SIZE	A	B	C	D
#8	.320	.092	.043	.037
#10	.372	.107	.048	.044
1/4	1/2	.146	.064	.063
5/16	5/8	.183	.072	.078
3/8	3/4	.220	.081	.095
1/2	7/8	.220	.102	.090
5/8	1 1/8	.273	.128	.125
3/4	1 3/8	.366	.144	.153

ROUND HEAD

SIZE	A	B	C	D
#8	.297	.113	.044	.067
#10	.346	.130	.048	.073
1/4	7/16	.1831	.064	.107
5/16	9/16	.236	.072	.150
3/8	5/8	.262	.081	.160
1/2	13/16	.340	.102	.200
5/8	1	.422	.128	.255
3/4	1 1/4	.526	.144	.320

HEXAGON HEAD

SIZE	A	B	C
1/4	.494	.170	7/16
5/16	.564	.215	1/2
3/8	.635	.246	9/16
1/2	.846	.333	3/4
5/8	1.058	.411	15/16
3/4	1.270	.490	1 1/8
7/8	1.482	.566	1 5/16
1	1.693	.640	1 1/2

SOCKET HEAD

SIZE	A	B	C
#8	.265	.164	1/8
#10	5/16	.190	5/32
1/4	3/8	1/4	3/16
5/16	7/16	5/16	7/32
3/8	9/16	3/8	5/16
7/16	5/8	7/16	5/16
1/2	3/4	1/2	3/8
5/8	7/8	5/8	1/2
3/4	1	3/4	9/16
7/8	1 1/8	7/8	9/16
1	1 5/16	1	5/8

Tables

PHYSICAL PROPERTIES OF METALS

METAL	SYMBOL	SPECIFIC GRAVITY	SPECIFIC HEAT	MELTING POINT *		LBS. PER CUBIC INCH
				DEG. C	DEG. F.	
Aluminum (Cast)	Al	2.56	.2185	658	1217	.0924
Aluminum (Rolled).....	Al	2.71	–	–	–	.0978
Antimony	Sb	6.71	.051	630	1166	.2424
Bismuth	Bi	9.80	.031	271	520	.3540
Boron.......	B	2.30	.3091	2300	4172	.0831
Brass.......	–	8.51	.094	–	–	.3075
Cadmium.....	Cd	8.60	.057	321	610	.3107
Calcium	Ca	1.57	.170	810	1490	.0567
Carbon......	C	2.22	.165	–	–	.0802
Chromium	Cr	6.80	.120	1510	2750	.2457
Cobalt	Co	8.50	.110	1490	2714	.3071
Copper......	Cu	8.89	.094	1083	1982	.3212
Columbium ...	Cb	8.57	–	1950	3542	.3096
Gold	Au	19.32	.032	1063	1945	.6979
Iridium......	Ir	22.42	.033	2300	4170	.8099
Iron........	Fe	7.86	.110	1520	2768	.2634
Iron (Cast) ...	Fe	7.218	.1298	1375	2507	.2605
Iron (Wrought) .	Fe	7.70	.1138	1500–1600	2732–2912	.2779
Lead	Pb	11.37	.031	327	621	.4108
Lithium	Li	.057	.941	186	367	.0213
Magnesium ...	Mg	1.74	.250	651	1204	.0629
Manganese ...	Mn	8.00	.120	1225	2237	.2890
Mercury	Hg	13.59	.032	38.7	37.7	.4909
Molybdenum...	Mo	10.2	.0647	2620	4748	.368
Monel Metal...	–	8.87	.127	1360	2480	.320
Nickel	Ni	8.80	.130	1452	2646	.319
Phosphorus...	P	1.82	.177	43	111.4	.0657
Platinum.....	Pt	21.50	.033	1755	3191	.7767
Potassium....	K	0.87	.170	62	144	.0314
Selenium.....	Se	4.81	.084	220	428	.174
Silicon......	Si	2.40	.1762	1427	2600	.087
Silver.......	Ag	10.53	.056	961	1761	.3805
Sodium......	Na	0.97	.290	97	207	.0350
Steel	–	7.858	.1175	1330–1378	2372–2532	.2839
Strontium	Sr	2.54	.074	–	–	.0918
Sulphur......	S	2.07	.175	115	235.4	.075
Tantalum	Ta	10.80	–	2850	5160	.3902
Tin	Sn	7.29	.056	232	450	.2634
Titanium.....	Ti	5.3	.130	1900	3450	.1915
Tungsten	W	19.10	.033	3000	5432	.6900
Uranium	U	18.70	–	–	–	.6755
Vanadium	V	5.50	–	1730	3146	.1987
Zinc	Zn	7.19	.094	419	786	.2598

* Circular of the Bureau of Standards No. 35, Department of Commerce and Labor.

CONVERSION TABLE METRIC TO ENGLISH

WHEN YOU KNOW	MULTIPLY BY: VERY ACCURATE	APPROXIMATE	TO FIND
LENGTH			
millimeters	0.0393701	0.04	inches
centimeters	0.3937008	0.4	inches
meters	3.280840	3.3	feet
meters	1.093613	1.1	yards
kilometers	0.621371	0.6	miles
WEIGHT			
grams	0.00228571	0.0023	ounces
grams	0.03527396	0.035	ounces
kilograms	2.204623	2.2	pounds
tonnes	1.1023113	1.1	short tons
VOLUME			
milliliters		0.2	teaspoons
milliliters	0.06667	0.067	tablespoons
milliliters	0.03381402	0.03	fluid ounces
liters	61.02374	61.024	cubic inches
liters	2.113376	2.1	pints
liters	1.056688	1.06	quarts
liters	0.26417205	0.26	gallons
liters	0.03531467	0.035	cubic feet
cubic meters	61023.74	61023.7	cubic inches
cubic meters	35.31467	35.0	cubic feet
cubic meters	1.3079506	1.3	cubic yards
cubic meters	264.17205	264.0	gallons
AREA			
square centimeters	0.1550003	0.16	square inches
square centimeters	0.00107639	0.001	square feet
square meters	10.76391	10.8	square feet
square meters	1.195990	1.2	square yards
square kilometers		0.4	square miles
hectares	2.471054	2.5	acres
TEMPERATURE			
Celsius	*9/5 (then add 32)		Fahrenheit

* = Exact

CONVERSION TABLE ENGLISH TO METRIC

WHEN YOU KNOW	MULTIPLY BY: VERY ACCURATE	APPROXIMATE	TO FIND
LENGTH			
inches	*25.4		millimeters
inches	*2.54		centimeters
feet	*0.3048		meters
feet	*30.48		centimeters
yards	*0.9144	0.9	meters
miles	*1.609344	1.6	kilometers
WEIGHT			
grains	15.43236	15.4	grams
ounces	*28.349523125	28.0	grams
ounces	*0.0283495231 25	.028	kilograms
pounds	*0.45359237	0.45	kilograms
short ton	*0.90718474	0.9	tonnes
VOLUME			
teaspoons		5.0	milliliters
tablespoons		15.0	milliliters
fluid ounces	29.57353	30.0	milliliters
cups		0.24	liters
pints	*0.473176473	0.47	liters
quarts	*0.946352946	0.95	liters
gallons	*3.785411784	3.8	liters
cubic inches	*0.016387064	0.02	cubic meters
cubic feet	*0.028316846592	0.03	cubic meters
cubic yards	*0.764554857984	0.76	cubic meters
AREA			
square inches	*6.4516	6.5	square centimeters
square feet	*0.09290304	0.09	square meters
square yards	*0.83612736	0.8	square meters
square miles		2.6	square kilometers
acres	*0.4046564224	0.4	hectares
TEMPERATURE			
Fahrenheit	*5/9 (after subtracting 32)		Celsius

* = Exact

Tables

METALS WE USE

SHAPES	LENGTH	HOW MEASURED	*HOW PURCHASED	OTHER
Sheet less than 1/4 in. thick	to 144 in.	Thickness x width widths to 72 in.	Weight, foot, or piece	Available in coils of much longer lengths
Plate more than 1/4 in. thick	to 20 ft.	Thickness x width	Weight, foot, or piece	
Band	to 20 ft.	Thickness x width	Weight or piece	Mild steel with oxide coating
Rod	12 to 20 ft.	Diameter	Weight, foot, or piece	Hot-rolled steel to 20 ft. length; cold-finished steel to 12 ft. length; steel drill rod 36 in.
Square	12 to 20 ft.	Width	Weight, foot, or piece	
Flats	Hot rolled 20-22 ft. Cold finished	Thickness x width	Weight, foot, or piece	
Hexagon	12 to 20 ft.	Distance across flats	Weight, foot, or piece	
Octagon	12 to 20 ft.	Distance across flats	Weight, foot, or piece	
Angle	Lengths to 40 ft.	Leg length x leg length x thickness of legs	Weight, foot, or piece	
Expanded sheet	to 96 in.	Gauge number (U.S. Standard)	36 x 96 in. and size of openings	Metal is pierced and expanded (stretched) to diamond shape; also available rolled to thickness after it has been expanded
Perforated Sheet	to 96 in.	Gauge number (U.S. Standard)	30 x 36 in. 36 x 48 in. 36 x 96 in.	Design is cut in sheet; many designs available.

* Charge made for cutting to other than standard lengths.

Index